FROM HIS HEART,
THROUGH MINE,
To Yours . . .

A Collection of Emails

about Experiencing God

By Jessica Sullivan

TATE PUBLISHING, LLC

DEDICATION

All glory, honor, and praise to Christ Jesus,
my Lord, my Savior, my Friend

<>< Jessica

In Loving Memory of

Robin Barr
who reminded me that the Lord speaks
in many ways and that
He chooses to use many different voices.

ACKNOWLEDGMENTS

Michele . . . Wow! What a joy it has been to partner alongside of you in this project! Thanks for being God's agent in making this all happen

Mom . . . Words could never express my gratitude to you. I feel blessed every day that God gave me you as my mommy. You live so selflessly and love so purely. I see Christ in you so much, Mom, and because of that, I pray to be more like you each day. I love you, Pod . . . (hehe, couldn't resist!)

Dad . . . I love being your Princess! Thank you for helping me to understand what it means to be a Princess, not only to you, but also to the Lord. Your perseverance through tough times has challenged me. I'm so proud of you . . . I love you, Daddy!

Garrett . . . Bo, you live life so passionately! I love that about you! You have given me so many memories, have made me laugh until my belly hurts, have helped me learn to take myself lightly, have challenged me to live without fear, and have inspired me live to life to the fullest and capture the blessings in each day. I couldn't have dreamed of having a brother like you! I see God's goodness and grace through you. I thank the Lord for giving you to me as my brother . . . and my friend. I love you, Bubby!! (Yes, I *did* just write that! Haha!)

Gordon, Pat, Erin, and Kacy . . . I praise God for our lifelong friendship and the way He was able to use that platform to let your light shine so brightly in my life, bringing me to His light. Thank you so much for introducing me to Jesus! I can't imagine my life without Him!

Jenna . . . Your friendship has been such a precious gift to me. Thank you for loving me unconditionally and giving me grace upon grace . . . I love you!

NB Friends . . . Thank you for sticking by my side through all the years. I praise the Lord for how each of you has sharpened me and helped me grow. You have given me so many cherished memories and many, many laughs. I love you!

Aggie Friends . . . Thank you for allowing the Lord to use you in countless ways to help me know and understand Christ on a deeper level. You have helped Him become so real to me! I love you and miss all our fun times together in Aggieland!

Lisa . . . How have you put up with me during this?! Thanks for your patience, your encouragement and the surrendered life you live before Christ. You challenge me and spur me on more than you'll ever know! P.S. Thanks for teaching me how to live from the heart and for reminding me to take sabbaticals every now and then. ☺

Paris Community . . . Oh my sweet friends, what would I have done without you? I will forever be grateful for the love and support you have given me during this process! I honestly wouldn't have persevered without your encouragement and words of wisdom. Thank you for your friendship, love, and patience! ☺ Thank you also for being Christ to me in so many ways.

The Young Life Community . . . I am so blessed to have been surrounded by such a great cloud of witnesses! May your love for Jesus continue to help you press on and keep fighting the good fight!

Dib . . . Thank you for reminding me of God's goodness and His unending grace, and that the enemy is at work in very sly ways.

Group 7 . . . For honest games of hot seat, friendships, and your approval. ☺

Jill . . . Well, you were right! Almost a year to date from the day you anointed me . . . I have come back to that moment over and over again. Thanks for being such a faithful friend and servant to the Lord. May God continue to bless you with Kingdom Connections!

YL Winter Training friends . . . Thank you for the keys of freedom . . . you will never know how much your words and prayers blessed me that night. I took your advice on the intro . . . ☺

Daddy Dan . . . Precious, precious, precious. Thank you, thank you, thank you!

Hisword2day . . . those on my e-mail list . . . Thank you so much for all of your love, prayers, and support! It has been *such* a joy and honor to share with you over the years. Thanks for reading, but mostly, thanks for all of the words of wisdom and encouragement you have sent back to me! You have been such a blessing to me!

Family and Friends . . . I wish I could list you all . . . Thank you for your love and friendship! You have helped refine and sharpen me, and through your life, love, and faith the Lord has given me a clearer picture of Christ. I'm humbled and blessed to know you and share life with you!!

Most of all, Jesus . . . I thank You for loving me, choosing me, and setting me free. Without you I truly am nothing. Thank you for giving me so much life . . . thank you for giving me Yourself. I will never fully understand, but I thank you and love you with all of me.

TABLE OF CONTENTS

May 30, 2003–My prayer for you–Colossians 1:9

June 5, 2003–Glimpses of His greatness–Deuteronomy 3:24
June 11, 2003–Update from TX!
June 11, 2003–Surviving life's fires–Daniel 3:26–27
June 12, 2003–Overflowing with thankfulness–Colossians 2:6–7
June 13, 2003–God's masterpiece–Isaiah 64:8
June 18, 2003–Heaven's work ethic–Colossians 3:23–24
June 19, 2003–What's in your hands?–Exodus 4:2

July 1, 2003–The Beatitudes–Matthew 5:3–10
July 3, 2003–Dependence Day–John 15:5
July 7, 2003–Jess in Oregon

August 4, 2003–But by His grace–1 Corinthians 15:9–10
August 5, 2003–Still a long way off–Luke 15:20
August 11, 2003–Holding hands–Isaiah 41:9–10, 13
August 12, 2003–What the Lord declares–Jeremiah 29:11
August 13, 2003–Trimming dead ends–John 15:1–2
August 19, 2003–The power of praise–1 Thessalonians 5:18
August 21, 2003–Because of You–Galatians 1:24
August 25, 2003–God's flock under your care–1 Peter 5:2–3
August 26, 2003–Discharging trust–1 Corinthians 9:16–17
August 27, 2003–Quieted by His love–Zephaniah 3:17
August 29, 2003–Surgery update

September 2, 2003–The hope of glory–Colossians 1:27
September 9, 2003–Go take possession–Deuteronomy 1:20–21
September 15, 2003–Hypochondria of the heart–Philippians 4:8
September 16, 2003–God thinking out loud–Deuteronomy 5:29
September 17, 2003–Acknowledging God–Deuteronomy 4:39
September 22, 2003–Paraphrasing David–Psalm 8:3, 9
September 23, 2003–His compassions never fail–Lamentations 3:21–23
September 25, 2003–Better to trust the Lord–Psalm 118:8
September 30, 2003–Display cases–1 Timothy 1:12–17

October 2, 2003–The voice of His word–Psalm 103:20
October 6, 2003–A perverse heart–Psalm 101:3–4
October 8, 2003–Believing and trusting the Lord–Romans 4:18–21
October 10, 2003–REJOICE!–Psalm 105:1–5
October 14, 2003–It's a great day to be alive–Psalm 118:24
October 16, 2003–The broken toaster–Psalm 51:10
October 21, 2003–The beat of a different drummer–John 7:3–4, 8–10
October 24, 2003–The Lord is near–Philippians 4:5
October 27, 2003–The Spirit prays–Romans 8:26–27

October 28, 2003–What have you entrusted?–2 Timothy 1:12
October 30, 2003–Miracles do happen–Genesis 18:14

November 3, 2003–Not to us, but to the Lord be glory–Psalm 115:1
November 4, 2003–Pen or Pencil?–Proverbs 27:1
November 6, 2003–Carry a lighter loan–Matthew 7:13–14
November 7, 2003–Best or rest?–Exodus 23:19
November 10, 2003–Sweet tea–Proverbs 13:19
November 12, 2003–Let your light shine–Matthew 5:16
November 14, 2003–Peace is a noun–John 14:27
November 17, 2003–God is faithful and loving–Psalm 145:13
November 20, 2003–Know and rely on God's love–1 John 4:15–16
November 21, 2003–A lesson from the deer–Psalm 13:5–6
November 25, 2003–You are so richly blessed–Psalm 107:1
November 26, 2003–Be a blessing to God–Deuteronomy 8:10

December 2, 2003–He appears faithfully–Hosea 6:3
December 3, 2003–Time–2 Peter 3:8
December 4, 2003–Be at rest for the Lord has been good–Psalm 116:7–9
December 15, 2003–Come let us adore Him–Matthew 2:11
December 17, 2003–A lesson in worship from the Magi–Matthew 2:11
December 18, 2003–The gifts of the Magi–Matthew 2:11
December 22, 2003–Highly favored–Luke 1:28–30
December 24, 2003–To us a Son is given–Isaiah 9:6
December 30, 2003–A prayer for you–Psalm 90:14

January 5, 2004–Life is not a white elephant gift–Ecclesiastes 5:18–19
January 6, 2004–Out of town
January 14, 2004–Thank you–Colossians 4:12
January 16, 2004–Embracing the cross–Matthew 16:24
January 22, 2004–To know Christ–Philippians 3:10–11
January 23, 2004–The Lord longs to be gracious to you–Isaiah 30:18
January 26, 2004–A glimpse of God's grace–Romans 1:20
January 27, 2004–Jesus today–Luke 4:18–19, 21
January 28, 2004–In the same boat–Luke 8:22–25

February 3, 2004–As Jesus went–Luke 8:42–44
February 5, 2004–Great is His love–Psalm 86:11–13
February 10, 2004–3 challenges for you–Psalm 119:56–58
February 12, 2004–Where's Jesus?–Jeremiah 29:13
February 17, 2004–Prayer requests for Jess–Luke 12:11–12
February 18, 2004–WOW, God! Thanks!
February 20, 2004–He always listens–John 11:40–42
February 26, 2004–Minutemen: dressed and ready–Luke 12:35–38
February 27, 2004–Are you willing?–Luke 13:34

March 2, 2004–Fertilizer–Luke 13:6–9
March 4, 2004–Known and identified by fruit–Luke 6:44
March 5, 2004–Keep your eyes on Jesus–Psalm 25:15
March 8, 2004–In Him–Acts 17:28
March 10, 2004–We are going–Luke 18:31
March 12, 2004–May God be gracious to you and bless you–Psalm 67:1–2
March 16, 2004–Lord, I want to see–Luke 18:41
March 24, 2004–Enriched in every way–1 Corinthians 1:4–9
March 29, 2004–Within your heart–Luke 17:21
March 31, 2004–Let go of your rocks–Matthew 11:28–30

April 2, 2004–Run your race–Hebrews 12:1
April 5, 2004–Visa update–Deuteronomy 32:3–4
April 7, 2004–A lesson from Pilate–Luke 23:24–25
April 9, 2004–Some verses for Good Friday
April 13, 2004–Leap for joy–Psalm 28:7
April 16, 2004–A bird's song to the Lord–Judges 5:3
April 19, 2004–Revive me–Psalm 119:107
April 22, 2004–A windy ride–Romans 8:28

May 5, 2004–Light & mountains–Psalm 76:4
May 7, 2004–Mountains and valleys–Psalm 23:4
May 12, 2004–Wherever you go–Joshua 1:9
May 14, 2004–Awesome deeds of righteousness–Psalm 65:5–7
May 18, 2004–Encouragement from the Centurion–Matthew 8:5–7
May 21, 2004–Into the details–Matthew 10:29–31
May 26, 2004–Thanks. . . . . Psalm 138:1–2
May 28, 2004–The fish's mouth–Matthew 17:25–27

June 1, 2004–The time has come . . . headed to Paris

FOREWORD

One of God's grace gifts in my life has been a "ringside seat" to the lives of thousands of children and teenagers who have come through our church's ministries. At times those gifts are even greater as the Lord allows a continuing relationship with some of these individuals into adulthood. Jessica Sullivan is one of the grace gifts I treasure most!

Never have I witnessed such a well-honed gift so effectively used in such a young person as the gift I have seen the Lord use in Jessica. She masterfully combines the gifts of teaching and writing to apply the sometimes complex truths of Scripture to everyday experiences of life. As I received her devotional thoughts via e-mail I often found myself saying, "That is me!" . . ."How did she think of that connection!" . . ."WOW!" . . ."Thank you Lord!" With each message Jessica helped me experience the truth of what the Lord teaches.

If you listen fully to the written words in this book and allow the applications to become yours experientially, I believe they will bring transformation in your personal life and in your relationship with the Lord. In these devotional thoughts you will see at least two truths very clearly: God's desire for an intimate, loving relationship with you personally; and God's glory. As a young adult Jessica already knows the truth which takes many of us years to learn—we are loved little people with a huge, glorious God!

So, as you read the messages of this book, ask the Lord to open the eyes of your heart to His glory and His desire to have an intimate relationship with you. If you choose to do that, the Lord will bring life change to you.

In truth there is one other thought that came to mind each time I received one of Jessica's messages—"Lord, thank you for the gift of grace you have given me and others in Jessica Sullivan." Before you reach the end of this book, you will be praying the same prayer!

Gordon Sudduth,
D.Phil., University of Oxford '97
Pastor, Oak Ridge Baptist Church
Executive Director, GraceLife Counseling & Research

NOTE FROM JESS

Hello Friend!

Today is a glorious day . . . I was awakened in the darkness just before the dawn and was blessed with a front row seat to a display of God's splendor and majesty as the sun rose over Paris on this beautiful winter morning. As I enjoyed this glimpse of God's beauty, I felt Him nudging my heart telling me that today was the day we were going to write this note to you. I must confess, I've been *so* nervous and intimidated to write you because, well . . . it is going to be (and now IS) an "introduction" to a book . . . a *book!* This reality still humbles and shocks me! I never, ever, ever, ever intended for these e-mails to be published into a book.

God apparently had other plans.

During the fall of 1999, God began kindling a desire in my heart to begin getting to know Him in a different way than I ever had before: through His Word. At that point, I would read the Bible, but never got too much out of it and didn't really enjoy my time in the Word. However, in His perfect way, God got me involved in a Bible study that really started speaking to my heart! I was learning so much and was excited to share what I was learning through the study. As a result I started sending e-mails to a small group of friends and family with quotes from the study. No verses or personal thoughts, just direct quotes from the study.

Then came the summer of 2000 . . . God had called me on a missions trip to Turkey and then to work in St. Andrews in Scotland. The people I served with in Turkey had a profound impact on my life. They had a love for Jesus and an intimacy with Jesus that I've rarely seen since. They really *knew* Him. They knew His heart, His thoughts . . . and His personality. I loved Jesus more than I could understand, but I wanted to know Him like my team did, in that deep, intimate, unfathomable way.

Again, in God's perfect way, He provided fertile grounds on the greens of St. Andrews to grow those seeds of interest and desire that had been planted in my heart on Turkey's soil. While in Scotland, I had ample time alone and literally spent the entire rest of the summer just getting to know Jesus in a new and intimate way. For the first time ever, I opened God's Word and it made SO much sense to me! The Holy Spirit truly opened my eyes to wonderful things in God's Word and I couldn't get enough of Jesus or His Word! I had never before seen how living and very active our God is! It was a fascinating and exhilarating summer . . . one that truly changed my heart and life forever.

During that summer and upon returning to the USA, my relationship with Jesus deepened and my heart became (and continues to become) increasingly stirred by the noble theme of God's love. I have seen the Lord move in ways I could never have imagined, heard His gentle whisper in the sweetest ways, and delighted in His Word more than the choicest food (and that's saying a lot because I *love* to eat!) As a result, the e-mails have evolved, and I now share how the Lord is teaching, growing, refining, encouraging, and loving me through His Word, other people, my experiences, and in the quietness of my heart. The sheer joy and excitement of experiencing and getting to know Jesus is what has always compelled me to type. One of my greatest joys is to share with others what God has shared with me and shown me! The Lord continues to amaze me with the glorious and wonderful ways He loves me and allows me to experience Him and know Him! How humbled I am every single day!

About two and a half years ago, people on my e-mail list began mentioning the idea of getting these e-mails published. I always just chalked such responses up to encouragement. Then one day God really got my attention and said, "Let's talk about this, Jess." So, I sat down on the stairs of my apartment and told Him, "Look, I don't want to publish a book . . . I have *absolutely no* desire to travel that road." He quickly responded with, "And who do you think you are Miss Priss?" I conceded, quite reluctantly though. "Okay, Lord," I said. "You're right. This is not my ministry and I am not my own. So, whatever is *Your* good pleasure, You make it come to pass. I can't believe I'm even praying about this, but if You want these e-mails to be published, great! Wow! I will walk that road, but I'm telling You today, I'm not going to do a *single thing* to make that happen. I promise You, I will walk *whatever* road You pave, but I'm not seeking it out. And IF this is the direction You want to take these e-mails and this ministry, then Lord, please change my heart . . . grant me a desire to write because You know better than anyone that I am not a writer!" (And I'm honestly not . . . I was never the kid who wrote in a journal, I despised poetry classes, and it took me ages to write papers in college. Without the Lord, writing just isn't my thing or my gifting!)

Over the past couple of years people have sent me information on publishing, given me editors to contact, etc. I took these as "prayer reminders," committed this concept of a book to the Lord, then deleted them from my inbox, threw the information away, or left it sitting in a pile of papers I'd never go through. "Lord, I told you, I'm not pursuing this . . . I will walk *whatever* road You take me down, but I'm not about to pave it!"

In December 2003 my mom printed a year's worth of these e-mails and put them into a binder to give to her sisters for a Christmas present. Then last summer (2004) my mom's friend, Michele, was visiting and saw the binder. She asked if I had ever thought about getting published to which my mom replied, "Jessica wants whatever the Lord desires, but she isn't going to seek that out. She figures if it is the Lord's will to have them published, He will somehow make it happen."

Sure enough He did! What you're holding today is that binder of e-mails! My mom had told me Michele wanted to send them to a publisher, but in my wildest dreams I never would've imagined that someone would actually publish them! But as only God would have it, Michele did send them off and Tate Publishing did want to publish them! When my mom phoned to tell me "They want to overnight a contract to you," I was flabbergasted! "WHAT?! ARE YOU KIDDING ME?!" Could this *really* be happening??? I questioned.

Excitement and fear rose to the surface of my emotions . . . excitement that God was moving and somehow, despite the state of this broken vessel, using me. Even still fear and timidity quickly overwhelmed me. I have really struggled with being a part of this project. I feel so inadequate but then that's me looking at me and not at Jesus. . . .

Over the past several months as these e-mails have been transformed into a book, God has ever so patiently and faithfully been working on my heart, reminding me that He has not given us a spirit of fear or timidity, but a spirit of power, of love, and of sound mind. And today I woke up to the beat of a different drummer! I was *excited* to write you! GO GOD! I knew today was the day.

As you read this book, you will walk through a span of a year and a half with me . . . at the beginning I had just graduated from Texas A&M and moved to Gunnison, Colorado to live with and work for my brother, Garrett. He owned a hot dog stand on Mt. Crested Butte and we had some wonderful and hilarious times together! During my time in Colorado, I heard God's call to go serve Him in Paris, France with Young Life International. Upon my return to Texas, I went through training and raised my prayer and financial support. The journey within this book ends on the day I moved to Paris. Today I am writing you *from* Paris and as I think back over the two years since I graduated, I am *blown away* at the goodness of our God! Walking through life with Jesus sure is an adventure, isn't it?!

Well, this note has taken on a completely different spin than I intended when I began typing! Yet somehow, in the midst of sharing this story with you, God has granted me a feeling of reassurance and a sense of peace. Thank you for letting me share my heart and for taking the time to read . . . you have no idea how much that means to me! You will soon discover that I am in no way, shape, or form a biblical scholar, rather just a simple girl sharing how she is experiencing, seeing, growing in, and finding the Lord.

Friend, I am humbled . . . humbled beyond words that God would allow me the opportunity to share with you my experiences of walking with Jesus. If through these emails you are encouraged, uplifted, convicted, challenged, or blessed, PRAISE BE TO CHRIST JESUS MY LORD! Truly, He is the Author; I am merely the typist. Words could never do Him justice, therefore, I pray that the Lord will overcome my shortcomings and speak from His heart, through mine, to yours . . .

In the love and abundant grace of Jesus Christ

<>< Jessica

"I pray that out of his glorious riches he may strengthen you with power through his Spirit in your inner being, so that Christ may dwell in your hearts through faith. And I pray that you, being rooted and established in love, may have power, together with all the saints, to grasp how wide and long and high and deep is the love of Christ, and to know this love that surpasses knowledge–that you may be filled to the measure of all the fullness of God."

Ephesians 3:16–20 NIV

Father, into Your hands I commit this book. May You alone be glorified and magnified . . . I love you, Jesus. Amen.

From: Hisword2day
To: Your heart
Sent: Wednesday, December 25, 2002 7:58 PM
Subject: Lesson from the manger - Luke 2:7

" . . . she gave birth to her firstborn, a son. She wrapped him in cloths and placed him in a manger, because there was no room for them in the inn." *Luke 2:7* **NIV**

Merry Christmas!! I hope this e-mail finds you surrounded by the love of family and friends as you enjoy this wonderful day. It definitely is a day worth celebrating!

As I watched and listened to the different sights and sounds this Christmas season, I was intrigued by the details of the Christmas story and how Christ was brought into this world. Reading the account of Jesus' birth in Luke tells us that He made His grand appearance into this world in a not-so-grand style, rather quite simply, humbly, and quietly. He didn't poof Himself into a glorious position of wealth and fame, which is what the Jews were looking for—a king in Solomon style: lavishly wealthy, full of splendor and having incredible power. Nor were there brass bands or fireworks to accompany His arrival. No entourage of people or bags of gold accompanied Him. Instead, He came in a way quite unexpected: as a helpless baby. He wasn't even born in the meager comforts of a home during the time. No. Instead, He was born in a stable surrounded by dirty animals, nasty stable smells, and loud stable noises without even a bed to rest in other than a trough—the very thing that animals ate out of. His entourage consisted of the heavenly hosts, a few Magi bearing tokens of their respect, and the animals resting in the stable.

I was really struck by the details and learned another lesson from this story. Just as Jesus arrived into the world humbly and quietly, so we can expect Him to continue to make His appearance into our lives in a similar manner. He won't announce His arrival into the scenes of our lives with bells or trumpets, nor will fireworks accompany His presence. And we're not only going to find Him in the clean halls of a church, within the security of a Bible study, or in the good part of town. No, we will find him in some quite unexpected places: on the "other side of the tracks," in the slums of a city, in the face of a homeless person, and in midst of adversity. The Lord will often make His appearance when and where we least expect it and in a way we'd never have imagined. Just think of the Jews. This was the LAST way that they would've thought the Messiah would've been brought into the world, but that's how God chose for it to happen. I know that I fail to look for Him in unconventional places and in unconventional circumstances, but we serve a God that is not conventional so we need to learn to look for Him in all places, even in the stables of life. We need to learn to find Christ in simplicity.

As we approach this New Year, I encourage you to start looking for Jesus in random places—places you may not normally seek Him out. See Him in a sunset, feel Him in a breeze, experience His power in a thunderstorm, witness His love through the eyes of a stranger, see how He provides you time to spend with Him, alone, as you wait in traffic, and tap into His love, strength, joy, and grace in the midst of adversity. You can even find Him surrounded by nasty smells and loud noises in the trough of life for He is everywhere and is with you wherever you go (Joshua 1:9)!

Have a very merry Christmas and may you be blessed by the true Spirit of the season. Happy Birthday, Jesus!

In His love and grace,

<>< Jessica

Prayer requests? Praises?

From: Hisword2day
To: Your heart
Sent: Wednesday: January 01, 2003 11:53AM
Subject: God's love: the direction for your heart—
2 Thessalonians 3:5

"May the Lord direct your hearts into God's love . . ." *2 Thessalonians 3:5* **NIV**

HAPPY NEW YEAR! I hope that you had a wonderful New Year's Eve and that you enjoy this brand new year. The start of a new year always brings so much excitement and anticipation for what the Lord has in store for the upcoming year. As I looked back on 2002, I was amazed at all that had happened, where I had been, whom I had met, things I had experienced, and how the Lord grew me through all of it. I honestly was astounded because He has blessed me so richly this year! Why He has done so is beyond me, but I am so thankful that He has allowed me to experience Him in so many different ways and through so many people, you included. Thank you for letting His love shine through you and for encouraging me through your faith. You have no idea how your love for Him has spurred me on!!

As we start this year off, my prayer for you is that the Lord directs your heart in God's love. No matter what situation or circumstances you encounter throughout this year—and you can be certain that there will be some tough times—know and believe that the God of love and peace will be with you (2 Corinthians 13:11). He will arm, strengthen, guard, protect, and guide you. Let your heart be open and tender to His love for it is by this unfailing love that He will direct your path. I just pray that you would follow where He leads you because if you travel along the path of His command, you will be in for the delight of your life! I mean it will be just AWESOME. After all, He knows your heart better than you do and knows what will truly make you happy. So trust Him to fulfill your every want, need, and desire. And you can trust that the path God chooses for you is always the best, even if the terrain along that path appears a bit complex and/or rough. Remember, He will never call you to do that which He can't do through you; He will never call you to go where He hasn't gone before or wouldn't go with you (Deuteronomy 31:8); and He will never lead you down a path of destruction because the plans He has for you are plans not to harm you, but to prosper you—plans to give you hope and a future (Jeremiah 29:11). Therefore, get excited about 2003! It will be a year filled with special moments, cherished memories, an abundance of joys, many lessons, and all of the Lord's blessings. It will be a year filled with experiences with Christ! This year will not go as you probably expect, but it will go exactly how He has planned.

Please know that my prayers will be with you this year. I will pray that God will direct your heart by His love and that He will instill in you the strength, faith, and obedience to go wherever He leads and to do whatever He calls you to do whenever He needs you to do it. I will pray that you will be who He created you to be. Most importantly, remember that His Spirit will dwell within you if you have invited Him to do so and you will reap the rewards of His love as a result. So may 2003 show you His greatness and His strong hand. There is not another god in heaven or on earth who can do the deeds and mighty works He does . . . and you get to experience all this and will often be the recipient of such deeds. Wow! I look forward to hearing about what the Lord is doing in your life so please feel free to share with me whenever! Have a wonderful year living and growing in the Lord! Make 2003 the year you aim for perfection, are of one mind, live in peace, and run in the path of His command.

Praying for your perfection,

<>< Jessica

Prayer requests? Praises?

Please feel free to share with others anything that I send you! What I send you comes from the Lord's heart through mine, so if you think anyone may benefit from what the Lord has been teaching me then by all means, share away! Print, copy, forward, whatever! Also, if you know anyone who would like to receive these e-mails, then just send me their address or have them send me a little e-mail and I will be honored to add them. And, if you would like to be taken off this list, please just let me know that too! Have a terrific first day of 2003!

From: Hisword2day
To: Your heart
Sent: Monday, January 06, 2003 12:56PM
Subject: Seeking Him = better spiritual vision–Jeremiah 29:13

"You will seek me and find me when you seek me with all your heart." *Jeremiah 29:13* **NIV**

This verse has been one the Lord has used in my life in so many different ways. It always brings such comfort and joy to my heart because it reminds me that when I do seek Him, I will find Him. He says in Jeremiah 29:14, "I will be found by you," declares the Lord, "and will bring you back from captivity . . ." What music that is to my heart!

However, God really convicted me of something this weekend. Reread Jeremiah 29:13 and pay close attention to the words "when you *seek* me." Seek in this passage is a verb, which means it requires action. This reaffirms that our relationship with the Father, Son, and Holy Spirit is *interactive:* it's mutually and reciprocally active. You seek Him, you find Him—guaranteed. I know that all too often I expect to find Him without seeking Him, and sometimes we do find Him when we're not seeking Him. But if we really want to experience all that the Lord has in store for us and see all of the small (yet big) ways He's working in, through, and around our lives, then we must seek Him with all of our of heart! It is only then that we have a better chance of finding Him in everything!

Let me give you an example. One of my roommates and best friends from college, Misha, has really poor vision. In fact, one time while we were living in the dorms a friend of ours played a joke on her. Jody (the person playing the joke) was in the same room as Misha and was in plain sight; she was just pressed close to the wall. Without her glasses or contacts, Misha can only see blurs and therefore, couldn't find Jody even though she was in the same vicinity, and Misha could hear her calling out her name.

Although my roommate's eyesight is undoubtedly poor, when she puts her glasses on or contacts in, she can see perfectly. Now this doesn't mean she always sees *everything* because we can certainly miss things even when we have 20/20 vision, but all the details come to life when she has her glasses on or contacts in. See, my roommate doesn't have to put on her glasses. No one forces her to—it's her choice. She knows that if she doesn't wear her contacts then her vision will just get progressively worse and so in order to avoid that and to experience life more abundantly, she puts her glasses on or wears her contacts daily.

Well, we can apply this concept to our daily lives. No one forces us to put on our "spiritual glasses," but if we don't we can expect to have spiritual vision similar to my roommate's physical vision: limited at best. See, if we don't put on our "spiritual glasses" by seeking the Lord through prayer, time in His word, and fellowship we will miss out on all the details and our ability to see Him will get progressively harder as our spiritual vision will become more hindered. He may be right next to us calling out our name, and we can't find Him because we haven't put our "glasses" on. We do not have 20/20 vision when it comes to spiritual vision because the schemes of the devil and the darkness of this world have greatly hindered our ability to see and to feel His presence. What's even scarier is that without our "spiritual glasses" on, not only do we miss out on seeing the Lord and feeling His presence, but we also miss out on seeing Satan and feeling his presence. He too may be in our vicinity yet we won't see him and can easily fall into one of his schemes.

The Bible says that Satan "prowls around like a roaring lion looking for someone to devour" (1 Peter 5:8) and when we can't see him or recognize his deceptive ways we're much more susceptible to being pounced on. It is only by God's power and grace that we can see and experience Him and can guard ourselves against the ways of the devil. The Lord will never force us to experience Him, hence why He tells us that when we seek Him we will find Him. By spending time with Christ and getting to know Him we are then able to find Him more easily in the circumstances of our lives. We can experience Him more abundantly through everything—trials and joys! Plus, as we guard our hearts with His Spirit, we allow Him to fight our fights for us.

So don't miss out on the Lord's presence nor His work in, through, and around you, and don't miss out on Satan crouching at your door. Seek Christ with all of your heart and you will surely find Him. After all, He declares that you *will* find him, and He will bring you back from captivity. Your captivity may include a broad range of things, but as you seek Him watch and be utterly amazed at how He can free you. Take some time to put your "spiritual glasses" on and to experience the abundant life He so longs to give you. Remember that in order for this relationship with

Christ to function as it should you too must act for it is a mutually and reciprocally active relationship.

I pray that you have a marvelous and exciting day of discovering Him in the details of life. Take action—seek Him with all your heart today and you will surely find Him.

In His love and grace,

<>< Jessica

Prayer requests? Praises?

From: Hisword2day
To: Your heart
Sent: Thursday, January 16, 2003 3:28 PM
Subject: The whisper of His power–Job 26:7–14

"He spreads out the northern skies over empty space; he suspends the earth over nothing. He wraps up the waters in his clouds, yet the clouds do not burst under their weight. He covers the face of the full moon, spreading his clouds over it. He marks out the horizon on the face of the waters for a boundary between light and darkness. The pillars of the heavens quake, aghast at his rebuke. By his power he churned up the sea; by his wisdom he cut Rahab to pieces. By is breath the skies became fair; his hand pierced the gliding serpent. And these are but the outer fringe of his works; how faint a whisper we hear of him! Who then can understand the thunder of his power?" *Job 26:7–14* **NIV**

Isn't this passage just awesome?! It rocked my boat because being out in Colorado really made this verse hit home with me as I get to see so much of God's glorious beauty and so many of the works of His hands on a daily basis. I am so blessed with being able to literally see the reality of this passage in front of me every single day! Yet what I see: the majesty of the mountains, the radiance of the sun, the splendor of the moon, the glistening of the snow, the beauty of the ice covered trees and rivers, and the coolness of the mountain air are just on the "outer fringe of His works." They are but a whisper of His presence, love, and power and give us just a mere glimpse at who He is. WOW! To think that I am only getting to experience a faint *whisper* of His thundering power and yet he SURROUNDS me in every aspect . . . this just blows me away! Job was definitely correct when He wrote, "Who then can understand the thunder of his power?" for our finite minds truly can't even begin to fathom His infinite power, wisdom, and above all, His infinite, unfailing love.

Well, something I was reminded of and something I want to remind you of today is that you don't need to be in Colorado or some place with extreme beauty to be able to experience the reality of this verse. You can feel it, see it, and experience it wherever you are and in whatever circumstances you may find yourself in currently. The Lord is with you wherever you go (Joshua 1:9) and He is in everything . . . you just need to put on your "spiritual glasses" in order to see Him. So put on your "spiritual glasses" and let Him blow you away as you delve into an experience and meeting with Him that will knock your socks off! Of course, sometimes you may just need a tune-up on your attitude or perspective to be able to see Christ in your present situation. And it may take some time for you to be able to see how and why things had to happen, but you must remember that the Lord has His mighty hand in everything and everything you go through has some bigger, eternal purpose behind it. Even if you can't seem to find Him in the midst of your circumstances or where you are, just keep in mind that you are God's workmanship, created in Christ Jesus (Ephesians 2:10). Therefore, just by being you, you are getting to experience the works of His hands because the intricacies of who you are and how you function are also another example of what we can find on the "outer fringe" of His power.

Today I encourage you to pray that God would open your eyes to see Him in this world, through your circumstance, and in yourself. Then realize that the awesomeness of this experience is only a peep at what you will experience when you are with Him in heaven and get to see more than just the "outer fringe" of His works and hear the full "thunder of His power." Also, if you find yourself in a situation where you feel hopeless and helpless remember that if all that Job mentions in this passage are but a mere whisper of Him and a mere glimpse at His power then may it remind you that He can do anything . . . He can meet any need (Philippians 4:19), change any circumstance, deliver you from your fears (Psalm 34:4), and He Himself will be your peace in and through everything (Ephesians 2:14).

The earth is full of His unfailing love (Psalm 33:5) so let yourself experience it and hear the whisper of His power! May the joy of your salvation be renewed in your heart today as God Himself, the God of peace, sanctifies you through and through.

In His love and grace,

<>< Jessica

Prayer requests? Praises?

From: His Heart, Through Mine
To: Your heart
Sent: Friday, January 17, 2003 1:42 PM
Subject: Barren trees–1 Thessalonians 5:18

"give thanks in all circumstances, for this is God's will for you in Christ Jesus." *1 Thessalonians 5:18* NIV

A few days ago during my ski break I was alone on a lift just enjoying the beauty of the day. It was superb . . . deep blue skies, barely any wind, and fresh snow on the "Hill" as it's referred to here. As I went along, I just began praising the Lord for His beauty captured in the moment and for surrounding me with so many reminders of His awesome power and unfailing love. About that time I noticed the trees. The aspen lose their leaves and stand there naked throughout the winter, while the evergreens remain wrapped in their blanket of leaves. Even though the beauty of the evergreens with snow atop their branches was a captivating sight, it was the barren aspen trees that caught my attention. As I looked at them I was struck at how they stood. It seemed as though they were lifting up their hands to the heavens in praise. I just thought that was the neatest thing because I felt like I was witnessing Isaiah 55:12 come to life as I saw the mountains and hills bursting into song before me and all of the trees clapping their hands as though they were praising their Creator.

However, what God struck me with next was what sent an arrow of conviction into my heart. It sunk in that the trees were barren. They appeared as though they had nothing. They had been stripped of all their "fruit," of what makes them beautiful (their leaves), and yet they praised Him still—their arms were lifted high to the heavens even during their season of desolation.

This sight also brought 1 Thessalonians 5:18 to mind and reminded me that even in times of what I see as bleakness and barrenness I need to continue to give thanks always. When I feel as though I have nothing or have been stripped of everything, I still need to praise Him. See, we need to be like these barren trees for there is a time and a season for everything (Ecclesiastes 3:1). God has a reason for every activity under the sun, and this time of what seems to be barrenness might be necessary in order for us to experience a season of "leaves." It might be necessary so that our blessings can come into fruition. I know that I for one all too often forget that.

With that said, today if you feel as though you resemble these desolate trees, if you feel barren and bleak, then I encourage you to resemble them on another level too . . . lift your hands up in praise to your Creator. Know that the God of all grace, who has called you to His eternal glory in Christ, after you have suffered a little while, will Himself restore you and make you strong, firm, and steadfast (1 Peter 5:10). He knows the plans He has for you and those plans might involve some bleak moments, but it is only so that He can give you a hopeful future. God never promised life would be easy, but He did promise us an abundant life. And although abundance rarely comes without its trials, it is through those trials and amidst adversity that there are blessings if we are willing to discover and then accept them.

Today I encourage you to give thanks in ALL circumstances for this is God's will for you in Christ Jesus. It may just be that praising Him despite and for your circumstances is what yields an eternal perspective for you so that you may be able to face your fears and your situation. Know that He loves you passionately and furiously and everything that happens in your life will somehow reveal that love. Have a delightful day praising Him!

His,

<>< Jessica

Prayer requests? Praises?

From: Hisword2day
To: Your heart
Sent: Tuesday, January 21, 2003 10:45 PM
Subject: The moon and you–Isaiah 60:1–2

"Arise, shine, for your light has come, and the glory of the Lord rises upon you. See, darkness covers the earth and thick darkness is over the peoples, but the Lord rises upon you and his glory appears over you." *Isaiah 60:1–2* **NIV**

This past summer my brother and I were driving back to Gunnison from Crested Butte after going to the movies. The moon happened to be in its full glory that night. Its brightness and the result of its light breaking through the darkness captivated both my brother and myself. In fact, its light was shining so brightly that you could see for miles in the valley and up to the tips of the mountaintops. At one point, Garrett turned off the headlights and said, "See, the moon's so bright that you don't even need your headlights. You can still see in the dark."

Well, the last several nights here in Colorado have been very similar to that summer's eve. The moon has been radiating with splendor casting its light on us in the darkness. It's been so breathtakingly gorgeous! A fact about Ole Mr. Moon that I find to be quite interesting is his source of light. Do you know where he gets his light? The sun. The moon reflects the sun's light in order to shine light in the darkness of the world. Pretty cool if you ask me. Even more so when we apply it to ourselves because, as Christians we are the same way—we serve the same purpose the moon does: to bring light into the darkness of this world. Furthermore, our source of light is the same: the Son. This passage reminds us that the world is indeed covered in darkness. Satan has done a brilliant job of blanketing the world with his darkness, especially over the eyes of people's hearts.

That's where you come in. The Lord rises upon you and His glory appears over you; He clothes you in the brightness of His love. He radiates His light off of you so that you can be a light and bring salvation to the ends of the earth (Acts 13:47 paraphrased). Paul and Barnabas quoted that from the book of Isaiah and it still applies to us now. You truly are a light in the darkness of this world because of His light. He has placed you on your platform so that your light may shine so brightly before others that they may see your good works and come to glorify your Father in heaven.

Your light has come and the glory of the Lord rises upon you with each new day so that others may also be able to see in spite of the darkness, just as my brother and I could see in the darkness because of the moon's light. So today I pray that you don't hide from His light, but instead let the glory of the Lord that rises upon you radiate into this sin-ridden world and into the darkness of people's hearts. You are resplendent with light from Him so arise and let your light shine! You may be the only light of God some people ever encounter. Have a delightful day and may the grace of the Lord Jesus be with you, God's people.

In His light and love,

<>< Jessica

Prayer requests? Praises?

From: Hisword2day
To: Your heart
Sent: Thursday, January 23, 2003 7:48 PM
Subject: Entertaining strangers and angels–Hebrews 13:2

"Do not forget to entertain strangers, for by so doing some people have entertained angels without knowing it." *Hebrews 13:2* **NIV**

Working at the hot dog stand here in Crested Butte, I meet a lot of people with a variety of personalities from all sorts of different backgrounds. Many of our customers are regulars, but most of them are people on vacation—people I've never met before. Complete strangers. I'm a people person so this is great for me! I just love getting to interact with people on any scale! Furthermore, most of the days here consist of blue skies and fair weather. They're typically cold, but without snow or cloud coverage—it's actually quite enjoyable. And I love being outside getting to soak up the Lord's beauty. However, there are those days that seem miserable. The wind is biting and the snow is dumping. My hands are freezing and my toes are numb. My body is aching from trying to keep warm and my mouth is so cold that I can't talk properly. These are not fun days to be outside all day long, and I will have to admit that they take their toll on me, especially on my attitude. I seem to not want to deal with people on the days when the weather is bad. Unfortunately, I allow the bitter cold wind to sweep away my openness and friendliness. Oh I'm still cordial and smile, but I was very much convicted that my heart isn't really there when the weather isn't ideal. I find that I'd rather someone not come up to the stand and order something so that I don't have to get my hands cold.

I read Hebrews 13:2 a few short days after we had a big snowstorm which I had to work in and another arrow of conviction was sent straight into my heart! As I read, God was saying to me, "Jessica! Do you not realize that I have provided you an opportunity to entertain strangers every single day? Despite the weather, My Princess, you are on a mission and you never know how your smile or attitude will wear off on someone. Don't pass up an opportunity to share My love with someone because you're cold. I understand how cold you are, but look deeper than your coldness and try to see the platform I've given you. You're getting a chance to entertain angels, Jessica!!! *Angels!*"

Wow. When put in that perspective, how could my soul not be steaming with joy? He's so right too. I have an amazing opportunity to meet so many people and share Christ's love with them on a very regular basis, and so do you. You may not work with or encounter people as often as I do, but people are in your life nevertheless. For example, there's the cashier at Wal-mart or the grocery store, the person you sit next to on the bus, the person you work with, a roommate, a husband or wife, a child, your neighbor, the mailman, the person you sit next to in class or on a plane, a complete stranger you pass on the street . . . all of these and more just very well might be angels in disguise. Don't pass up an opportunity to entertain them. Now keep in mind that to entertain strangers doesn't necessarily mean throwing a big dinner party or dazzling them with gifts (although that may sometimes be how we're called to entertain people). Small acts of kindness can leave just as much of an impact on people. So smile at a stranger. Pay a compliment to your co-worker. Ask a cashier how his/her day is, and mean it. Give someone a hug with feeling behind it. Tell people how much they are loved by you. Whatever way you "entertain" people, do so with God's love. These are just a few examples of little acts of kindness that can "entertain" people's hearts and can allow Christ's resplendent light to shine through you and dazzle people with His love and grace. Although you may never encounter certain people again, Christ can still have an impact on their lives through you in the brief moment that you are with them.

Don't let the changing weather of life persuade you to miss a chance to share Christ's love. Look deeper than the surface of your situation and see if God might not be providing you a platform from which He will shine His light off of you. He may be giving hugs from heaven through you today. So remember, you are on a mission wherever you are. Therefore, as you encounter people today, tomorrow, and always, try to recognize that you are being given an amazing opportunity from the Lord to entertain strangers and by doing so, you just might be entertaining angels without knowing it. What an awesome thought! The bitter winds of life are sure to blow, but don't let them sweep away an opportunity to love on others. Have an awesome day and may you grow in peace and the knowledge of His passionate love for you!!

Fully surrendered,

<>< Jessica

Prayer requests? Praises?

From: Hisword2day
To: Your heart
Sent: Tuesday, January 28, 2003 9:04 AM
Subject: Trusting God faithfully–Daniel 6:23

" . . . And when Daniel was lifted from the den, no wound was found on him, because he had trusted in his God." *Daniel 6:23* **NIV**

I recently listened to a sermon on Daniel, and God really seemed to be speaking to my heart through His word and those of the pastor. What an amazing story of faith and deliverance Daniel has! Did Daniel have his faults and did he fail God miserably at times? Sure he did, but there's still a lot we can learn from this pillar of faith so today we're going to learn a little lesson from Daniel on what it means to trust God and to call upon His name.

As we read the story of Daniel, we learn that Daniel was an extraordinary man. He had been appointed as one of three administrators who were to oversee the 120 satraps and essentially, to maintain King Darius' kingdom. However, we are informed that Daniel was not just any person or administrator. In fact, he so distinguished himself among the other administrators and satraps by his exceptional qualities that the king planned to set him over the whole kingdom (see Daniel 6:3). Can you imagine how smoothly this went over with the other guys? Not so smoothly. Think about presidential elections. Each candidate tries to find as much muck on the other candidates as they can possibly conjure up in order to discredit them. My imagination leads me to believe this is the type of thing these guys were trying to accomplish against Daniel. However, much to their disappointment, they could find no corruption in his conduct of governmental affairs because he was trustworthy and neither negligent nor corrupt. They realized that if there was going to be any basis for charges against Daniel it was going to have to do with the law of his God. It was going to have to deal with his faith. And so they set about devising a plan to make it illegal for Daniel to worship his God. In the end they were successful, as the king was quite presumptuous and willingly obliged to a sneaky plot to make himself god for a month. How absurd! God for a month. I mean, if you're God, you're God, period. Nevertheless, King Darius issued a decree forbidding anyone to pray to any god or man other than himself for one month. (Can we say arrogant!?) And if you were found to disobey this decree, you would be thrown into the lion's den. Scary stuff.

Once again, however, Daniel proved to be an extraordinary man. Even when faced with the threat of a lion's den for praying to his God, he remained faithful. When Daniel learned about the decree, he went home to his upstairs room where the windows were open to Jerusalem and three times a day he got down on his knees and prayed, giving thanks to his God, just as he had done before (Daniel 6:10). Wow. Not only did he remain faithful, but also he did so openly. That means for all to see. And they did. As a result of his open faithfulness, he was thrown into the lion's den, just as the decree warranted. Now was Daniel doing this to make a spectacle of himself or just to go against the crowd? No. The Bible says that what he did was what he had always done. He wasn't trying to be different; he was just remaining faithful, not changing a thing.

Before I go any further, I feel I need to ask, would you? Would you continue to pray as you'd always done despite the threat of being thrown into a den of lions? Don't be quick to read on. Instead, take a moment to reflect. If you were faced with death, would you remain faithful and continue to seek and trust your God? Put yourself in Daniel's shoes. What would you do? Okay, now here's the question that really stung me when God placed this one on my heart. Let's say it wasn't even death you faced, but just some sort of persecution, maybe rejection from a friend or society, or not fitting in as well, would you remain faithful when faced with this lion's den? Be honest. My answer hurt. How about yours? Death: sure I would. At least I say that, but I've never been faced with a situation even similar to Daniel's. Persecution and rejection? Now these I have been faced with and sad to say all too often I have failed the test. I've remained quiet when an opportunity came for me to reveal my faith or to praise my God. And I've practiced my faith behind closed doors and windows for fear of being thrown in the lion's den of rejection or persecution . . . I've lacked trust. Have you?

Well, here's where we need to pay close attention. Daniel was thrown into the lion's den with a stone sealing the entrance and was left there with no protection other than his shield of faith for the entire night. Can you imagine what must have been going through Daniel's mind as he was being marched into that den of death? My goodness! But his shield proved strong. The next morning Daniel was lifted from the den and no wound was found on him. Why? Because he had trusted in his God. Not because he made a deal with God, as I so often do, but because he had wholeheartedly, faithfully, and fervently trusted Him. Psalm 91:14–15 says, "Because he loves me," says the Lord, "I will rescue him; I will protect him, for he acknowledges my name. He will call upon me, and I will answer him; I will be with him in trouble, I will deliver him and honor him." Now did Daniel experience this or what?! The Lord sealed the mouth of the lions and satiated their hunger to protect Daniel. He delivered Daniel and greatly honored him. He did all of this because Daniel loved God and because he called upon His name. He acknowledged God, openly despite his circumstances. And God was glorified through Daniel being thrown in the lion's den. As a result of Daniel surviving, King Darius issued a decree that in every part of his kingdom people must fear and reverence the God of Daniel.

Daniel was weak and helpless on his own in the lion's den, but in his weakness, God's power was perfected and magnified. Just as God was with Daniel in his lion's den, He will be in the lion's den of your life as well. Your shield of faith is much more powerful than you can imagine. I dare you to trust it. The same truth applies to you as it did to Daniel. If you love Him, He will rescue you. He will protect you when you acknowledge His name. When you call upon Him, He will answer you and He will be with you in your times of trouble. He will deliver and honor you. If you trust Him, you too can be delivered from your lion's den without a scratch on you. How encouraging is that?!

Notice, I said, "can be delivered" because I must remind you that we're not always rescued based on an earthly definition of rescue. Can God rescue you from anything? Of course He can, but He doesn't always. He *is* able to do anything. *Nothing* is too hard for Him. But you can read so many examples in the Bible or in history books in which God doesn't deliver people, in an earthly sense. Paul: God delivered him over and over again, but one time he succumbed to death. Jesus: He was left hanging on a cross crying out to His Father "My God, My God, why have you forsaken Me?!" And countless other believers in history have been subjected to death as a result of their faith. I can't tell you why. All I know is that He is sovereign and that He has a perfect reason for why He does what He does because His ways are perfect (2 Samuel 22:31). He was glorified through all of these situations. What an honor to be used to glorify His kingdom! Something else to consider is that in reality, the Lord did deliver them. It was just a heavenly deliverance rather than an earthly one. In other words, He delivered them from this world and brought them Home. Now that's true deliverance! I love my life, but I tell you what, I'd much rather be in heaven than here. I'm so anxious about what awaits me there! This world doesn't even compare to what heaven is like!

One of the things that we can learn from Daniel's story is that your faith can and will be used against you. Expect it. It may be the only way people know how to get to you. However, take Daniel's example and remain faithful in the midst of persecution. Keep those windows open and your knees bent! ☺

Another thing we can learn from Daniel's story is that when faced with trouble, we need to trust the Lord. The Lord never promised us that we would evade trouble. In fact, we might face more of it for trusting Him, but what He did promise us is that He'd be with us in trouble (Psalm 91:15). And furthermore, that He would deliver us. I can't promise you what that deliverance will entail—removal from our situation, entrance into heaven, or some other form of deliverance—but He will deliver us.

And lastly for this lesson, God doesn't deliver us because of some deal we make with Him. He doesn't rescue us because of what we can do for Him. No. He protects, rescues, and delivers us because we trust Him. Simple as that. The reason why He will do all of those things is because we love Him and acknowledge His name. Isn't His love amazing?!

Today I encourage you to put up your shield of faith. Whenever you are faced with a lion's den, remain faithful, seek His heart, and *trust Him.* Your faith in Christ can be used against you, but also remember that it always works *for* you. Have an amazing day and may you be strengthened and confirmed in His love.

Praying for your perfection,

<>< Jessica

Prayer requests? Praises?

(Sorry this was so long today! However, thanks for taking this journey with me!)

From: Hisword2day
To: Your heart
Sent: Thursday, January 30, 2003 9:05 AM
Subject: Compassion in a sunrise–Lamentations 3:19–23

"I remember my affliction and my wandering, the bitterness and the gall. I well remember them, and my soul is downcast within me. Yet this I call to mind and therefore I have hope: Because of the Lord's great love we are not consumed, for his compassions never fail. They are new every morning; great is your faithfulness." *Lamentations 3:19–23* NIV

Wow! What a great passage! I read this yesterday morning just after waking up as it was the scripture related to my devotional that day. I'm always encouraged and strengthened by this verse, but yesterday it had a neat twist to go along with it.

Just after reading these verses, I went into the kitchen to get some coffee. To walk to the kitchen from my room you pass a window that overlooks the valley below and you can see the other mountain range off in the distance. It truly is an amazing sight so I always take a peek . . . why not get a glimpse of His beauty as you start off your day, right? ☺ Well, yesterday's view was especially captivating. We had pretty gray skies so the light was really flat yet it was still really beautiful. But what was so special about yesterday was what God painted on the canvas of those mountains. I woke up early enough to see the latter part of the sunrise (crazy, I know!) and it was breathtaking! Clouds surrounded the tops of the mountains, and a faint blanket of fog covered the valley. However, there was one area that the clouds didn't touch. Instead, this area was filled with light. The mountains were brushed with a light pink glow as they reflected the sun's light. It was just a relatively small spot encircled by clouds, yet it was a captivating sight. Garrett even came to tell me to look at the sunrise. It was absolutely brilliant!

As I sat mesmerized by the beauty of this scene, this verse seemed to come to life right before my eyes. Even though I may have afflictions of sorts (we all do): I'm tired, distraught, confused, whatever might have been weighing heavy on my mind, I was delightfully reminded that His compassions are new with every morning . . . and I literally saw that in a sunrise! God called this truth to my mind and it truly did give me all kinds of hope throughout the day. He portrayed a picture to me that said, "Even though you may sometimes feel surrounded by clouds and grayness, you are not consumed, my precious child. My light will still reach you and my glow can still reflect off of you. For my compassions never fail and they are new every single morning! Look right before your eyes! I love you with an everlasting love, Jessica."

So today if you or someone you know has been going through some gray days, remember that with each new morning you're about to embark on a journey filled with love, grace, blessings, and compassion from the Lord. He may remind you of this in a sunrise, through a person, in a situation, or in some other way. Ask the Lord to help you discover His compassions. The earth is full of His unfailing love, so go on a treasure hunt today and seek His faithfulness where you might least expect it. If you will allow the Lord to consume you, then you will not be consumed by your current circumstances nor will you ever be. Invite Him into your life today. You may know Him and have a relationship with Him, but Paul reminds us that we still need to die to ourselves *daily* (1 Corinthians 15:31). Do that today and then wait in anticipation for the way that you will experience His love and grace. You are the apple of the Lord's eye so He's going to follow through on His promises and you will see His compassion with each new morning. Call to mind the truth in this passage in the midst of whatever you're going through and let it bring you hope throughout your day! Have a blessed day and pray for the eyes of your heart to be open to see His love in anything.

Seeking Him,

<>< Jessica

Prayer requests? Praises?

From: Hisword2day
To: Your heart
Sent: Tuesday, February 04, 2003 9:07AM
Subject: Submit to God—Job 22:21–22

"Submit to God and be at peace with him; in this way prosperity will come to you. Accept instruction from his mouth and lay up his words in your heart." *Job 22:21–22* **NIV**

I just think this is an awesome verse for us to keep in mind both today, and always. I encourage you to start every day with a simple prayer of submission that just lets the Lord know that you are His today . . . you are willing to go where He will call you and to do whatever He may have planned for you . . . with a joyful heart. (Plus, praying this prayer will help you to keep your focus throughout the day. It will remind you of your purpose and Who is with you always.) In this way prosperity will come to you, maybe not prosperity of this world, but prosperity of the heart, soul, mind, and body. It will be a heavenly prosperity! And what could be better?! So as you walk today's journey, accept instructions from the Lord as they come to you through His word, your experiences, and especially in the quietness of your heart and may you store up His words in your heart and treasure them more than your daily bread. Storing up His words in your heart is like having a gold mine within yourself! Have a wonderful day and enjoy being at peace with Him! ☺

In His love and grace,

<>< Jessica

Prayer requests? Praises?

From: Hisword2day
To: Your heart
Sent: Thursday, February 06, 2003 11:19 PM
Subject: Thorns and humble pie–2 Corinthians 12:7–10

"To keep me from becoming conceited because of these surpassingly great revelations, there was given me a thorn in my flesh, a messenger of Satan, to torment me. Three times I pleaded with the Lord to take it away from me. But he said to me, 'My grace is sufficient for you, for my power is made perfect in weakness.' Therefore, I will boast all the more gladly about my weaknesses, so that Christ's power may rest on me. That is why, for Christ's sake, I delight in weaknesses, in insults, in hardships, in persecutions, in difficulties. For when I am weak, then I am strong." *2 Corinthians 12:7–10* **NIV**

Have you ever wondered why you are the way you are sometimes? Why you do certain things? Or why you don't do certain things? Have you ever wondered why you had to endure something? Have you ever wondered why you are so weak at times? If you're anything like me you have wrestled with these questions over and over again. I have asked myself these questions, and many more, out of sheer frustration, and in pure shock at other times. In short, I've struggled with my own thorns—a lot. I've even pleaded with God to take them away, often times for more than just the three times that Paul did. Sometimes God has removed these thorns and other times He has not. When He has chosen to not remove the thorns though, He's sustained me with His abundant grace and taught me how to live with them and use them. I've come to see through myself that we humans have this funny way of becoming really confident in ourselves. We take great pride in how wonderful we are—when we're wonderful that is. I find that when things are going along just hunky dory and I don't see myself messing up too much (I know I goof more than I even realize!), I begin to drift away from God and am in need of a big slice of humble pie. And let me just tell you, the Lord certainly knows the perfect recipe to humble me! One main ingredient is the memory of my past sins. The gallows of the past nearly strangled me to spiritual death years ago, but God's grace mercifully saved me. I know that God has forgiven and forgotten my past, but the memory of things I've done or have not done can humble me more than anything! They put me in my rightful place . . . on my knees! Plus, the memories, as painful as they may be at times, restore the joy of my salvation because I know that I do not deserve it at all! These reminders of my shortcomings, both the old and current ones, make me cherish the relationships I have with my precious Jesus.

Some of these thorns have traveled with me, as some of your thorns may have as well. However, the Lord has brought me a long way from desperately pleading with Him to remove these thorns to being able to praise Him for my past, my habits, and my weaknesses. And if He has not done so already He can do the same for you . . . all you have to do is let Him! I'll tell you, it's been a long and bumpy road, but Jesus has used my weaknesses to A) humble me B) make my treasure my salvation and C) spread His love and grace onto others as I have so lavishly received it. It's hard to turn to Him and praise Him for what you may consider to be your thorns, but believe me once you do, you will experience how His grace is sufficient for you and how your weaknesses are simply a magnifying glass for His power. Furthermore, you will begin to be able to boast all the more gladly about your weaknesses and actually *delight* in them, in insults, in hardships, in persecutions, and in difficulties, for you will realize that when you are weak, then you are truly strong for His grace IS sufficient for you.

So now I encourage you to ask yourself what your thorn(s) are. Once you identify them, ask yourself how you have struggled with them. You may not be able to identify your thorns and that's okay—you will in due time. If you have become aware of them, have you pleaded that the Lord take them away? How? What was the Lord's answer to you? How did He respond to your plea? I know He responded, because the Bible tells us that our prayers never fall on deaf ears, so how? Did you listen? (Ouch, that one hurt when I asked myself!)

Your thorn may not be your past. It may be your present, or it may consist of what Paul mentions: weaknesses, insults, hardships, persecutions, and difficulties. Whatever your thorn(s) may be, ask the Lord to give you the Spirit of wisdom and revelation so that you may know Him better through them. Also, pray that the eyes of your heart may be enlightened in order that you may be able to know the hope to which you were called, the riches of His glorious inheritance, and His comparably great power. With this said, I am not insinuating that we are given a license to continue in our sins, habits, or weaknesses but I am pointing out that the Bible says that where sin abounds, grace abounds even more. (Romans 5:20) Now, if you have accepted Christ, you have died to sin;

therefore, how can you live in it any longer? (Romans 6:2) Surrender these thorns to Him . . . whether they are something you struggle with personally or are your circumstances (insults, persecutions, difficulties, etc.) and know that you will be traveling this road together with Jesus. Turn to the Lord and *allow* His grace to be sufficient for you.

Will you accept His gift of abounding grace today? I pray that you do! As a result, you will be able to enjoy your slice of humble pie a little more gladly for you can rest assured that Christ's power will rest in you. Just remember that your thorns *do* have a purpose. They may be God's way of guarding your heart from ever wandering too far from Him, and they always allow you to see the Lord's power in full swing as you watch Him make up for your shortcomings, weaknesses, and circumstances. How exciting! I pray that today you will let your thorns restore to you the joy of your salvation—it is definitely something worth being joyful over! Have a brilliant day abiding in His love and grace!

Praying for your perfection,

<>< Jessica

Prayer requests? Praises?

From: Hisword2day
To: Your heart
Sent: Friday, February 07, 2003 8:55
Subject: The harmony of God's grace–Ephesians 1:7–8

"In him we have redemption through his blood, the forgiveness of sins, in accordance with the riches of God's grace that he lavished on us with all wisdom and understanding." *Ephesians 1:7–8* **NIV**

Beautifully put! How reassuring it is to me to know that through Him we have been redeemed and forgiven! "To redeem" means to recover, reclaim, retrieve, repurchase, buy back, pay off restore, buy off, or ransom. Now apply that to yourself and how Jesus has redeemed you from this world and from your sins . . . how He has redeemed you from yourself and from walking straight into the arms of Satan. Pretty incredible isn't it?! Furthermore, He forgave us. This is such sweet music to my ears! There have been some things that I wouldn't have forgiven myself for if I were in Jesus' shoes . . . I've just been downright stupid at times and have defiantly ignored His commands and His love. However, the forgiveness He has bestowed upon you and me is in accordance (in harmony and agreement) with the riches of God's grace. What a blessing this is! It means He wants to redeem and forgive us . . . wow!

Now reread what Paul writes—it's important to note this. Redemption and forgiveness are lavished on us with all wisdom and understanding and in accordance with the riches of God's abounding grace. Because they are in harmony with God's grace, our redemption and forgiveness (and all our blessings for that matter!) must have a purpose. After all, God is sovereign and as Paul reminds us, He has lavished His grace on us with all wisdom and understanding . . . He knows what He's doing and why. There is a deeper meaning and an eternal purpose for the blessings He so abundantly gives. So today I pray that you will search within your heart. If you have accepted these beautiful gifts (and many more) than I encourage you to rejoice over your redemption and forgiveness. If you've not, then I pray with all of my heart that you will.

Get excited about experiencing the riches of God's grace and remember that blessings are not just things that make you smile in life . . . they are often the things that make you cry.

In His love and grace,
<>< Jessica
Prayer requests? Praises?

From: Hisword2day
To: Your heart
Sent: Monday, February 10, 2003 4:55 PM
Subject: Rising on the wings of the dawn–Psalm 139:7–10

"Where can I go from your Spirit? Where can I flee from your presence? If I go up to the heavens, you are there; if I make my bed in the depths, you are there. If I rise on the wings of the dawn, if I settle on the far side of the sea, even there your hand will guide me, your right hand will hold me fast." *Psalm 139:7–10* **NIV**

Do you ever have those days that just wear you down, but still keep you laughing because of all of the haphazard events that happen throughout the day? Well, yesterday was one of those days for me. My brother, Garrett, is on a hunting trip for the weekend, which means I was in charge of running the hot dog stand. (Me in charge? Scary thought, I know.) No problem though, right? Wrong. To begin with, we needed taco meat. Well I had cooked just enough meat Saturday night to last us for Sunday. Somehow though it was burnt to a crisp Sunday morning. I mean black, crunchy, burn-the-container burnt! My co-worker and I laughed and just decided, "Oh well, no taco meat today." Then the weather. Oh the weather! Can we say bitter cold, windy, *and* snowing . . . all at once! It was a ferocious day outside, which of course makes standing around rather miserable. No biggy though . . . I'm used to numb fingers and toes by now. Next came the kitchen work at the end of the day. It was time to make the big batch of taco meat for today which we make 30 lbs. at a time. We got it cooking and it was looking good . . . we just needed to add the spices which was my job. (Now get ready for a good laugh.) Somehow, instead of grabbing the chili seasoning, I grabbed the cayenne pepper. So instead of using half a container of chili seasoning, I poured half a container of cayenne pepper into the meat! Oops! It was some kind of SPICY! (Are you laughing as hard at me as I did?! Thought that might amuse you. Fortunately, I was able to remedy my rather large mistake this morning by mixing that rather spicy batch with a new batch of meat . . . without spices.) Then, to top the day off I got home to find water running down our drive. The water pipes had busted! There was no water at our house . . . again. (Same thing happened a month ago.) All I had wanted to do when I got home was to take a shower, do a load of laundry, grab some dinner, and hit the hay. Well, the shower idea was out, I couldn't do laundry, and it's pretty hard to cook without water, much less brush your teeth or go to the bathroom. I voted to stay at a friend's house. However, as I was leaving, I discovered that, "Oh, wonderful . . . the drive is frozen over" which makes driving downhill quite an unexpected adventure . . . and means I can't get back up to the house via car! Lovely! At that point, I was exhausted, frustrated, and hungry. And the combo of those three things hitting at the same time isn't a pretty combo with this gal!

It was also at that point that I decided it was time for some praise and worship music to accompany me on the drive to my friend's house in order to put me in the right frame of mind about the chaotic day. I knew that I needed to thank God for everything because I have learned that somehow blessings will come from everything, even a day like yesterday. His word promises us that all things work for the good of those who love Him (Romans 8:28). Plus, I knew that He was with me and taking care of me, so I just wanted to thank Him for being there and for not making me go through that fun-filled day alone. Anyway, one of the songs I listened to is by Watermark and its lyrics reminded me that He always knows where to find me. Gosh was that music to my ears . . . quite literally! ☺ It just put my heart at ease because I was so sweetly reminded of the truth in this passage of Psalm 139. He *does* know where to find me and I can't flee from His Spirit, nor His presence. He is with me always, in the darkest of times and in the best of times, during the most chaotic of days and during the quietest, most uneventful of days. His right hand is holding me fast during whatever I experience and wherever I am. Oh my heart be still! I just sat there and said "Thank You! Thank You! Thank You!"

See, the Lord knows how to tug the strings of your heart. He knows what makes your heart sing. He knows how to reach you and remind you of His love, grace, peace, presence, power, and truth. He knows you. And isn't that a wonderful comfort! Well, God knows that nature is a huge way to reach me. I can just see God and His attributes in the beauty of His handiwork. So this morning the Lord sent me a huge hug from heaven! It was a stunning morning! The trees were laced with traces of snow. The blue skies were dazzled with wispy pink and orange clouds. And the air had the delightful fragrance of a fire. This is when God drove this point home: "Jessica, here I am. I do know how to reach you so enjoy this morning! Rise on the wings of the dawn, my princess. I was with you yesterday, and I still am today. I love you, my beloved!"

I send this to you today to remind you that whatever circumstances you might find yourself in today, or tomorrow, whether they're good, bad, frustrating, calm, exciting, mundane, sinful, or holy, the Lord your God is with you. You can't flee from His presence or His Spirit no matter how hard you try or how much you feel you deserve for Him to desert you. He loves you too much. Therefore, I encourage you to rest assured that wherever you go He is with you. His hand will guide you and hold you fast. He knows your heart and He knows how to reach you. You may have to look for Him sometimes, but Jeremiah 29:13 reminds us that when we seek Him with all of our hearts, we will indeed find Him. With that, I urge you to *let* Him show you His unfailing love in all the many ways He knows how to reveal Himself and His love. He can and will find you *anywhere*. Go seek out the treasure He has in store for you today and may you rest in peace knowing that He is with you wherever you go.

In His unfailing love

<>< Jessica

Prayer requests? Praises?

From: Hisword2day
To: Your heart
Sent: Friday, February 14, 2003 11:55 AM
Subject: Living in Love–1 John 4:11–12

"Dear friends, since God so loved us, we also ought to love one another. No one has ever seen God; but if we love one another, God lives in us and his love is made complete in us." *1 John 4:11–12* **NIV**

Happy Valentine's Day! I love today's holiday because it's a day to celebrate love and all the many blessings that love brings into our lives. Today I thought this verse was rather fitting to send. God has loved us with an unfailing, passionate, furious love and since He loved us we ought to give that love to others for freely we have received this love so freely we should give it. Why bottle it up?! Pour out what the Lord has poured into you and watch in amazement at how that blesses others!

Another key point in this verse is that no one has seen God. We don't see His being, but we can see His love in SO many ways, and since God is love (1 John 4:8,16) that is how He can be seen in this world. Max Lucado once wrote "love can be known only by the actions that it prompts."* What a true statement that is! Are your actions prompted by love? If you want others to know Christ and see Him through you, then love one another for the Lord can definitely be know by the actions that He prompts. In fact, the actions prompted by love (God) in the early Christians is what attracted people to Christianity—the generosity and loving care Christians extended not just to their families and friends, but to complete strangers and to those in need. These early Christians' actions pointed straight to the love of Christ. Let your actions point straight to the love of Christ and attract people to Him. His love truly is magnetic so don't silence His quiet whisper when you feel Him nudging you to do something . . . even a small act of kindness can be a hug from heaven for someone.

Furthermore, as this verse reminds us, if we love one another (even those who we don't want to love) God lives in us and His love is made complete in us. What an awesome, awesome thought! God's love can me made complete in us. WOW! To think we're part of the equation for such a thing! AMAZING!

So dear friends on this Valentine's, I pray that since God has so loved you, you would so love others. Let the love that you have received from your heavenly Father prompt you to lavish others with love. As people are sending and receiving love and care packages, bouquets of flowers, and reminders of love, I encourage you to send packages, bouquets, and reminders of the Lord's love and grace so that His love may be completed in you. Know and rely on the love God has for you—it's unfailing! Have a very happy Valentine 's Day and remember to tell your loved ones how much you love them and how much God loves them. For as a friend recently reminded me, if today were your last day on earth you would want those three little words to be ringing in the ears of those you love.

In His love,

<>< Jessica

Prayer requests? Praises?

* Max Lucado, *A Love Worth Giving*

From: Hisword2day
To: Your heart
Sent: Monday, February 17, 2003 5:55 PM
Subject: Cuddling up to Jesus–John 13:25

"Leaning back against Jesus, he asked him, 'Lord who is it?'"
John 13:25 NIV

John is our speaker today. John and the other disciples are feasting with Jesus at what we know as the Last Supper. This is a bizarre night for them. First, Jesus washes their feet, much to their amazement. Then He begins to predict His betrayal, a concept the disciples are bewildered by. They have no clue what He is referring to. Surely not one of them would betray their beloved Jesus! How? What was there to betray? They are at a loss. Well, one of them, whom Jesus loves, is reclining next to Him (John 13:23). We know this disciple to be John and because of his proximity to Jesus and some other cultural factors, Simon Peter motions to him to ask Jesus which one of them would betray Him. Here is where we pick up: John is questioning Jesus. However, today we're not going to focus on *what* John was asking or even *why,* although both are extremely important and worth looking into. Instead, we're simply going to focus on the fact *that* he asked, and in particular, *how* he questioned his precious Jesus.

In order to better understand this passage and today's lesson, I think it's crucial to understand just how confused the disciples were at this point in time. See, Jesus was at a height in popularity. His followers were growing in numbers. The disciples were performing miracles in Jesus' name. People were lining up in the thousands simply to hear Jesus speak. All this was going on, and then to hear Jesus talk about someone betraying Him? No, it couldn't be! And anyway, how was this person, whoever he was, going to betray Him? They didn't understand Jesus' mumbo jumbo about all this "going to God's house to prepare a place" for them. He was in His prime! What must He be talking about betraying and leaving?!

Here's what gets me: in their confusion and bewilderment, they actually took the initiative to ask Jesus what He meant. Granted they didn't understand His reply, and He knew they wouldn't and didn't. But He also knew that they would in time. My question is: how many of us don't stop to ask the Lord why or what He means by something we don't understand? I know I'm a culprit. Life happens and I don't understand it, but instead of going to Jesus, I look within myself or turn to others before turning to the Lord. Now, turning to others is a blessing and I think it's a great thing to do, but we need to get something straight. Does Jesus, the author and perfector of our faith who is the Alpha and Omega, the knitter of our innermost being, and the One who knows what we need before we even ask Him . . . does He know the answers to life's questions or does Joe Schmoe? Jesus is your answer. He can use others to deliver the answers to you and to deliver comfort and encouragement to you, but ultimately He is the One with the answers. Therefore, I applaud John on his actions to simply ask Jesus when he was lost, confused, and bewildered. It's an action we should mimic more often. Just simply stop and ask. You may not understand His answer now, but in time the Holy Spirit will reveal it to you.

Now we get to my favorite part of this verse: *how* John asked Jesus. Reread it with me. "Leaning back against Jesus, he asked the Lord . . ." Leaning back against Jesus. Oh how wonderful that must have been! To recline next to Him, and then to lean against Him. Can you imagine?!

Well, my dear friend, you should because you can. The physical being of Jesus may not be here to cuddle up to, but you can certainly nestle your heart and soul into His loving embrace anytime you want or need to. When you are confused, frustrated, bewildered, lost, angered, broken, or just curious about something in your life, whether it's spiritual or personal, lean back into the arms of Jesus and ask Him. Ask the Author of life and the Giver of peace to give you discernment on certain issue. Ask Him to help you understand why something happened. Ask Him to give you comfort, strength, clarity, wisdom, and peace to get through the times you don't understand. Then when you ask, expect to get an answer . . . in due time. I must remind you that you may not understand now, and you may never until heaven, but trust that He will get you through times when you feel at a loss, spiritually, emotionally, physically, or intellectually. All you have to do is ask.

At today's banqueting table, as you're reclining next to Jesus, follow John's example: lean up against Him and ask Him all of your questions—from the silliest to the deepest and most complex. Jeremiah 33:3 tells you to call to the Lord and He will answer you and tell you great and unsearchable things you do not know. So cuddle up to Him, call out to Him, and let Him answer you. Let Him grant you the Spirit of wisdom and revelation to understand. Let Him give you peace when there comes a time you are not to understand . . . those times will come according to Acts 1:7. Whatever your circumstances, please lean on Jesus . . . He is the only person or thing worth leaning on in this life. He is your strong tower. Let Him be just that.

In His loving grace,

<>< Jessica

Prayer requests? Praises?

From: Hisword2day
To: Your heart
Sent: Tuesday, February 18, 2003 4:17 PM
Subject: Jesus' troubled spirit–John 13:21

"After he had said this, Jesus was troubled in spirit and testified, 'I tell you the truth, one of you is going to betray me.'" *John 13:21* **NIV**

I've read through this passage on the Last Supper numerous times before. However, as I read through it yesterday something else stood out to me. So today we're going to continue with our lesson in John, but we're going to look at another character—Jesus.

Reading through the gospels, the attributes generally associated with Jesus Christ are strength, wisdom, power, peace, glory, etc. We seem to gain strength from knowing He was all of these and more. And rightly so. Yet, we tend to push under the rug the idea that Jesus also experienced moments of sadness, anger, confusion, helplessness, weakness, and brokenness. We know that He did indeed experience not only power and strength, but humility and weakness for two reasons. First, Hebrews 4:15 tells us that "we do not have a high priest who is unable to sympathize with our weaknesses, but we have one who has been tempted in every way, just as we are—yet was without sin." And secondly, we can read about it over and over again in the New Testament. Jesus wept over Lazarus's death (John 11:35). On the Mount of Olives He pleaded in desperation for "this cup" to pass from Him before surrendering to the cross. (Luke 22:42) We're also told that this night He was in such anguish that "he prayed more earnestly and his sweat was like drops of blood falling to the ground" (Luke 22:44) Then on the cross, Jesus cried out "My God, my God, why have you forsaken me?" (Mark 15:34) And in the verse above (John 13:21) we read that Jesus was troubled in spirit. So yes, Jesus experienced anxieties in life. He knew what it meant to feel sorrow, anxiety, frustration, desperation, etc., and because of this He understands the curve balls that life throws at us. In fact, He warns us of these things and tells us to not be bogged down by them in Luke 21:34 because he knows from experience how easily it can be to be dragged down into the pits of despair.

So today I just wanted to send you this reminder that Jesus not only knows the joys and wonders of life, but He also knows what it feels like to be in the ditches of life too. He cannot only *sympathize* with you when you're feeling down, He can *empathize* as well. Therefore, if you're experiencing a troubled Spirit for whatever reason (or when you do) I pray that this verse will bring you strength and comfort for you do have a high priest who knows what you're going through because He Himself has been through it too. He is the Father of compassion and the God of all comfort, who comforts us in all of our troubles. Trust the Lord to keep you strong to the end and lean on Him to be your tower of strength daily! Know that you can relate to Jesus on all levels and have a marvelous day doing so!

All glory to Him,

<>< Jessica

Prayer requests? Praises?

From: Hisword2day
To: Your heart
Sent: Tuesday, February 25, 2003 8:50 AM
Subject: God's response then and now—Exodus 3:7–8

"The Lord said, 'I have indeed seen the misery of my people in Egypt. I have heard them crying out because of their slave drivers, and I am concerned about their suffering. So I have come down to rescue them from the hand of the Egyptians and to bring them up out of that land into a good and spacious land, a land flowing with milk and honey . . . '" *Exodus 3:7–8* **NIV**

I've been reading in Exodus lately and when I read through this passage, I could just almost hear the Lord saying something similar about us today. We may not be literally in chains and have slave masters over us to oppress us and treat us as ruthlessly as the Egyptians did the Israelites, however, you and I *can* be bound by different chains and can be held captive to the point of suffering. The chains we often find ourselves bound in are those of the heart and mind. We become slaves to our emotions, relationships, circumstances, habits, and various other things, which can often be like cruel slave drivers tormenting us and leaving us feeling miserable. And oh how Satan loves to put these shackles on us! Why? Because he can so easily deceive us due to the fact that we don't recognize them as "chains" holding us captive and keeping us from experiencing the freedom we have in Christ.

Let me clarify something. We're not always going to have perfect lives. We're going to run into obstacles and mishaps daily! There are lessons to be learned through all of them. What we must be ever so careful to decipher is which situations have the potential to put chains around our hearts. Many times we won't realize we're trapped until after the fact. If and when that's the case, cry out to the Lord. He will have the same compassion on you that He did the Israelites. After all, if you belong to Christ, you belong to God and this passage reminds us that He pays close attention to His people. If there's one thing I know about the Lord it is that He is passionately in love with you. What happens to you happens to Him. He doesn't like to see His children miserable so He's going to be attentive to your cry.

He can see the misery you're in and He is ever so concerned about your suffering, whatever type of suffering that may be. Furthermore, He will also come down to rescue you from your captivity. It may take some time and you'll need to trust Him and cooperate with Him—something we're not always fond of doing, but He *will* bring you out of your bondage and into the land of freedom.

Today I encourage you to trust the heart of God and to learn to lean on Him when you feel bound by the shackles of life. He doesn't like to see His people tormented by slavery and we are all too often slaves to this world and slaves to ourselves. Remember that Christ came to set you free. He was the key to unlock your chains. Now you just need to walk out of them, which is easier said than done. Believe me, I know.

Don't stay in the comfort of your chains. They really do inhibit you from experiencing the abundant life God so desperately wants you to enjoy. Trust the Lord to come down and rescue you. Let Him. He hears you crying out even when you don't hear Him responding. So today ask the Lord to give you the Spirit of wisdom and revelation so that you might be able to see what enslaves you. Then ask Him to help you become free. Oh how He loves to hear His beloved ask that! Have a superb day walking in the freedom of Christ!

Praying for your perfection,

<>< Jessica

Prayer requests? Praises?

From: Hisword2day
To: Your heart
Sent: Friday, February 28, 2003 9:26 AM
Subject: My God–Matthew 28:20

" . . . And surely I am with you always, to the very end of the age."
Matthew 28:20 **NIV**

Tuesday was a pretty rough day for me. I was informed of some rather shocking news and it definitely put a damper on my day. On top of that, my brother was out of town, which meant I had to work at the hot dog stand all by myself. Now I really don't mind doing that, it was just one more little thing to have to deal with that day. Work really is a blast! (For those of you who don't know . . . I'm in Colorado living with my brother and working at his hot dog stand on Mt. Crested Butte—yes, using that college degree). ☺ The people who work around us at the other stands are just great and are tons of fun. The traffic guys keep us laughing all day long, and there's always the radio or a CD playing. Well, that particular day the radio was set to oldies and let me tell you, they were playing some great songs! They just put my heart and mind in a lighter spirit and helped me to enjoy the day. One song in particular caught my attention: "My Girl." As I was dancing and singing along to the song, "I got sunshine on a cloudy day. When it's cold outside, I got the month of May . . . I guess you'd say, what can make me feel this way . . . my girl. Talkin' 'bout, my girl. I don't need no money, fortune, or fame. I got all the riches, baby, that one man can claim," God whispered to my heart, "Listen." And then it hit me. I tried out some different lyrics and here's what I heard God singing to my heart that day: "You've got Sonshine on a cloudy day. When it's cold outside, you're got the warmth of May. I guess you'd say, what can make you feel this way, your God, talkin' 'bout your God. You don't need no money, riches, or fame. You've got all the riches, baby, one woman can claim . . ."

What music that was to my ears that day, quite literally! See no matter what kind of day you're experiencing, or what situations you will endure Jesus is with you always, to the very end of the age. He is with you on your gloomy days and with you on your wonderful days. He can make your gloomy days much brighter and cheerier because you have Sonshine beaming down from heaven into your heart. When the cold, bitter winds of life come whipping through, you've got someone who can make your heart so much warmer. Your fortune comes from the richness of His love invested in your heart. You don't need your name written in history books. You just need it written in *His* book, which it is if you have a relationship with Jesus Christ. How encouraging is all of that?! It certainly put a new twist on my day!

When life brings you some gloomy days, remember that you have His light to brighten up your day, His warmth to kindle your heart, the riches of His love, and know that you are famous in heaven. May it bring you so much comfort and joy to know that He is with you always no matter what, even when you can't feel, hear, or see Him. Have a wonderful day in His light and love!

His,

<>< Jessica

Prayer requests? Praises?

From: Hisword2day
To: Your heart
Sent: Wednesday, March 05, 2003 5:00 PM
Subject: How to seek the Lord–Proverbs 2:1–5

"My son, if you accept my words and store up my commands within you, turning your ear to wisdom and applying your heart to understanding, and if you call out for insight and cry aloud for understanding, and if you look for it as for silver and search for it as for hidden treasure, then you will understand the fear of the Lord and find the knowledge of God." *Proverbs 2:1–5* **NIV**

Wow! What a passage! Ever wonder exactly *how* we should seek the Lord? I mean He tells us to seek Him and we will find Him, but just *how* are we to seek Him? Well, here is your answer. As I read this, it really got my attention. What I realized was that I don't store up God's commands within me. I so often don't turn my ear to wisdom nor do I apply my heart to understanding. I fail to call out for insight or to cry aloud for understanding. And then here's what really sent a zinger of conviction to my heart: I don't look for it as I would for money or silver. And I certainly don't search for it as I would for a hidden treasure. But what more of a treasure could we dream of than knowledge and understanding of the Lord?! However, I find that people get caught up in seeking money, acceptance, grades, sports, success, prestige, friends, and relationships etc. more than seeking God. What's more is that I know I'm guilty of this all too often.

How about you? Would heaven's jury find you as guilty as they find me?

If you find yourself in the same boat as me, be encouraged for the Lord is *constantly* reaching out to you. He *wants* you to seek Him. He *wants* to be found by you. He *wants* for you to know and understand Him. But He's never going to force any of that on you. You must want it and when you want it with your whole heart, then you shall have it. However, we can't simply *want to* seek, find, and know the Lord. We have to *do* it and we must desire this as much as if not more than anything else. So take today and give your heart an evaluation. You can want and seek so many things in life, just remember who should be your priority. Today I leave you with the challenge to accept God's words and to store up His commands within you, turning your ear to wisdom and applying your heart to understanding. Call out for insight and cry aloud for understanding, and look for it as for silver and search for it as for hidden treasure. Then, my brothers and sisters, you will understand the fear of the Lord and will find the knowledge of God. What a treasure hunt this will be! Have a wonderful day seeking the Lord!

In His love and grace,

<>< Jessica

Prayer requests? Praises?

From: Hisword2day
To: Your heart
Sent: Sunday, March 16, 2003 11:45 PM
Subject: Mountain-moving faith–Matthew 17:20–21

" . . . I tell you the truth, if you have faith as small as a mustard seed, you can say to this mountain, 'Move from here to there' and it will move. Nothing will be impossible for you." *Matthew 17:20–21* **NIV**

I recently read this passage for a devotional and since I'm smack dab in the middle of mountains, it brought a new reality home to my heart. Garrett and I can look out any window in our house and see mountain range after mountain range. Driving to work we come around a curve and wham! There's a majestic mountain rising up before us. We're literally surrounded by them! It's such a beautiful sight to be able to gaze upon such wonderful pieces of the Lord's creation and see the works of His hands in such splendor. As I marveled at the mountains I thought to myself, "Wow. Faith as small as a mustard seed (and that's itsy bitsy) can move one of these *enormous* mountains." Well, looking at the mountains and actually realizing their size, to be quite honest, it seems impossible. However, God's definitely shown me that He is more than capable of doing such things. After all, the mountains are the works of His hands and they belong to Him (Psalm 95:4–5) so of course He can.

Something else God helped me realize that day was that just as the earth has mountains scattered on its terrain so we have mountains scattered on the terrain of our lives: things that seem to be so huge and permanent that there's no way of getting around them, no way of moving them. And if you've traveled any road in life you have known all to well what it's like to turn a corner and wham! There's a daunting mountain looming right before you. These mountains are named Pride, Anger, Complacency, Selfishness, Self-control, Depression, Stress, Anxiety, Faithlessness, Hopelessness, Relationships, Habits and many, many other names. I know I've definitely come upon some mountains in my life! But what's encouraging and worth noting on the tablets of our hearts is that the smallest amount of faith can move these mountains. With faith and trust in the Lord *nothing* will be impossible for you. Even though this mountain you are currently facing seems to be fixed in place, faith can move it. With God's help you can do anything, and I mean *anything*. You can overcome any habit. You can survive any depression. Your hope can be restored. Your faith can be revived. Your pride can be humbled. Your anger can be controlled. Your selfishness can be turned into selflessness. And on and on.

However, I must bring out one extremely significant point that is of the utmost importance if we are to understand this passage and how it can apply to our lives. Notice the wording of the verse. The Bible says *move* not *remove*. Our mountains of weaknesses or struggles aren't always going to go away; they won't always be *removed*. What God does promise us though is that they will be *moved*—God will help us live with them. Does that mean that the Lord can't or won't remove certain mountains from our lives? No, of course not. Nothing is impossible or too hard for the Lord (Genesis 18:14). But we are so quick to think that our way of dealing with things is the best and more often than not, that's not the case. The best thing for us isn't always to remove certain circumstances from our lives. Why, we may never know, but it is not for us to know and understand what the Lord has set by His own authority. We must realize that once we accept Christ, we then have the power of the Holy Spirit (Acts 1:8) and let me tell you, that's some kind of power! With this power we'll be able to survive the trek, up, around, or through our mountains in life. And with this knowledge, we must claim and cling to that power and trust that He is sovereign and that He knows the reasoning behind what seems like such madness at times. If nothing else, these mountains, or what we consider to be our "balls and chains" should help us cling to the Lord even more because they remind us that we desperately *need* Him to fight our battles alongside us.

Today I encourage you to look outside the window of your heart and see what mountains are surrounding you. Search your heart and ask the Lord to help you see what mountains are looming in your midst. You may already be confronted with one and might be fighting what seems like a losing battle. If this happens to be you please know that I am praying for you and that you must try to believe in your heart of hearts that you are NOT fighting a losing battle. Always keep in mind that it's darkest before the dawn and that your dawn may be about to arrive. Don't lose faith, *I beg you*. The smallest amount of faith can make monumental differences in your life and heart. It can move those mountains of struggles. Whatever mountains you're faced with now or in the future inscribe the truth of this passage on your heart. Cling to your faith more than ever because it's the only thing that's going to help you move those mountains. Nothing will be impossible for you if only you have faith.

In His strength and compassion,

<>< Jessica

Prayer requests? Praises?

From: Hisword2day
To: Your heart
Sent: Sunday, March 23, 2003 6:54 PM
Subject: Complaining–Lamentations 3:39

"Why should any living man complain when punished for his sins?" *Lamentations 3:39* **NIV**

But boy do we know how to master that art! We default the blame onto God before trying to see what product this unpleasant circumstance (whether it be spiritual, emotional, physical, or mental) may be of our own choosing. We are the ones who choose to partake in sins and choose not to follow God's will. Recently I've realized that I am the queen of this! I complain way too much when it's my own fault for the situations I find myself in. I have wreaked lots of emotional and spiritual havoc in my days and I'll be the first to admit that I've tried to blame it on God. Somehow, because He's all-powerful (because He's God), it's His fault that I am where I am. Yet, if I get real honest with myself it's my own decisions, my own actions, my own choices that have put me in the circumstances I complain about or that I have a difficult time dealing with. Now granted, there are going to be some (many) situations in life that we have no direct tie to. Sometimes we're just put in situations beyond our control. However, even when this happens there's always a reason, mind you. God is most certainly sovereign and all-powerful and He knows why things happen the way they do. All too often though I find that we are ever so quick to point the finger of blame at God and ever so hesitant to hold up the mirror of reflection to ourselves. I bet if we did take a peek at the mirror of our heart and lives we'd find that many of the situations we find ourselves in, the unpleasant ones in particular . . . are ones that we put ourselves in. So before cursing God and getting angry with Him, try holding that mirror up and see if what you're complaining about or struggling with isn't a result of your decisions coupled with your actions. It may not be at all, but don't fail to see that you are to blame from time to time. I know for me, it's most of the time.

Now I might have made you feel rotten just now, but that wasn't my intention. My intention is to encourage you and spur you on into a deeper relationship with the Lord. In order to do so this is one battle you'll have to surrender. Recognize that you are at fault many a times but that even though your sins may have put you in certain situations, if you know Christ, God has forgiven them and remembers them no more. Now this doesn't mean you don't have to live with the consequences of your sins. You inevitably will. However, hold near to your heart that as high as the heavens are above the earth, so great is His love for you who fear Him and that as far as the east is from the west, so far has He removed your transgressions from you (Psalm 103:11–12). He doesn't hold your sins against you. We serve a God who doesn't know how to hold a grudge. He loves you beyond measure. He loves you no matter what you've done or been through. He loves you regardless. So delight in His love and seek His forgiveness for your past, your present, and your future. He will so graciously give it. He already has. Receive and *embrace* that forgiveness. Pray that the Lord will help you stray from willful sin and that He will help you recognize areas that you are prone to sin in. (Has that been the cry of my heart recently!) He's with you always and has never let you fight a battle alone. So if the circumstances you find yourself in are battles, and ones you've put yourself in, just remember you're not fighting this fight in vain. He's still with you. Hold up the mirror of reflection and see what lies within your heart. Then look in His heart and see how much love for you dwells within.

May the grace of the Lord Jesus Christ, and the love of God, and the fellowship of the Holy Spirit be with you all,

<>< Jessica

Prayer requests? Praises?

From: Hisword2day
To: Your heart
Sent: Wednesday, March 26, 2003 8:49 AM
Subject: God watering your heart–Hosea 6:3

"Let us acknowledge the Lord; let us press on to acknowledge him. As surely as the sun rises, he will appear; he will come to us like the winter rains, like the spring rains that water the earth." *Hosea 6:3* NIV

I found this verse to be very appropriate for our lives. Speaking from experience, I so seldom acknowledge the Lord in *all* things. I'll acknowledge Him when it's easy. Sure, of course, when life's going smoothly it's "Praise the Lord!" However, when life's storms seem to be blowing, "Praise the Lord" isn't exactly what you hear resounding from my lips or my heart. Sound familiar? It is in those times, the times when life's storms are blowing, that we must truly *press on* to acknowledge Him. We must seek to do so and strive to, as it isn't always easy to do so. Why must we? Because this verse rings true . . . as surely as the sun rises, He will appear. He will be present. He will make His presence known. Just as the rains must come to water and nourish the earth so that it can survive and plants can grow, so our lives benefit from the rainy days we encounter. Often times God has planted seeds in our hearts and it takes a storm to provide those seeds the opportunity to grow. Taking a godly perspective, we can start to look at the storms that rage in our hearts and lives as God coming to us like the winter rains, like the spring rains to water and nourish our hearts so that we can survive and grow.

As storms come and go I encourage you to press on to acknowledge the Lord. He is as constant as the rising of the sun and He will appear on every scene of your life. He comes to us as the rains . . . to water our hearts with love. One closing thought: our hearts are very similar to Texas wildflowers . . . the more rain they get in the fall and winter, the prettier and more abundant the wildflowers will be in the spring. Applying this to our lives, the more "rain" we get in certain seasons of our lives, the more beautiful and abundant our harvest will be in the upcoming season.

Have a delightful day acknowledging the Lord and being showered by His love!

In His abundant love,

<>< Jessica

Prayer requests? Praises?

P.S. We finally have internet connection at our house so I will have more time to reply to your e-mails now. ☺ Yippee!

From: Hisword2day
To: Your heart
Sent: Sunday, March 30, 2003 9:22 PM
Subject: Priceless love–Psalm 36:5–7

"Your love, O Lord, reaches to the heavens, your faithfulness to the skies. Your righteousness is like the mighty mountains, your justice like the great deep. O Lord, You preserve both man and beast. How priceless is your unfailing love! . . ." *Psalm 36:5–7 NIV*

This evening Gunnison, Colorado witnessed one of its most amazing sunsets ever!! As most of you know, I am absolutely *mesmerized* by sunsets. (And that would even be an understatement—ask my mom.) In order to get "the best seat in the house (town)," I drove to a parking lot where I could watch the sun setting over the mountains and just gazed upon the beauty of the Lord for the duration of the sunset. As I was watching, jaw gaping wide, a Third Day song came on the radio and the words of Psalm 36:5–7 were the lyrics. Talk about a passage coming to life right before your eyes! AMAZING!

I've been struggling with a lot of issues out here and it seems that my time with the Lord has been suffering as a result. Well, a few days ago I made a conscious effort to make it a point to spend some quality time with the Lord . . . *quantity* wasn't the issue here, it was *quality.* And what a blessing that has been! God has definitely allowed me to feast on the abundance of His house and to drink buckets from the river of delights He so graciously gives us! Tonight, as I sat enthralled by the unfolding sunset, it was as if God were humming this song to my heart. "Jessica, my beloved child, look at the heavens. See the expanse of them before you. My love reaches even higher and wider. My faithfulness blows the boundaries of the skies. I never fail to bring the sun to rise and set every day, do I? Neither do I fail to be faithful in your life. And look at the mountains in front of you. See em? My righteousness is that huge! Even bigger! My justice runs as deep as the oceans . . . Can't you see my love?!"

Yes, I could see it! So much so that it reminded me of how priceless His unfailing love truly is. I hope you do the same. I encourage you to look for His unfailing love in the heavens. You'll find that they truly do declare His glory! And find His faithfulness as He stretches His hand out over the skies and places all the stars in the night skies and calls them each by name. Find the majesty and grandeur of His righteousness. Feel the depths of His justice. Then relish in the fact that what you are experiencing is all an expression of His love. And that, my friends, is truly a priceless gift. Many things have a price tag attached to them. My education? Thousands of dollars. (Thanks mom and dad!) A study Bible? $60-something. A Bible study? $20-something. The wages of sin? Death. Your salvation? Christ's blood. But God's love? *Priceless*. There would never be enough money in the world to buy His love. Even if there were, God wouldn't want money. He wants love. He wants you to delight yourself in Him and as you do, He gives you your heart's desires (Psalm 37:4). Won't you give Him His?

In His unfailing love,

<>< Jessica

Prayer requests? Praises?

From: Hisword2day
To: Your heart
Sent: Friday, April 11, 2003 11:28 AM
Subject: Fear of the Lord–Deuteronomy 10:12–13

"And now, O Israel, what does the Lord your God ask of you but to fear the Lord your God, to walk in all his ways, to love him, to serve the Lord your God with all your heart and with all your soul, and to observe the Lord's commands and decrees that I am giving you today for your own good?" *Deuteronomy 10:12–13* **NIV**

A little overwhelming? At first glance, just maybe. Do you walk in *all* His ways? I'm struggling with that one. I walk in *some* of His ways. How about serving the Lord with *all* your heart and soul? Sometimes. But I often wholeheartedly serve myself over serving God. And observing the Lord's commands and decrees? Well, when it's convenient, right? Wrong! We should keep our oath even when it hurts (Psalm 15:4). So, yeah, in short, I certainly wouldn't be making a score to brag about on this test. How about you? Certainly sounds like He demands a lot. Well, before we jump to the conclusion that the Lord demands more than we can offer, let's break this down and see if we don't come to a different conclusion.

First of all, we need to clarify one very important point in this passage. What in the world does it mean to "fear the Lord?" I mean we read things like "Blessed is the man who *fears* the Lord" (Psalm 112:1), "He whose walk is upright *fears* the Lord," and "He who *fears* the Lord has a secure fortress" (Proverbs 14:2, 26). We also read, "The *fear* of the Lord is the beginning of knowledge" (Proverbs 1:7), and of course this passage: "What does the Lord your God ask of you but to *fear* Him?" (Deuteronomy 10:12). (All italics mine)

But what does fearing God mean? Well, I started my investigation by asking myself what I associated the word fear with and what its definition is. What I concluded was that fear automatically brings up thoughts of being scared, terrified, alarmed, dismayed, anticipating misfortune, something dreaded, anxiety, etc. Yet this can't be what God intended when He had the writers of the Bible pen "fear the Lord." Surely He doesn't want us to be frightened by Him and scared away. From what I know of Him, He wants us to come to Him, not run from Him in terror. Nevertheless, how many of us live in this type of fear of the Lord? I find that many times people (myself included) are scared and alarmed of God. We are dismayed and anticipating misfortune (for example, "the wrath of God") and on and on. Been there, done that, bought the t-shirt? Yeah, me too.

Well, the good news for us is that this is not generally the fear He intended for us to have towards Him. Is it understandable why we are sometimes (often) scared of Him? Sure. After all, we can read in Numbers 14:34 that it's possible to have God against us. And in Deuteronomy 6:15 we read that God can strike misfortune on us by burning His anger against us and by destroying us from the face of the land. Then there's always the example of Job who certainly had a dose of misfortune and experiencing something dreadful. His whole family and livelihood were stripped from him! Was God getting back at Job? Gosh no! God was using Job to prove a point to Satan, but God *did* allow all of that to happen. So, yeah, there's reasonable cause for people to have this type of fear towards God. However, the definition for fear most often used when referring to fearing God is one with a meaning of reverence. More often than not, and maybe every time, (I don't know because I am certainly not a Biblical scholar!) to *fear* God means to "honor God and order our lives in accordance with His will because of our *reverence* for Him."* This type of fear causes one to have a "loving reverence for God that includes submission to His lordship and to the commands of His word."* What does it mean to revere God, to show Him reverence? To revere someone or something means "to regard with the deepest respect and awe" (Webster). And reverence means "the act of revering; a bow or curtsy."

I had never thought of bowing or curtsying in correlation to reverence, but a little research helped make the relationship very clear. Bowing and curtsying have been forms of salutation for centuries. They are generally thought to be symbols of respect, courtesy, politeness, and yielding or submitting to another person. Think about the movies—especially ones set in a different era. Two people pass on the street and they bow and/or curtsy to each other as if saying "hello." You see a distinguished Englishman bow to the lady he wishes to dance with. In return, she does a curtsy which says, "Yes, I'll dance with you." By doing a curtsy she is yielding to his offer to dance. In medieval times, and throughout history, when members of the noble orders were in the presence of their lord, lady, or noble they paid homage to him or her by bowing their head and body in honor and respect. Still today, players at Wimbledon must bow or curtsy before the royal box where the Duchess usually sits.

Similarly Christians show their respect with a bow—a bowing of the knees. One of the deepest forms of honor and respect we can show the Lord is to come before Him and bow before His royal box where the Prince of Peace and King of Kings finds His resting place. When we bow our knees, we are coming into the presence of our Lord and King and taking one step closer to truly fearing the Lord. We are yielding to His invitation to dance with us.

See I don't think that these verses in Deuteronomy 10 are giving us statutes we can't live up to. I believe the point is simple: to fear the Lord. The rest of the verse clarifies *what it means* to fear the Lord and *how to fear* the Lord. It's all just different ways of saying "fear the Lord." I'm guessing that those original hearers of these words being spoken thought much like we do. "What? Fear the Lord? Are we not told, 'Do not fear for I am with you?' (Isaiah 43:5 NASB) And yet now you're telling us to fear the Lord? How do those precepts coexist?" First, the two types of fear are different. When God says, "Do not fear," He is saying, "Do not be afraid or terrified" . . . However, when He says "Fear the Lord," He means "Honor Him with reverence and respect." Second, to me, (and again I am no expert) God seems to be saying in the rest of this passage, "Here are some tips on *how* you fear Me: walk in all My ways, love Me, serve Me with all your heart and with all your soul, and finally, observe My commands and decrees that I give to you *for your own good.*"

So don't be *afraid* of God. Revere Him. Yes, acknowledge the part of God's character that can be wrathful. He certainly is capable of being that and if we fail to recognize that part of Him than we won't be honest with ourselves nor will we really know the Lord our God. However, remember that your heavenly Father is slow to anger, abounding in love, and forgiving sin (Numbers 14:18). The fact that He can be enraged (although it takes a lot) should draw us into a deeper reverence for the Lord. It should make us respect and honor Him all the more. After all, out of His great love for us He suppressed His anger and sent His only begotten Son to die a criminal's death so that we might truly live. That alone is reason enough to go into the presence of the King of Kings and bow before His royal box to pay Him homage today.

Fearing the Mighty and Awesome,

<>< Jessica

Prayer requests? Praises?

*According to the NIV Study Bible Notes

From: Hisword2day
To: Your heart
Sent: Tuesday, April 15, 2003 2:56 PM
Subject: A level path, a scenic view–Proverbs 4:25–26

"Let your eyes look straight ahead, fix your gaze directly before you. Make level paths for your feet and take only ways that are firm." *Proverbs 4:25–26* **NIV**

A couple of days ago I went for an evening jog with Drake, our lab, to enjoy the wonderful Colorado evening. It had been a warm day and the sunset was going to be spectacular so I wanted to be outside to enjoy it. I figured an evening jog would be the perfect solution. A little exercise and some awe-inspiring scenery—what could be better? So I set out on my run taking a back road and running right alongside the road in the dirt so my knees would be more comfortable. I knew that taking these back roads would provide the best view of the sun setting over the mountains and I was very excited because just as my brother chases fresh snow, I chase sunsets. ☺ However, I quickly discovered that the dirt path I was running on was unleveled which meant I was missing out on the majestic scenes surrounding me because I was absentmindedly staring down at my feet. Lovely as my shoes may be (ha ha), they pale in comparison to the beauty of a sunset in The Rockies. When I looked up and realized what I had been doing and missing out on I just thought to myself, "Jessica, look up! Run on the road for crying out loud! Don't miss this! This is too amazing!"

And that's when God whispered these words of Proverbs into my heart. "Let your eyes look straight ahead, fix your eyes directly before you. Make level paths for your feet (quite literally) and take only ways that are firm." Wow. In that instant, God reminded that as I run the race He has set before me, I often fail to take the firm path, many times for comfort's sake. I might be right *alongside* the *level* path, but instead of running *on* it I'm running on the *unleveled* path, which causes me to fixate my eyes downward, not straight ahead. As a result, I miss out on so much of life's scenery surrounding me. I miss out on seeing the marvelous works of the Lord, simply because I won't look up.

What about you? Don't be quick to answer. Ponder these questions even if just for a moment. Have you ever failed to look up? Have you ever missed out on enjoying the Lord's beauty because you had your gaze fixed downward instead of upward? Is it more comfortable for you to run on the unleveled paths in life? Have you missed out on His majesty surrounding you? I certainly have (and one too many times).

I don't want to miss out any more though. Do you? If you answered as I did, then I encourage you to ask the Lord to help you lift your eyes to the heavens and fix your eyes straight ahead. He has so much to offer you!!! Ask God to show you the level paths in life so that the eyes of your heart won't be fixated downward, but upward. God's glory was bursting forth with joy right before me on my run. Similarly, His glory is bursting forth with joy right before you in the race the Lord has marked out for you in life. I desperately don't want any of us to continue missing out because our eyes aren't looking up and straight ahead. Talk about some incredible scenery we'd be missing out on! Just as my running shoes paled in comparison to The Rockies, The Rockies pale in comparison to what God has in mind for the scenery of your life!

My dear friend, I want you to listen very closely because it may be faint, but you can hear the Lord saying, "My precious child, Look up! Run on the road for crying out loud! Don't miss this! This is too amazing!" So, look up, my brothers and sisters! Delight your hearts in the Lord and cloak yourself in His love. Make level paths for your feet and take only ways that are firm. Don't take the dusty side roads. You weren't meant to travel those. Your path is the path of the righteous, and it is level (Isaiah 26:7). Let your eyes look straight ahead and fix your gaze directly before you. Essentially, you will be fixing your eyes on the Lord because, after all, He goes *before* you (Deuteronomy 31:8). And what could be more beautiful, more intriguing, more spectacular, more awe-inspiring, more breathtaking, more marvelous, more amazing, and more captivating than the Lord your God?

May His good Spirit lead you on level ground today and always.

By grace His child and your sister,

<>< Jessica

Prayer requests? Praises?

From: Hisword2day
To: Your heart
Sent: Thursday, April 17, 2003 12:34 PM
Subject: God's museum and His presence–John 1:3

"Through him all things were made; without him nothing was made that has been made." *John 1:3* **NIV**

Ever feel like Jesus has taken a leave of absence? You come up to the Royal Box and there's a sign that says, "Be back in 5." I have certainly felt the absence of God more than once in my life. It's normal. Don't feel bad for feeling that way. I bet it would be safe to say that we've all been in those shoes before. However, no matter how we feel, it doesn't change the fact that He's always present. Whether we see, feel, or hear Him, He's there. As constant and sure as the rising and setting of the sun He is with you *always.*

This verse happened to be my verse of the day on my Palm Pilot today. And of course being in the majestic setting of the Colorado Mountains the reality of this verse hit very close to home. I stopped to ponder on this truth and was overcome with sheer joy at the splendor of His radiance shining forth in His creation. It really made me realize that although I may not feel Him with me at times, He is. If I ever need a reminder of His almighty presence, all I need to do is look out my window and there I will find vivid reminders of His invisible attributes and presence.

If you're in need of a reminder of His presence, love, power, joy, peace, loving kindness, perfection etc, look out your window. Take an evening constitutional (I just love that word!). Go for a bike ride and feel Him breathe a cool wind upon your back. Watch a couple of dogs play. Look into the eyes of a child. Or simply sit on your porch and enjoy a front row seat at the exhibition of the Artist of the Universe! His eternal power and divine nature will become manifest right before your very eyes!

As you look at the world that surrounds you I pray that the words of John will sink very deeply into your heart. Through Him *all* things were made. The birds and the trees, the sunrises and sunsets, the mountains and plains, the rivers and oceans, the breeze and the stillness, the moon and the stars . . . none of these came to be without Him. Isn't it just awesome to think that we are living amongst the works of His hands?! (We *are* the works of His hands.) And remember that the work of any artist usually reveals something about the artist him/herself. Similarly everything that God has created says something about His attributes (Romans 1:20). Only His works aren't hung on the walls of a museum. The world is His canvas; it's His museum. It's the compilation of the works of His hands. You've got a lifetime pass to walk the halls of His museum! Take advantage of enjoying it! Don't let it go to waste. Use it every single day! Every sunrise and sunset is different so you'll get a new show of watching The Artist at work on a masterpiece!

Take a moment to enjoy the simple gift of today. I pray that the beauty of the world surrounding you will help you to see and feel the splendor of His holy presence with you always.

His servant, your sister,

<>< Jessica

Prayer requests? Praises?

From: Hisword2day
To: Your heart
Sent: Wednesday, April 23, 2003 2:01 PM
Subject: More than just puppy love–Romans 5:8

"But God demonstrates his own love for us in this: While we were still sinners, Christ died for us." *Romans 5:8* **NIV**

God has recently been teaching me just how deeply, profoundly, passionately and furiously He loves us. He's been making demonstrations of His love through various situations, objects, and of course, His word. And He's really showing me this through Drake, my brother's black lab.

First, you need to understand Drake. Drake is a two-year-old lab and happens to be the most docile, mellow, laziest lab you'll ever meet! (No lie!) Generally speaking, Drake is a very well- behaved dog. He listens to you and knows what he's allowed to do and what he's not allowed to do; however, he is still a dog and *definitely* has a tendency to misbehave on occasion. Well, Drake and I went to the park the other day to go play. On this particular day he had *quite* the tendency to misbehave. He wasn't listening, at all! He ran off when I called him and then got in the water that I kept telling him not to get into. (As I was saying "no" he was dashing for it at full speed). Then he had stinky (wet dog) syndrome for the rest of the day.

He also loves to beg and IF we give him what he's desperately begging for, he doesn't appreciate it. He takes what he's told not to. He eats what is unhealthy for him (in particular "people food" because he doesn't know it's harmful to him—he just knows it tastes good). He sheds all over the place. He tears apart shoes. And boy is he LAZY! Garrett and I reprimand him, but only because we love him and don't want him to get hurt or sick. We want him to listen so that he doesn't run out into the street and get nailed by a car. We don't want him to eat certain items because they'll eventually cause him problems and might even kill him. Yet within just a few minutes of him being a "bad boy!" (I wait just long enough to let it sink in that he did something wrong), I'm wooing all over him, petting him, hugging him, kissing on him, and confessing my undying love for him. No matter how bad he's been, I can't help but love him. Sometimes I just *can't* get mad at him—as much as he deserves it and as much as I should, I can't. I'll just laugh rather than discipline him because of the predicament or mess he's made. And I *really* can't get mad or stay mad at him if he comes and snuggles up to me, rests up against me, or lays his sweet little head in my hands or lap. I melt! I've got a severe case of puppy love!

And does this not mirror us with God? To put it lightly, we don't listen, even when He's screaming at us to do, or not do something. We eat the forbidden fruit. We do things that are unhealthy for us because it feels good and we can't see any harm in it. We beg and IF we get what we've been so desperately begging for we rarely appreciate it or acknowledge that He blessed us. And wow can we be LAZY. And isn't it so like God to do what He has to get His point across—to reprimand or discipline us—then to immediately start loving on us? Not even two seconds after we're "bad" He's confessing His undying love for us. He's blessing us with every spiritual blessing and showering us with hugs and kisses from heaven. Sure He reprimands us, but only because He loves us (Hebrews 12:6). Plus, I bet there are times that He simply can't get mad at us either, no matter how much we deserve it! Can't you imagine the roar of God's laughter at the predicaments and messes we get ourselves into?! And do you even know how much you make God's heart melt? You are the apple of His eye so when you snuggle up to Him, recline next to Him, or put your sweet head in His hands, He simply melts, so much so that He'd send His Son to die on the cross even while you're "misbehaving." I'd say His love for us is a bit more than just "puppy love," wouldn't you?

Before I close, I want you to note when, where, why, and how He loves you. Not when you're perfect. Not after you've reached the point of repentance. Not because you've got so much to offer Him. No. He loves you when you're sinning, where you are in your life, repented or not, rich or poor, healthy or sick, faithful or not, young or old, because you are His beloved child, the apple of His eye. And how does He love you? By sending Christ to die on the cross *while you were still sinning.* Engrave this on the tablets of your heart . . . He doesn't love us because we're sin*less.* He loves us despite the fact that we're sin*ful.*

Don't reject that love either. This is something that we're prone to doing. My friend sent me an e-mail in which he told me that he was reminded that he is too much like his dog, Chopper, who nips and growls when he's being shown love and affection. Why? Chopper doesn't want to be moved from his comfortable position or he doesn't realize he's being showered with love. Just as Chopper doesn't like to be moved from his comfortable position or doesn't realize he's being showered with love, we often don't want to be moved or we don't realize that our Master is about to bless us with love and affection and so we squirm away or "nip" at God. Let's try not to be like Chopper. Rather, let's embrace God's love by remembering how His love was demonstrated to us. Know that He can't help but love you and that *nothing* can separate you from the love of Christ. Nothing. Not even "misbehaving." It was while you were "misbehaving" that He demonstrated the depths of His love for you.

I hope and pray that this Easter reminded you of the truth and depth of His love, and that you may come to know it, experience it, and rely on it.

In His love and grace,

<>< Jessica

Prayer requests? Praises?

From: Hisword2day
To: Your heart
Sent: Monday, April 28, 2003 2:41 AM
Subject: Only by prayer–Mark 9:29

" . . . This kind can come out only by prayer." *Mark 9:29* **NIV**

Jesus arrives on the scene to find the teachers of the law arguing with His disciples. A man had brought his demon-possessed son to the disciples to heal him, and yet they could not. They'd previously driven demons out from others, but this one they simply could not. Jesus, of course being Jesus and all, did so with ease. He commanded the spirit to leave the boy and never to return again and "The spirit shrieked, convulsed him violently and came out" (Mark 9:26). The bewildered disciples asked, "Why couldn't we drive it out?" (Mark 9:28) Jesus' response: "This kind can come out only by prayer." (Mark 9:29) Notes in my study Bible tell me "The disciples apparently had taken for granted the power given to them or had come to believe that it was inherent in them. Lack of prayer indicated they had forgotten that their power over demonic spirits was from Jesus."

Friends, I want you to recognize something. We take for granted one of the main powers Christ has given us—prayer. Tell me if you don't agree. We are much like the disciples and think *we* can fix problems or situations. We think we can drive out "demons." (We'll discuss what I mean by "demons" later.) Our human instinct tells us we must *do* something. We can't just sit there, we must actively take charge. Don't you agree? *Why is it that more often then not our first instinct is to rush out and do something about a situation before really praying about it? Why is it we spend more time worrying or talking about a situation or trying to change it than we do praying about it?* Maybe because we don't trust God enough. Maybe because we haven't realized the truth behind what Jesus said to the disciples: Certain things can *only* be accomplished by prayer. Certain things can only be accomplished by Me (my paraphrase).

We face all kinds of demons. They come in many shapes and sizes and disguises. Just what do I mean by "demons"? Things that seem to possess you. Things that plague you and send your heart and spirit into "convulsions." We may not see the same kind of demons that the Bible refers to, but that's not to say that they don't still exist. We tend to experience demons in a more deceptive way. Unforgiveness. Disbelief.

Anxiety. Addictions. Depression. Anorexia. A series of stressful days. Bad habits. Negative attitudes. Worry. Stress. Uncontrolled anger. Sin. These, and many, many more, are very normal, common things, which we do not think of as demons and which is why they can be so harmful and hard to deal with. We tend to think we can handle them, we're supposed to handle them and being humans, we set out to handle them— often times, before ever praying about them. Yes, many of the things I mentioned are medical conditions. However my point is not at all to criticize these conditions or circumstances or those who struggle with them—I've struggled with several of them myself! I simply wanted to state that these are forms of what demons might look like today.

Speaking from experience and from what I've gathered from listening to others who have dealt with some of these issues, these struggles are like dealing with demons. It is as though one or more of these issues truly does seem to possess them at times. They can't control them or their feelings, hate dealing with them, and wish they could get rid of them. The issues plague them. We all have at least one "demon," whether we know what it is or not. We all struggle. Sometimes there are things we can physically do for someone or ourselves. Many times God calls us to *do* something. Yet we must *never* forget that the power we have to *do* something comes from God alone. Apart from Him we can do nothing. (John 15:5) And prayer is a vital way to stay connected to the Lord so that when He calls you to *do* something you *can* and *will* know what to do. That "something" might be only to pray for the person or situation.

I say "only" as in that's the "only" task He's given you, not to diminish the power of praying. I've often heard people say, and have said myself, "I wish there was something I could say or do, but the least I can do is pray for _____." What?! The *least* we can do?! It's the *most* we can do! It may seem small and insignificant, but the most powerful and important thing we could ever do for someone, or for ourselves, is pray! Prayer releases the power of the Holy Spirit and allows the Holy Spirit to intercede for us (Romans 8:26). It willingly allows God to go to work. Not only that but reread what Jesus said in Mark 9:29. "This kind can come out only by prayer." Certain things can only be accomplished through prayer.

It seems like a "sure, sounds good" scenario, but I can testify to it. I've experienced the reality of what Jesus was telling His disciples that day. I struggled with forgiving two particular people in my life for several years. I just couldn't quit holding a grudge against them, they'd hurt me so badly. I realized that I hadn't truly forgiven them because whenever someone would mention either of these people I couldn't resist the opportunity to say something crass and talk about how they'd hurt me. Feelings of anger welled up within me—not the footprints that forgiveness leaves. Then I happened to read something that sent an arrow of conviction to the bull's eye of my heart. It talked about how to forgive people. And it started with praying for them. Not *about* them, but *for* them. Praying that God would bless them and that God would extend His love and grace to them that day. Talk about absurd! Praying for blessings for people I sincerely wanted cursed?! I didn't want to do it, and I wasn't sure that I was ready to do it, but I knew I was called to do it as a Christian. These feelings had driven a wedge in my relationship with Christ and to get rid of that I was willing to do *anything*. Plus, it wasn't setting a good example for Christ when I was spitting out rude comments about someone simply because they'd hurt me. I can't imagine what Christ has the right to complain about with me and look what He did?! I needed to treat these two with the same love with which He treats me—the same love Christ extends to them. And you know what? It honestly worked. I can't really explain how, but it worked. Christ did it. Not me. I prayed. He changed my heart.

Furthermore, I struggled with an eating disorder, not terribly severe, but bad enough. I didn't realize I was even struggling with one until a doctor gave me a sharp wake up call, which also made me realize that as I was doing this to my body, I was destroying God's temple. I didn't want to do that anymore, but I didn't know how to escape because I didn't know how I got to where I was or why I was even captured by this disorder. There was absolutely nothing anybody else could *do* for me. There was really nothing I could *do* for myself. But they could pray. I could pray. I couldn't really change the way I thought. My vanity had gotten the best of me. Plus, habits are hard to break and my eating patterns had become just that: a habit.

So I began to pray. Hard. Specifically. Through scripture. My prayer every single day was "Lord, help me to see that I am fearfully and wonderfully made. I am the work of Your mighty awesome hands. And Lord, let me not strive to put up this facade the world wants to see. Let me be who, and look like whom YOU created me to be and look like. My desire is that people would see the beauty of You inside of me, not what beauty may possibly exist in my flesh." After three months of fervently praying about this, I was able to gradually walk away from those chains. I still have to pray that prayer, but I'm no longer captured by this struggle and *it's all because of prayer.* I *did* nothing. Christ did everything. Prayer was the only useful weapon I had in this "Jessi Freedom War." It was the atomic bomb to this demon in my life.

Prayer is the most vital weapon we have against the enemy. The prince of this world can strip us of every single ability we have to *do* something against him and about a situation, but as a friend recently reminded me, he can't stop us from praying. Sure Satan can do things that *could* drive us from praying by putting us under extreme trials and tribulations, but he can't stop us from doing so. He can't disconnect the communication lines between us and God. Only we can. And in these D-Day type battles we face, communication lines are everything so keep them open and functioning! Prayer is such an important part of our relationship with Christ. It strengthens that relationship between us and Jesus. Satan wants nothing more than to ruin that relationship or the one we can have with Him. Don't let him win! Don't let him interfere or you'll be missing out on something! See prayer is not only our way of communicating directly to the Lord; it's His way of communicating to us. Let Him whisper of how He delights in you. Let Him tell you the battle plans. Let Him tell you He loves you.

Pray hard. Pray specifically. Pray through scripture. Pray powerfully. Pray alone. Pray together. Pray aloud. Pray silently. Simply put, PRAY! And by doing so I hope you begin to grasp what Jesus told the disciples. Certain things can only be accomplished by prayer. No, not "Prayer can only accomplish certain things." Prayer is more powerful than that. Christ is more powerful than that. After all, is anything too hard for the Lord (Genesis 18:14)? You're talking to the One who can do anything and through whom you can do all things so prayer can accomplish much more than just certain things. Go ahead. Drop prayer bombs on someone else's demon. Drop prayer bombs on your own. Then watch as prayer accomplishes more than you could ever dream of! Begin to grasp the power of your prayers!

Have a wonderful day and may it be filled with prayer!

Prayerfully yours,

<>< Jessica

Praises? Prayer requests?

P.S. I did not at all touch on all the aspects of prayer and how significant it is to your relationship with Christ! I merely touched on this particular aspect of prayer and how God spoke to me through this verse.

From: Hisword2day
To: Your heart
Sent: Tuesday, April 29, 2003 1:27 PM
Subject: As you help by your prayers–2 Corinthians 1:10–11

"He has delivered us from such a deadly peril, and he will deliver us. On him we have set our hope that he will continue to deliver us, as you help us by your prayers. Then many will give thanks on our behalf for the gracious favor granted us in answer to the prayers of many." *2 Corinthians 1:10–11* **NIV**

Yesterday I wrote to you about what I call the "Mark 9:29 principle": certain things can only be accomplished by prayer. Well, I think that our dear brother Paul understood what Jesus was talking about. He didn't believe that only certain things could be accomplished through prayer, through Christ. Nope. He knew and had experienced that there are some things *only* prayer can accomplish, only Christ can do. He reiterates Jesus' point through his writings, which are riddled with references to prayer. He talks about his prayers for fellow believers, the prayers of many that have helped and blessed him, and he continuously stresses that we should pray for each other. All of which strongly suggest that he believed in the significance, power, and importance of prayer. Furthermore, I believe there is a remarkable lesson we can learn from Paul, which he portrays in these verses.

What strikes me so much about this passage is what Paul writes about how he was delivered from his perils of which "he felt were so life-threatening that he regarded his survival and recovery as tantamount to being raised from the dead."* He of course gives full credit to the Lord, but he recognizes the crucial part that prayer played in his past and would play in his future deliverance. He knew that prayer would sometimes be the only weapon to fight certain battles and the only way people would be able to help him in dire circumstances. And he wholeheartedly relied on those prayers. "He has delivered us from such a deadly peril, and He will deliver us. On Him we have set our hope that He will continue to deliver us, as you help us by your prayers." He knew prayer had a vital role in this battle. It was his "secret" weapon or reinforcement, critical for his survival.

Well, lately I've been getting a lesson in the significance, power, and importance of prayer. Two people who I love dearly and am very close to are struggling with two of the "demons" that I mentioned in yesterday's e-mail. Oh how I wish I could *do* something to help them! I wish I could snap my fingers and make their struggles go away. Yet my efforts have been shot down and have made me realize that praying for them is the *only* thing I can *do* for either situation.

One person has rejected my help, won't let me help. Not only that, but my love has been rejected as well. I was feeling very disheartened by this experience when I received a phone call from a very dear friend of mine who reminded me that simply because someone won't let me help doesn't mean I can't. She told me about a situation that she was experiencing similar to mine and said, "Jess, they can reject my love, my help, my words, and my efforts, but they can't stop me from praying for them. I can always pray for them." And that is so very, very true! You may not be able to do something for someone either because it's beyond your ability to do so or because they won't let you, but you still can. You can still intercede for them through prayer, which in reality is the most you could ever do for them anyway!

The other person is going through something that I simply cannot do anything about. It is a battle within and one that can only be fought by this person and God. Although I cannot help fight this battle for this person, I can help provide ammo for the fight. How? Simple: prayer. Our prayers for others help more than we ever will realize! We're asking the Maker of heaven and earth, the Lord of Lords and King of Kings to intercede on their behalf and fight their battles for them! Talk about some serious reinforcements for the battle! WOW!

Prayer is so crucial. It's paramount to anything we could ever *do* for people. Our efforts pale in comparison to those of the Lord! With that said, I encourage you to pray for someone else today. Someone you know who's going through something or simply someone who is on your mind today. You never know when your simple prayers may be the very keys needed to unlock someone else's chains and deliver them from their "deadly perils."

Just as you don't forget to pray for others, don't forget to ask people to pray for you. Do you ask people to pray for you? Specifically and honestly? I know I don't. I give a "church" prayer request for consistency, faithfulness, obedience, etc. And not that those aren't valid requests and we don't need to pray about those things—we most certainly do and they are awesome things to ask people to pray for! But don't let that be all if there's more you need others to pray for. I am often so hesitant to ask people to pray for the war waging within me or for certain situations. Maybe I'm shameful or prideful and don't want others to know I'm struggling with something. That makes me realize that maybe I don't truly comprehend just how vital prayers are and how incredibly powerful they are. However, I know I need to let people know how they can pray for me specifically and honestly. After all, there are certain things that only prayer can accomplish.

Can you relate? Do you not want to "burden" people with your requests? Or are you afraid to ask people to pray for you? Well, you're not alone. We've all been there if not now, at one time or another. However, something we need to realize is that it is a complete *honor* to be able to pray for people. For someone to come to you and ask you to pray for them is truly nothing but an honor! Think about it. When you ask someone to pray for you or someone you know, you are asking him/her to go before the Lord Almighty on your behalf. You're giving that person an excuse to go talk to the King of Kings! Wow . . . wow! And that's the same mentality we should maintain when we are asked to pray for others. We're being given an excuse to go into the presence of our heavenly Father! Let's stop half-heartedly saying, "Of course I'll pray for you." Let's quit half-heartedly signing our e-mails with "You're in my prayers." Mean it. Pray, even if it's just the very moment they ask. The Lord will continue to deliver others from whatever their circumstances may be *as you help them by your prayers.* Don't underestimate the power of your prayers. They just might be someone's secret weapon or reinforcements, critical for the battle or skirmish they are fighting.

Know in your heart that your prayers will be answered, maybe not exactly as you prayed, but they will never go unanswered. Somehow, some way God answers every request made known to Him. And when your prayers are answered, then many will give thanks for the gracious favor granted in answer to your prayers. How simply awesome! Help someone today. Pray for him/her. Have a terrific day and may the grace and peace of the Lord rest in your hearts and minds!

Prayerfully yours,

<>< Jessica

Prayer requests? Praises?

*According to the NIV Study Bible Notes

From: Hisword2day
To: Your heart
Sent: Thursday, May 01, 2003 10:27 AM
Subject: Your backbone of faith–2 Corinthians 1:24

" . . . because it is by faith you stand firm." *2 Corinthians 1:24* **NIV**

Ever realized just how important your backbone is? How vital it is to your being? How crucial it is for you to be able to physically do anything? It's the support system for your entire body. You injure it and you could be paralyzed for life, partially or completely. Your backbone provides the solid support you need in order to stand firm. Without it you do not stand at all.

Well, your faith is tantamount in importance to your relationship with the Lord just as the backbone is to the body. It is by grace, through faith that you can have salvation (Ephesians 2:8) believing in the death and resurrection of Jesus Christ. It is by faith that you persevere (read the hall of faith in Hebrews 11 and see if you don't agree!). It is through faith that you have fullness of joy. It is by faith that you pray. It is by faith that you understand that God is the Creator of this world and your life. It is by faith that you please God. (Hebrews 11:3, 6). By faith you hear God's small whispers and have the obedience to follow His footsteps. It is by faith that you attain the righteousness that comes from God (Philippians 3:9). The life you now live in the body you live by faith in the Son of God who loved you and gave Himself for you (Galatians 2.20).

Simply put by Paul, it is by faith that you stand firm. Life will deal you a lot of shaky times causing the Richter scale of your life to go off the charts! That is why it is so important that you cling to your faith and cling to your relationship with the Lord. For it is by faith and faith alone, that you will be able to withstand the fierce earthquakes of life. Without faith life will knock you down in an instant.

Never forget from whom your faith comes. Remember how vital your faith is to your life. It is crucial for you to be able to do anything. Apart from Him you can do nothing. (John 15:5) Injure your faith and you could paralyze your heart. Fortunately we serve a God who can help us overcome our paralysis! (Isn't He just wonderful?!) I hope and pray that we will realize that our backbone of faith provides the solid support we need in order to stand firm and continue our walk with the Lord. Without it we do not stand at all. (Isaiah 7:9)

Start living out your faith. Start living in your faith. Start letting your faith be your backbone. Having troubles with faith? Ask the Lord to help you overcome your unbelief. It's biblical! ☺ (Mark 9:24) Remember that by an amount of faith as small as a mustard seed you can move mountains. Simply amazing! I encourage you to stand firm in your faith and may you be strengthened and confirmed in it as you do!

In His love and grace,

<>< Jessica

Prayer requests? Praises?

From: Hisword2day
To: Your heart
Sent: Friday, May 09, 2003 11:13 AM
Subject: Our daily bread–Exodus 16:4

" . . . I will rain down bread from heaven for you. The people are to go out each day and gather enough for that day. In this way I will test them and see whether they will follow my instructions."
Exodus 16:4 **NIV**

The journey of the Israelites from Egypt into the Promised Land is quite a fascinating trip filled with so many details and lessons for us to learn from! Today we will look at one of these details and the principles that correlate with it. I'm constantly amazed at how the Lord can teach us a lesson today from an event that took place thousands of years ago. What an awesome God we serve!

When the Israelites left Egypt they were totally dependent on God for everything: food, clothing, housing, protection, direction, and water. You name it and it was God's job of providing. This left the people with the job of trusting—something they failed at time and time again (and an example of which we will see in today's scripture). The Israelites had been grumbling against Moses and Aaron about food, saying that if they'd stayed in Egypt under the cruel bonds of Egyptian slavery, they would be eating meat and all the food they wanted (Exodus 16:2–3). A portion of God's response to their grumbling is our verse today. I find it interesting that God very clearly states that the people were only to gather what was needed for that day, not to store up for the next day. Only on the sixth day were they to gather enough for two days. Moses relayed this message from the Lord instructing the people to not keep any extra for the next day, but to only take what was needed for that day (Exodus 16:19).

Think about what that means and implies. Like God says, it was a way to test them and see if they would follow His instructions—in other words, to see if they would trust Him enough to provide. God knew it would require a lot of trust and faith on their part to believe that He would remain faithful and true to His promise and His people, even though He always had. Telling His people to gather enough for just the day implied that God would provide for the next day and indeed He did.

Nonetheless, some of the Israelites paid no attention to Moses and kept part of the manna (the food God provided daily) until the morning. Do you know what happened to that extra food . . . the food they were told not to keep? It was full of maggots and began to smell. NASTY! Apparently, manna has a severely short "shelf life." And apparently the Israelites had very limited faith in their God.

You've probably heard the old saying, "Don't put all your eggs into one basket!" Our culture tells us to always have a back-up plan, to never put all of our trust and faith into one thing. Something could always happen and we need to be prepared, just in case. Well, it appears that some of the Israelites lived by this very same principle. They took more manna than God told them to. They weren't about to put all of their eggs into one basket! But why not? After all God had done for them, after all the miracles and acts of faithfulness they'd seen Him perform why wouldn't they put all of their eggs into one basket? We could talk about all kinds of reasons. They were in the wilderness, a desert where food wasn't readily available . . . and they were alone. However, to put it simply and concisely the real reason was a lack of trust. They didn't trust the Lord to provide what He promised He would. God said He'd give them their daily bread and that He did.

Neither do we trust God to meet our needs for today. Many of us complain to God about the discomfort of walking through what seems like a desert in trusting Him and would rather live in the comfortable bonds of slavery (sin/our past). We'd rather stay in bonds to feast on trivial, momentary pleasures than to walk through a desert to get to freedom and true abundance. Many of us don't trust God to do what He's promised or to continue doing what He's been doing as we travel this journey through life. We lack trust. We don't have complete faith that He will provide for us *today* and, therefore, we don't throw all of our eggs into His basket. He *will* meet our needs for today. Today may mean this very day for you, as it did for the Israelites. However, I believe that "today" can also apply to a particular season in your life. And you can and should trust God to provide for you today . . . this very day and/or for this season.

God told the Israelites He'd rain down bread from heaven for them . . . well not only did He keep His promise then, but He keeps that promise today. What do I mean by that? God has given us our daily bread—Jesus. He is the "bread of life" (John 6:35,48). He is the "true bread from heaven" (John 6:32). He is the "living bread that came down from heaven" (John 6:51). God has rained down "living bread" from heaven and has met all of our needs in Christ. And He will continue to do so . . . if only we will trust Him. We must learn to trust Him on a day-to-day basis before we can trust Him on a week-to-week, month-to-month, year-to-year basis. Jesus nailed it when He said, "Give us this day, our daily bread." He seems to be saying, "Meet our needs *today,* Father. Give us what we need *today.* Tomorrow You will continue to provide because You are faithful and are not slack concerning Your promises, so today Lord, meet our needs."

Will you pass the test and listen to His instructions? Will you trust Him to give you your daily bread? I hope and pray that you will. Live by the manna principle . . . trust Him with today. Don't worry about next week, be content with being provided for today. Let Him meet your needs today and then trust Him to continue to meet your needs tomorrow. He knows what you need before you even ask (Matthew 6:8) so trust Him to provide. Do your part . . . trust . . . and He'll do His part . . . provide. The Lord does not change (Malachi 3:6). He will not go back on His word to provide for you. Whatever it is He needs to provide for you may not be what you want, but He will always meet your needs. Wholeheartedly trust Him to open up the floodgates of heaven and to pour down blessing upon blessing . . . to rain down bread from heaven. Remember He did it for the Israelites, He has in Christ . . . and He will rain down whatever "bread" it is that you need today. Put all of your eggs into the basket of trusting Him. You don't need a back-up plan with the Lord.

May He lead you in His unfailing love. Have a blessed day!

His servant, your sister,

<>< Jessica

Prayer requests? Praises?

From: Hisword2day
To: Your heart
Sent: Monday, May 19, 2003
Subject: By Way of the Wilderness–Exodus 13:17–18

"When Pharaoh let the people go, God did not lead them by way of the land of the Philistines, although that was nearer; for God thought, 'If the people face war, they may change their minds and return to Egypt.' So God led the people by the roundabout way of the wilderness toward the Red Sea . . ." *Exodus 13:17–18* **NRSV**

When the Lord was leading the Israelites out of Egypt He led them through a barren land. What's more is that He did so intentionally. As this passage tells us the Lord led the people by the roundabout way, a very indirect route, the Way of the Wilderness. The Way of the Wilderness is the name of a road, like County Road 48 for example, and the Way of the Land of the Philistines is another name of a road, like I-45. Had they taken the Way of the Land of the Philistines they would have reached their destination, the Promised Land, in oh 2–3 weeks. However, taking the roundabout Way of the Wilderness led them on a 40-year trek through barren wilderness, a land of deserts and rifts, of drought and darkness where no one travels and no one lives (Jeremiah 2:6). Definitely not a place I would choose to travel through. Yet, God chose the desert road over the highway for them. Furthermore, God continues to employ this road today.

What do I mean by that? Well, God takes us on some journeys through the desert. He takes us via a roundabout way . . . by Way of the Wilderness. Have you ever found yourself in one of life's deserts? Ever felt like you were in a barren, dry, isolated, and lonely point in your life? Like your life was full of rifts and darkness? I'll be honest with you. I've been there. I've traveled through several deserts in my life. Some of these journeys have seemed to last for an eternity, others for a day or two, but all of them have taught me some invaluable lessons. What I find that I so often complain about during these times is the fact that I'm in a desert. I am very much like the Israelites . . . complaining about where I am, my life's condition, and how long it's taking. What I fail to remember is that God's loving hand is guiding it all.

God has a reason for every activity under the sun, even walking across the desert. It just may be that the reason we're going through a desert is so that God can take us from slavery to freedom, as He was doing with the Israelites. He was taking them out of bondage to the Egyptians to freedom in a land flowing with milk and honey. Similarly, God may be taking us out of bondage to something (sin, relationships, work, friendships, ourselves, school, illness, etc.) to a land of blessings. However, we may not get to this land of blessings on the direct route. We may need to travel the indirect route . . . the Way of the Wilderness, the desert.

Yet even the deserts of life have their blessings. I recently listened to a sermon about the Israelites experience in the desert that reminded me of this. The pastor relayed to us that when we're all alone in these barren, isolated "deserts" we're getting to spend some quality one-on-one time with God. We're getting a chance to learn to love God for God and not for His blessings. Yeah, let's reread that. We're getting a chance to learn to love God for God and not for His blessings. Ever catch yourself loving the Lord for how He blesses you and not for Who He is? I've been caught red-handed and can attest from experience that the desert will help you break that habit. When you become like the Israelites and are stripped of your comforts, feel as though you have no blessings in your life (although you always do and sometimes just can't recognize them), and must rely on God for virtually everything then you learn to love God for Who He is and not just for how He blesses you. What a priceless gift. Why? Because you will travel many deserts in your life and being able to experience the Lord's love amidst those bleak times will provide you with so much strength and endurance and will allow you to experience abundant life when abundance can't be found.

Furthermore, the reason the Israelites had to travel the Way of the Wilderness is because God was looking out for them. He was always thinking in their best interest. A little look into history tells us that the Way of the Land of the Philistines was inhabited by some fierce warriors. Had the Israelites traveled this route they would have inevitably encountered some brutal attacks and as this verse tells us, they wouldn't have endured, nor was it likely they would have survived. So yes, God took them on a roundabout way, but for a very good reason. God knew that they didn't know how to fight. Even though they went out armed for battle (Exodus 13:18), they didn't know the first thing about warfare. They'd been slaves for generations. Plus, God knew that an encounter with war would encourage the Israelites to return to Egypt and the bondage of slavery. The last thing God wants for His people is to be in chains! So out of His great love for them, He led them on the Way of the Wilderness. He took them through a desert. And out of His great love for you He will sometimes lead you through a desert as well. The last thing He wants for you is for you to be in chains. He knows what you can handle and it might just be that what seems like the most direct route would entail too much for you to handle so He spares you from that warfare. It may take a bit longer, but at least you'll make it to the land flowing with milk and honey rather than returning to your chains. So yes, God will take you on some roundabout ways, but He's always got a reason, in fact He's probably got several! One of those reasons is because God is looking out for you. He is always thinking in your best interest.

As I close today, I want to remind you that God will intentionally lead you into some deserts in your life. Be prepared. Does He do so to punish you? Heavens no! He does so to *bless* you. He may be trying to lead you out of some sort of slavery to get to the "promised land" in your life. He may be trying to teach you about Himself and the only way He can do so is to isolate you so you'll be almost forced to get to know Him. Although you're never forced, you'll always have a choice. By taking you through a desert there aren't as many distractions so maybe your choices will be a bit clearer, maybe the Lord will be more visible to you. He also might be leading you through this desert for your own protection, for your own good. I don't know and you may not know, but God knows why He's put you where you are so trust Him. As you travel through your life's deserts, remember that just as He was always present with the Israelites He will always be present with you. Seek the blessings to be found in the desert and remember His unfailing love for you!

In His love and grace,

<>< Jessica

Prayer requests? Praises?

From: Hisword2day
To: Your heart
Sent: Friday, May 30, 2003 6:15 AM
Subject: My prayer for you–Colossians 1:9

"For this reason, since the day we heard about you, we have not stopped praying for you and asking God to fill you with the knowledge of his will through all spiritual wisdom and understanding." *Colossians 1:9* **NIV**

I just wanted you to know that my prayer for you this weekend is that the Lord would fill you with the knowledge of His will through all spiritual wisdom and understanding . . . may you be filled with a spirit of wisdom and revelation so that you might know Him better. What an incredible witness you will be for the Lord as you come to know Him better and become filled ever so consistently with the knowledge of His will! He's blessing you today. Get ready for it! Have a wonderful weekend and enjoy being filled with the mind and heart of Christ . . . how simply amazing it is to know that He has chosen *us* to be His witnesses and children! Wow!

In His unfailing love and abundant grace,

<>< Jessica

Prayer requests? Praises?

From: Hisword2day
To: Your heart
Sent: Thursday, June 05, 2003 11:20 AM
Subject: Glimpses of His greatness–Deuteronomy 3:24

"O Sovereign Lord, you have begun to show to your servant your greatness and your strong hand. For what god is there in heaven or on earth who can do the deeds and mighty works you do?" *Deuteronomy 3:24* **NIV**

This verse hit a special place in my heart yesterday evening. The reality of this verse just amazed me! My mom and I were driving back from San Antonio and I caught a few fleeting looks at the sunset. The sky was not painted with vibrant colors, nor was it dazzled with radiant beams of light. Yet its simple beauty captured the attention of my heart. As I gazed at this glimpse of God's radiant glory, I was reminded that the Lord truly has merely *begun* to show us, His servants, His greatness and strong hand. For what god is there in heaven or on earth who could create such a masterpiece that our God does?!

What really strikes me in this verse is the word "begun." Notice that this passage doesn't read "The Lord has shown His servant His greatness . . ." Rather it reads that He has *begun* to show us His greatness and strong hand. He has only just started! All the miracles, reminders of grace, touches of love, sights of beauty, and moments of strength that we have seen and experienced are merely but a glimpse of His glory, greatness, power, and strength! Wow! To think that the Lord is in progress and only at the very beginning! He will be showing us His greatness for the rest of our lives with the grand finale being in heaven. There we will not just *begin to see* His greatness and strong hand. We will *see* them . . . we will see the Lord in the fullness of His glory! Gives us something to look forward to, doesn't it?

As I close, I pray that the Lord would give you a spirit of wisdom and understanding so that you might know Him better. Look around you and gaze at the glimpse you're getting of your God. Remember though that this is only but a fleeting look, a preview. There's SO much more to come and He desperately wants to share Himself with you! Get ready for an awesome spectacle of the Lord's greatness and power! For truly, what god is there in heaven or on earth who can do the deeds and mighty works your God does? *Your* God. He's personal and intimate with *you.* My glimpse was a sunset. What's yours today?

May your heart rejoice as the Lord shows you more of who He is.

In His everlasting love,

<>< Jessica

Prayer requests? Praises?

From: Hisword2day
To: Your heart
Sent: Wednesday, June 11, 2003 10:04 PM
Subject: Update from TX!

Hello friends!

Long time no write! I do apologize for that! Life has been busy as all get out! I wanted to send y'all a little update on me and what's coming up for me in the near future.

First of all, I moved back to Texas. I said my good-byes and left the wonderful state of Colorado, although hopefully not for good. My last few weeks were well spent on the rivers, camping and hiking in Utah, running along the mountain paths, reading, and delighting in God's beauty surrounding me. Garrett and I enjoyed not working and truly took advantage of the rest and relaxation spare time allows!

Being back in Texas has been nice . . . hot, extremely hot, but wonderful seeing friends and family again. (I really did go through a little shock adjusting to the weather!) Since being home, I've spent some time with friends back in College Station, visited my family in Mississippi, started working again at the salon I worked at in high school, and watched one of my best friends get married. (Aw!)

However, the most exciting news as of yet is what the near future seems to be holding. I wrote to you from Colorado to tell you that I was praying about an opportunity to serve the Lord with Young Life in Paris, France. After much prayer and many encouragements from heaven, I have felt that this is indeed the next step in my journey. So if it continues to be the Lord's will, I will soon be moving to Paris for 2–3 years where I will be working with youth in an international school sharing Christ's love with them. There are many details to be worked out and much more that I want to share with you so I will be writing you in the near future to give you more details. I ask that you please be praying for me during this time as I will need to be diligent and faithful in my time and walk with the Lord. And I ask that you be praying for my team members and the kids we will be working with in Paris . . . that the Lord be preparing their hearts and blessing their lives. Thank you, thank you, thank you!

So, in a very small nutshell that's what's been going on with me. I hope and pray that the Lord has been most gracious to you and your family and friends! We have so much to be thankful for! Have a wonderful day delighting in His love!

In His abundant love,

<>< Jessica

From: Hisword2day
To: Your heart
Sent: Wednesday, June 11, 2003 12:44 PM
Subject: Surviving life's fires–Daniel 3:26–27

"Nebuchadnezzar then approached the opening of the blazing furnace and shouted, 'Shadrach, Meshach and Abednego, servants of the Most High God, come out! Come here!' So Shadrach, Meshach and Abednego came out of the fire, and the satraps, prefects, governors and royal advisers crowded around them. They saw that the fire had not harmed their bodies, nor was a hair of their heads singed; their robes were not scorched, and there was no smell of fire on them." *Daniel 3:26–27* **NIV**

What a testimony Shadrach, Meshach, and Abednego are to us! Knowing that their faithfulness to the Lord was a one-way ticket into a fiery furnace, they still refused to abide by the king's decree to worship a golden image. They remained faithful and, as a result, walked out of that fiery furnace unscathed even though Nebuchadnezzar had ordered the fire to be heated seven times hotter than usual. (Ouch! That's hot!) It's amazing to me that although these three guys were surrounded by blazing hot flames, they were not burned. Shadrach, Meshach, and Abednego came out of the fire, but they didn't just survive it, they walked away *unharmed*—without even a hair of their heads singed!

Although they walked away unscathed, I'll bet you anything that they didn't walk away unaffected. They had met God in that fire. They experienced His power and His faithfulness. They not only believed that the Lord could rescue them, they witnessed Him doing it. They learned a lot about the Lord their God that day in the fire.

Similarly, we will be thrown into fires as well. They might not be literal, but the reality of life's flames can be all too real and just as harmful. Yet I believe that we can learn a lesson from our three friends. We can be surrounded by flames and not be burned. Although God might not save us from being thrown into life's fires, He will meet us in there. He can sustain us amidst the blazing flames and as a wise pastor once said, "You *can* go through the fires of life and not get scorched."

If you seem to be in a fiery furnace right now I pray that the story of Shadrach, Meshach, and Abednego will encourage you. God didn't spare our three amigos from experiencing the furnace, but He met them in there and spared their lives and He'll do the same for you. When you find that flames of desperation, helplessness, confusion, fear, and/or pain are leaping all around you, know that when you walk through the fire, you will not be burned; the flames will not set you ablaze (Isaiah 43:2). The Lord your God is right beside you and can sustain you through this fire.

Just as fire refines silver and tests gold so He may be refining or testing you. You may walk away from your fires refined, tested, and/or unscathed, but *never* unaffected. You will learn a lot about the Lord your God in your fiery furnaces. You will meet God in your fires. You will experience His power and His faithfulness. And I pray that you will witness Him rescuing you. Remain faithful even when facing the blazing heat of one of life's fires.

In His love and grace,

<>< Jessica

Prayer requests? Praises?

From: Hisword2day
To: Your heart
Sent: Thursday, June 12, 2003 6:36 AM
Subject: Overflowing with thankfulness–Colossians 2:6–7

"So then, just as you received Christ Jesus as Lord, continue to live in him, rooted and built up in him, strengthened in the faith as you were taught, and overflowing with thankfulness." *Colossians 2:6–7* **NIV**

What a great verse to live by every day! Continue to live in Him and abide in His love. Be rooted and built up in Christ, strengthened in the faith and overflowing with thankfulness.

Overflowing with thankfulness. Does that phrase linger in anyone else's mind as much as it does mine? That really struck something in my heart. Not only did it provide some great guidelines, it convicted me immensely!

When I picture something overflowing I see it bubbling over with excess. Take a glass of water for example. When it's overflowing, it's gushing water over the edge, flooding over; it's filled to capacity and then spread beyond its limits (Webster). Let's take this picture of overflowing and apply it to the vessels of our hearts and thankfulness.

Does it resemble your heart?

How can you tell? Listen to yourself. Matthew 12:34 says that out of the overflow of the heart the mouth speaks. Simply listening to yourself is one way to help you determine if your heart is overflowing with thankfulness. Do you hear more praises and thanksgiving or more grumbling and complaining? (Really think on this.) After listening to myself, I'd have to say that this picture of overflowing by no means mirrors my heart when it comes to thankfulness! On certain days it does, but on a regular basis I'd have to say that it's more like I'm overflowing with thank*less*ness even though I have every reason to be overflowing with thank*ful*ness! All of us have abundant reasons to be thankful each and every day! Sometimes we don't recognize those reasons, but if you're living and breathing, you've got more than enough reasons! After all, God has opened up the floodgates of heaven and poured down so many blessings that we don't know how to handle them all!

So today I encourage you to continue to live in Christ. Be rooted and built up in Him, strengthened in the faith, and then, it is my belief that you can't help but be overflowing with thankfulness. The Lord your God loves you so passionately and so intimately. He longs to be gracious to you. He rises to show you compassion every single day.

By His grace,

<>< Jessica

Prayer requests? Praises?

From: Hisword2day
To: Your heart
Sent: Friday, June 13, 2003 5:55 AM
Subject: God's masterpiece–Isaiah 64:8

"Yet, O LORD , you are our Father. We are the clay, you are the potter; we are all the work of your hand." *Isaiah 64:8* **NIV**

Ever watched pottery being made, made it yourself, or been in a handmade pottery shop? If you have you'll recall that no two pieces of pottery are exactly the same. Sure there are similar pieces with similar shapes, sizes, and functions, but they are never identical. Each piece is a unique masterpiece of the potter.

You too are a masterpiece. With God as your potter, you are one of His unique, priceless masterpieces. There is no one in the entire world just like you and there never will be either. Sure, there are people in the world who might be similar to you . . . similar in shape, size, etc. And there might even be people who have some of the same talents and/or spiritual gifts as you, but there is *no one* identical to who you are and *no one* whose purposes are identical to the purposes you serve in your life. There is no understudy for you. You and only you can accomplish what God has planned in advance for you to do.

I know I sometimes struggle with being me, but when I step back and realize that I am God's workmanship, created in His image, I am humbled and put back in my place. Who am I to criticize the Lord's work? After all *He* is the potter and *I* am the clay, not the other way around. I may not see myself as a masterpiece and you might not see yourself as one, but it doesn't change the fact that we are. So be encouraged: you are the wonderful work of the Lord's hands, created in Christ Jesus to do good works. After all, we are who we are by His grace and His grace to us is not without effect (1 Corinthians 15:10). Therefore, there's a reason you are the way you are, look the way you do, and have the personality and qualities that you have. As a result, you will make an impact in your life for the Lord. You matter more than you can realize. Simply put, you are fearfully and wonderfully made. You are a wonderful work of His hands and He is constantly molding you into His image.

You are a masterpiece.

Fearfully and wonderfully made by my Potter,
<>< Jessica
Prayer requests? Praises?

From: Hisword2day
To: Your heart
Sent: Wednesday, June 18, 2003 6:46 AM
Subject: Heaven's work ethic–Colossians 3:23–24

"Whatever you do, work at it with all your heart, as working for the Lord, not for men, since you know that you will receive an inheritance from the Lord as a reward. It is the Lord Christ you are serving." *Colossians 3:23–24* **NIV**

Does this sound like a work ethic to anyone else? Heaven's work ethic for earth: whatever you do work at it with all your heart, as working for the Lord, not for men. But there's an incentive for us to do so. We have an inheritance awaiting us. How cool is that?! So today I just wanted to encourage you to work at whatever it is that you're doing with all your heart. Remember that in all that you do you are serving the Lord. Whether that's a job, a homework assignment, serving in ministry, dealing with a difficult circumstance, or walking through those refining fires, you are serving Christ. You're not serving a boss, a parent, a professor, or yourself . . . although you might be temporarily, you're not eternally. Isn't that wonderful to know?! So don't get discouraged by how futile, monotonous, or hopeless your job, school, relationship, or circumstances might seem. Take heart in knowing your work and striving have eternal implications and rewards—rewards in heaven.

For whether you realize it or not you are working to receive something far greater than you could ever dream of attaining this side of eternity. You are working to receive an inheritance from the Lord. Can you just *imagine* what that must entail?! When I try to fathom what an inheritance from the Lord might look like my mind runs wild with ideas! How amazing it will be! Definitely makes me want to work at even my most difficult, trying situations with all of my heart so that I may be a little more worthy to receive that reward.

As I close I just want to encourage and challenge you to take up this work ethic today. Work at *whatever* it is that you're working at not for this world, society's approval, parents' approval, or personal gain, but for the Lord, for you know that your work will be rewarded with an inheritance from the Lord. You are serving the Lord today and eternal rewards are awaiting you.

Grace be to you,
<>< Jessica
Prayer requests? Praises?

From: Hisword2day
To: Your heart
Sent: Thursday, June 19, 2003 12:28 PM
Subject: What's in your hands? Exodus 4:2

"Then the Lord said to him, 'What is that in your hand?' 'A staff,' he replied." *Exodus 4:2* **NIV**

If we take a brief look at the scenario here we find that God is asking Moses to go back to Egypt, assemble the elders of Israel, and with the elders go talk to the king about letting the Israelites take a three-day journey into the desert to offer sacrifices to the Lord (Exodus 3:18). God was calling Moses to go into a territory he felt extremely uncomfortable going back into and Moses was therefore, a little hesitant, nervous, and might have been even scared. So he asks the Lord, "What if they do not believe me or listen to me and say, 'The Lord did not appear to you'?" God's response is our verse for the day. "What is that in your hand?" A simple staff is all Moses had, but with God's touch it was no ordinary staff! God instructed Moses to throw the staff on the ground and immediately it turned into a snake. He went to pick up the snake, upon God's instruction, and *voilà!* It was a staff again. Not only was this staff the original transformer, it could part an entire body of water! Something that seemed so ordinary was actually quite extraordinary when used for God!

As I ponder this situation with Moses, I am reminded that we will face similar situations. God will call us to do something far beyond our means or to go into territories which make us feel extremely awkward and uncomfortable, or even scared and nervous. We will hesitate because we may feel inadequately equipped for the task at hand. That's when God asks us this very same question, "What is that in your hand?" (What is it that you have to offer me?) For Moses it was an ordinary staff. For the boy on the shoreline of the Sea of Galilee it was five small barley loaves and two small fish. For you it might be your personality. It might be a skill or ability you have—typing, language, building, cutting hair, studying, writing, running, biking, fishing, kayaking, speaking, etc. Or it could be your resources—opening up your home to others, providing transportation to others with your car, meeting the needs of others, etc.

However, much like Andrew at the feeding of the 5,000, we ask, "But how far will such a small amount go among so many people?" We feel that we must come to God and offer Him so much, but really He expects us to come with so little. After all, He did create us and therefore He knows what we have and so that's what He asks of us—what we have in our hands. You may feel like what you have to offer is so insignificant, so small, and so ordinary. You may ask yourself, _What can really been done with what I have?_ However, you must remember that whatever you have is not insignificant to the Lord, otherwise, he wouldn't have given it to you. Furthermore, when used for the Lord, whatever you have can be used to do quite extraordinary things! God specializes in turning the ordinary into the extraordinary! Don't believe me? Then let the past encourage you: twelve baskets of leftovers are how far the little boy's five loaves of barley and two fish went. The waters were parted and Israelites were freed when Moses used what was in his hands.

Now just imagine what God can do with what is in your hands!

Fighting the good fight,

<>< Jessica

Prayer requests? Praises?

From: Hisword2day
To: Your heart
Sent: Tuesday, July 01, 2003 8:02 AM
Subject: The Beatitudes–Matthew 5:3–10

"Blessed are the poor in spirit, for theirs is the kingdom of heaven. Blessed are those who mourn, for they will be comforted. Blessed are the meek, for they will inherit the earth. Blessed are those who hunger and thirst for righteousness, for they will be filled. Blessed are the merciful, for they will be shown mercy. Blessed are the pure in heart, for they will see God. Blessed are the peacemakers, for they will be called sons of God. Blessed are those who are persecuted because of righteousness, for theirs is the kingdom of heaven." *Matthew 5:3–10* **NIV**

I'm reading a wonderful book by Philip Yancey, *The Jesus I Never Knew**, and in it he discusses the Beatitudes, a part of the Sermon on the Mount that has perplexed mankind since it was preached. What did Jesus mean and how, living in this world, are we to live by its precepts? Are we really blessed for being poor, persecuted etc?

Yancey poignantly reminds his readers that, "In a life characterized by poverty, mourning, meekness, a hunger for righteousness, mercy, purity, peacemaking, and persecution, Jesus Himself embodied the Beatitudes." With that and many of Yancey's other thoughts in mind, I went back through the Sermon on the Mount and discovered that Yancey was right: Jesus wasn't telling us to live up to impossible standards, rather Jesus was telling us "what God is like" and how God sees this world. Looking at the Beatitudes alone we will discover Jesus wasn't merely preaching to us; He was giving us His viewpoint on life. For the Beatitudes would truly become a reality in His life.

And Jesus truly feels *blessed* to have experienced His life! The Greek word for blessed in this particular passage is, as Yancey states, more like a short cry of joy, "Oh, you lucky person!" Now picture Jesus doing the same thing in response to His life, in response to the cross, "Oh how lucky I am!" Can you imagine?! Wow. This thought baffled me because I live a much, much, much more comfortable, less persecuted life than Jesus led. Oh but when hard times come I can honestly say that you won't see me leaping for joy shouting, "How lucky I am!" I don't *feel* blessed. And yet I know in my heart of hearts that I am.

I've realized that blessings from God aren't always immediate. However, if blessings are not to be found here on earth, they surely are to be found in heaven. ("Rejoice and be exceedingly glad, for great is your reward in *heaven.*" Matthew 5:12 NKJV emphasis mine) And oh what a joy it will be to receive them when we get there! It is my belief that Jesus was trying to convey that very point to us. I bet Jesus didn't always *feel* blessed for what He was experiencing. Yet He knew that He was. He knew as in He had experienced it. After all, He's been on the other side of eternity. He came from heaven to earth so He knows what is meant by "great is your reward in heaven." He's seen and is *testifying* to what awaits the blessed. Because He had much to endure, He was reminding Himself of what awaited Him.

Today I encourage you to reread the Beatitudes. Reread the entire Sermon on the Mount! Read it with the perspective that Jesus is speaking from experience and giving us His point of view. He's talking about His own life as much as He is ours and speaking to Himself maybe just as much as He's speaking to us. I often say things to others that I myself need to hear. This might be the case here. Jesus was preaching to the multitude, all the while reminding Himself that He too was blessed—that the rewards in Heaven, His rewards, were well worth the discomforts of His life in this world.

Jesus speaks of what He has seen and heard (John 3:32). Will you let His testimony give you strength and hope? Will you believe Him?

Truly blessed,

<>< Jessica

Prayer requests? Praises?

*Philip Yancey, *The Jesus I Never Knew*

From: Hisword2day
To: Your heart
Sent: Thursday, July 03, 2003 7:53 AM
Subject: Dependence Day–John 15:5

" . . . apart from me you can do nothing." *John 15:5* NIV

Tomorrow is a great day of celebration in the US of A, in fact it's the greatest secular holiday in the U.S. Flags will line the streets of small-town America everywhere, parades will be held, patriotic songs will be sung, and phrases like "God bless America!" will be seen on billboards, signs, and banners. It's Independence Day. A holiday whose name is self-explanatory: we celebrate this nation's independence.

As I'm surrounded by reminders of tomorrow's holiday, I'm also reminded of my pastor's words from Sunday's sermon, "Independence Day can be dangerous because it can blind us." I couldn't agree more. Don't get me wrong, I'm so proud to be an American! I will wave my flag tomorrow. I'll sing "God Bless America" and will probably wear something red, white, or blue. I do not at all disagree with this holiday. I celebrate it! We just need to be careful not to celebrate it too much. Celebrating a nation's independent status should not carry over into our personal lives. However, because this world so cherishes and applauds independence and the "independent person," it is quite easy to become blinded to the dependence we need to have on God in our daily lives. We are very much taught to be independent, especially in this culture. However, Christ teaches a different sermon. He teaches dependence. " . . . apart from me you can do nothing."

And let me remind you if you have accepted Christ into your heart and have given your life to Him then you have accepted Jesus' words. You have done just the opposite of what the Second Continental Congress did. Rather than signing a "declaration of *independence*," you have put your heart's John Hancock on a "declaration of *dependence*." How simply wonderful it is if you've done that! How blessed you are and will be *for eternity!* Indeed, how lucky you are!

So tomorrow, as this nation celebrates the anniversary of its proclamation of independence, may you also celebrate your proclamation of dependence on the Lord, not as a nation, but as an individual, as a Christian. If you've not yet made that proclamation of dependence on the Lord then may it be Independence Day on the calendar, but Dependence Day in your heart.

Happy 4th!

In and through Him,

<>< Jessica

Prayer requests? Praises?

From: Hisword2day
To: Your heart
Sent: Monday, July 07, 2003 2:41 PM
Subject: Jess in Oregon

Hi there!

I just wanted to send you a little note to let you know where I am and what I'm doing. I'm currently in Portland, Oregon and will be for the next three weeks for New Staff Training for Young Life! (my training for Paris) Yippee! God has been doing a lot, needless to say, in order for me to be here. SO I want to thank all of you for your continued prayers for me and this ministry! Also, I wanted to let you know that I may be out of contact for the next few weeks. I have limited access to the Internet and little free time so there's no telling when I'll get to e-mail. If you write I promise I'm not ignoring you! I just might not have received it yet!

Despite this, please write, because I'd love to hear from you and I will write you back when I have a chance! If I don't get to send any scripture e-mails out during this time, they will again resume when I return. However, I hope to be able to write . . . it's such an outlet and blessing for me! I need to! But if I can't type, my journal will be scribbled with ink so you'll be able to read about what God's been teaching me at some point or another. ☺

I also have a huge favor to ask of you. I need your prayers . . . no, I *really* need your prayers. I'm going through a lot of tough things right now—feelings of inadequacy, doubt, being overwhelmed, and just realizing that my relationship with Christ is in some desperate need of reconstructive surgery! Just please pray for me. Pray that my heart would be open to what I will be learning here and what the Lord wants to teach me through the training, through my experiences, and through my time with Him. Please pray that I would take my inadequacies to Him and realize that He's the adequate one and always will be. Pray that I wouldn't be overwhelmed by the task at hand, but would be overcome by His love, grace, and peace. And pray that as I walk into these refining fires that I would take heart as I meet Him in there. Thank you so much. You have no idea how much your prayers mean to me!

Anyway, just wanted to send you a quick note to let you know how things are progressing and where I am and to ask for your prayers. Thanks again! I hope and pray all is well with you!!!

In His abundant love,

<>< Jessica

Prayer requests? Praises?

From: Hisword2day
To: Your heart
Sent: Monday, August 04, 2003 6:39 PM
Subject: But by His grace–1 Corinthians 15:9–10

"For I am the least of the apostles and do not even deserve to be called an apostle, because I persecuted the church of God. But by the grace of God I am what I am, and his grace to me was not without effect . . ." *1 Corinthians 15:9–10* **NIV**

Have you ever struggled with God's calling on your life—with finding out what it is? Or have you struggled with whether what you think is God's calling *really* is? Do you ever feel inadequate for a particular task in your life (a job, parenthood, marriage, friendship, etc.)? Do you ever question why the Lord has you where you are or why you are the way you are? Do you ever question your past? Can you relate to Paul here: I do not even deserve . . . ?

I would have to answer a big fat "YES!" to all of these questions. In fact, these were the feelings and questions swirling around in my heart before I left for Young Life training, which is why this passage became my theme verse! I repeated it to myself time and time and time again, for although I am not an apostle, my heart very much mimics the cry of Paul's heart. I know that I deserve to be the least of Jesus' disciples. I don't even deserve to be called "His!" I mean if we could only count the nails I've hammered into the cross! Yikes! In knowing that though, I cling to Paul's next statement. *But by the grace of God, I am what I am and His grace to me was not without effect.* Oh what sweet music that is to my soul!

Friends, I want you to let this verse resonate in your heart. The Lord is going to use you as you are, for what you are, where you are, and where you've been to make quite an effect! By His grace, you are what you are and because of that He's going to make such an impact on this world through you! He's made you just the way you are for a *very* specific reason. Remember, there's no understudy for you! So that might mean that by His grace you're a student, parent, son or daughter, sibling, grandparent, lawyer, doctor, teacher, preacher, volunteer, secretary, janitor, salesperson, office worker, a leader or a follower, passive or assertive, extroverted or introverted, organized or unorganized, talker or listener, writer or reader. See God knit you together in your mother's womb and organized your DNA in such a way that you could be who and what you are. Therefore, *by His grace* you have certain likes and dislikes. Delight in them! *By His grace* you have certain strengths and weaknesses. Recognize them! *By His grace* you have certain passions. Pursue them! *By His grace* you have a certain past and have certain experiences. Be thankful for them. No aspect of your life is insignificant; the Lord can use *every* aspect of your life to have an effect on this world. Paul, who persecuted the church, can be your example!

With that said I feel as though I must share with you something the Holy Spirit has definitely been teaching me. Though by His grace I am what I am I must *allow* His grace to have an effect. His word promises that it will, but will we let it have the full measure of effect that God intends? I've found that in order for this to happen, we must surrender who and what we are and what we've experienced to Him and then allow Him to use these things rather than begrudge Him or hide them from Him. For me that means I must surrender my inadequacies and unworthiness. I must lay them at the foot of the cross and let Him equip me. Furthermore, I must surrender my past sins. I need to let myself accept His forgiveness and then let Him use my past sins to help me reach out to others in the name of Christ. By His amazing grace the Lord will use my inadequacies and sins to make such a strong impact for His kingdom and He'll use yours too! Indeed, His grace through you and me will have powerful effects in this world!

So I encourage you to remember that you are God's workmanship, created in Christ Jesus to do good works, which God prepared in advance for you to do. God's totally equipped you for the job of being you. However, you have the choice to accept the position. You can accept who God made you to be and how He knit you together and use it to glorify and magnify His name, or you can choose to resent yourself, and resent Him for making you as you are and thus not let His grace to you be used to the fullest. Which will you choose to do?

I hope and pray you will be who God created you to be, not who He created your best friend to be. For by the grace of God you are what you are and His grace to *you* is not without effect. Let God use you! Surrender areas of your life you've been clinging to and let His grace go to work! I think we'll all discover that the surrendered life is the most fulfilled, affected, and effective life, for barriers are broken down and you're free to run in the path of His commands!

By His grace given me,
<>< Jessica
Prayer requests? Praises?

From: Hisword2day
To: Your heart
Sent: Tuesday, August 05, 2003 12:44 PM
Subject: Still a long way off–Luke 15:20

"But while he was still a long way off, his father saw him and was filled with compassion for him; he ran to his son, threw his arms around him and kissed him." *Luke 15:20* NIV

The story of the Prodigal Son has always been one of my favorites. Jesus tells a story of a son who prematurely takes his share of his father's inheritance and then leaves his father's house to squander his wealth in "wild living." Soon his wealth is gone, and he's left with nothing, not even food to eat. So he swallows his pride and decides that he will return to his father and say to him, "Father, I have sinned against heaven and against you. I am no longer worthy to be called your son; make me like one of your hired men." Hoping that his father will accept him, he sets off on his journey home.

And this is where we meet our traveler today. "But while he was still a long way off, his father saw him and was filled with compassion for him; he ran to his son, threw his arms around him and kissed him." Now there's a detail in here that I'd never really noticed before. However, today the Holy Spirit allowed it to stick out to me as if it were in bold print! Notice the timing . . . but while he was still *a long way off* the father ran out to meet his son. The son had not yet made it back to his father; he was merely on his way there. But out in the distance comes a man, his father, running to meet him. The son had to be in shock! He didn't deserve such an act of loving kindness. He wasn't even hoping for one! He was expecting to come all the way to his father's doorstep and then grovel at his feet. Instead, his father ran out to meet his son where he was and showered him with love and compassion, even though he'd done nothing to warrant such acts.

Friend, read this and let the truth of this passage sink deep into your hearts: **Your heavenly Father will meet you where you are.** We've all been the Prodigal Son at one time in our lives. We might not have squandered wealth on prostitutes and drunkenness, but I'll bet you anything we've all squandered the blessings the Lord has given us in some form or fashion. I certainly know I have! I do it to some degree every day! If you're like me, when you've gone away from the Lord (or just feel far away) and finally realize that you want to return to that intimacy with Him, you feel so much like the son here and you think "I'll just go make a deal with the Lord ('Make me like your hired men.') Then He'll have me again." As if we can do anything to earn the right to be in His house! Instead, as we're headed back Home, our Father sees us from far away, is filled with compassion, and runs out to meet us. If only we will turn around and merely *start* heading back in His direction, the Lord will run out to meet us *where we are* even when we're still *a long way off.* Oh my heart be still! Thank you, Jesus!

So know that you don't have to be at a certain place in your life for your Father in heaven to love you and want you. You don't have to make it to His doorstep; **He comes to meet you where you are just as you are.** You don't and can't do anything to warrant the love the Father has for you. He simply loves you and that love for you covers a multitude of sins. You may still feel like you're a long way off, but I encourage you to turn around and let God come meet you where you are. Wherever you are, whatever you're dealing with or struggling with, turn around and let the Lord come shower you with compassion and love as He throws His arms around you and kisses you. The Lord absolutely delights in and celebrates you!

By the love and grace of Jesus Christ,

<>< Jessica

Prayer requests? Praises?

From: Hisword2day
To: Your heart
Sent: August 11, 2003, 11:06 AM
Subject: Holding hands–Isaiah 41:9–10, 13

"I took you from the ends of the earth, from its farthest corners I called you. I said, 'You are my servant'; I have chosen you and have not rejected you. So do not fear, for I am with you; do not be dismayed, for I am your God. I will strengthen you and help you; I will uphold you with my righteous right hand . . . For I am the Lord, your God, who takes hold of your right hand and says to you, Do not fear; I will help you." *Isaiah 41:9–10, 13* NIV

Have you ever felt like you're at the ends of the earth? Do you ever feel as though you're in a dark, faraway corner of your life? This weekend has been one of those times for me. I was a wreck Saturday night. Confused, scared, dismayed, upset . . . you name the emotion and I was feeling it! Fortunately though, the Lord had brought me to this passage earlier in the day and I clung to it for dear life. It was my lifeline, if you will! I was so reassured and comforted to know that the Lord was (and always is) up there holding my hand, walking alongside me. I felt dismay in every way and my strength was depleted. I desperately needed the Lord's help and oh how He has provided it! His word rings true. He has indeed been with me and calmed my fears. He has reminded me that He is my God. He is sovereign and, therefore, I need not be dismayed. Furthermore, He has *definitely* strengthened me. I can feel His righteous right hand clinging onto me, not letting go. He reached out and grasped hold of my hand to walk through this very difficult time with me. Knowing and experiencing all of this has blessed my heart so much, for when I couldn't stand on my own His righteous right hand was upholding me. I stood there clinging to my Jesus much like a child clings to her daddy's arm. Thank you, Jesus!

My reason for sending this today is to remind you that if you feel like you're in a dark corner of your life just know that the Lord is there. You are His servant. He has chosen you, not rejected you and therefore He will be with you whatever you go through, wherever you go. You do not go through dark valleys alone. He walks through them with you, holding your right hand. Is that not just the most comforting thought!? So do not fear what your circumstances may bring forth. Do not fear for Jesus is with you. He reaches down from His throne in heaven and takes hold of your right hand so that *He* can strengthen you and help you. Reach out and let Him take hold of your right hand. Intertwine your fingers with His and know that you are so deeply loved. He *will* strengthen you. He *will* help you. He *will* be with you always, therefore, do not be dismayed.

May the blessings of Christ's peace and love fill your hearts and minds today as you walk hand-in-hand with Jesus.

By His grace and love,

<>< Jessica

Prayer requests? Praises?

From: Hisword2day
To: Your heart
Sent: Tuesday, August 12, 2003 7:50 AM
Subject: What the Lord declares–Jeremiah 29:11

"For I know the plans I have for you," declares the Lord, "plans to prosper you and not to harm you, plans to give you hope and a future." *Jeremiah 29:11* **NIV**

Last night I was on the phone with a very dear friend of mine and we got to talking about this verse. She shared with me how the Lord recently spoke to her through this verse . . . something that really struck her heart. She'd never really paid much attention to this before, but for some reason the word "declares" really stood out to her. She went on to explain to me just how profound this word was to her in this context, how powerful and assuring it was. For declare is not a passive word. It's a very sure, assertive, explicit, and strong word. Because of that she can picture the Lord raising a fist in the air as He proclaims with definite authority and assurance, "I *know* the plans I have for you!!!" (With that thought in mind can't you just hear Him shouting that out in a bold, confident tone?) "Declares" seems to signify that this statement is not just a passing thought, rather it's a proclamation in which the Lord emphasizes that He knows the plans He has for you and that those plans are for peace and not evil, are to prosper you and not to harm you.

I just thought that was the neatest thing! Your version of the Bible may use a different word for declare, yet the truth remains: the Lord *knows* the plans He has for you. I would venture to say that He knows them in an experiential knowing kind of way. That is, He's been there . . . I mean, He has gone before you (Deuteronomy 31:8) therefore, He is very sure of the plans He has for you for He is quite familiar with them. He understands them. Isn't that reassuring? We may not understand them, but He does. So take heart in knowing that the Lord of all creation, the King of Kings and Lord of Lords knows the plans He has for you and those plans are to prosper you and give you hope and a future. Try to picture Him as my friend did: confidently proclaiming this with His fist in the air, and excitement in His voice. Does that thought get anyone else excited for what He has planned?

Have a terrific day and may you experience blessed reassurance in the plans He has for you, His beloved.

By grace His child, your sister,

<>< Jessica

Prayer requests? Praises?

From: Hisword2day
To: Your heart
Sent: Wednesday, August 13, 2003 8:01 AM
Subject: Trimming dead ends–John 15:1–2

"I am the true vine, and my Father is the gardener. He cuts off every branch in me that bears no fruit, while every branch that does bear fruit he prunes so that it will be even more fruitful." *John 15:1–2* **NIV**

I currently work at a salon so I hear all kinds of talk about hair. Besides the chatter of what colors to use, which product would be best, and what type of cut would work, I mainly hear the stylists talking about how to keep their client's hair healthier. The number one quote I hear pertaining to this is, "We need to get those dead ends off." Ends of the hair are usually drier than the rest of the hair shaft. As a result, they are more brittle and prone to breaking off or becoming split ends. Now, you don't want dead or split ends—they need to be cut off because it's like they are contagious! Once the ends splits or become dry and brittle, the rest of the hair shaft is in greater danger of doing the same. And who wants a head full of dead ends? ☺ Therefore, even if you're growing your hair out, it's a good idea to get a trim regularly. (Trimming your hair doesn't make it grow quicker; it protects it from breaking off higher on the hair shaft, thus allowing it to grow healthier and stronger.)

When it comes to your heart and life, God is your stylist. The Lord knows that the dead ends in your life are very much like the dead ends of hair—dry, brittle, and contagious. And He certainly doesn't want those to grow and cause your heart to become brittle. He doesn't want you to become one of those branches that bears no fruit and is broken off. No! He wants you strong and healthy with as few brittle areas as possible so that your faith can grow healthier and stronger . . . so that you will be even more fruitful. As a result, He comes in and snips away at the dead, split ends of your life, not because He's mean, but because He loves you. God trims away your dead, split ends so that you don't break off. That's the last thing He wants! He wants you to remain in Him and therefore, by trimming your heart's split ends, He's protecting you from being cut off and helping you to remain healthy and strong or to become healthier and stronger.

As He prunes you, may you delight in the love and care He's showering on you. I pray that you would see His love and grace in it . . . that it's for your good and for the good of the Kingdom. That which bears no fruit He cuts off, and if there's an area in your life like that He will cut it off to prune you—not to harm you, but to protect you. He wants to give you that blessed future He has planned for you and wants you to experience what it's like to bear fruit so let Him trim away your dead ends and watch as your life begins to bear more fruit for His kingdom!

In His love and grace,

<>< Jessica

Prayer requests? Praises?

From: Hisword2day
To: Your heart
Sent: Tuesday, August 19, 2003 7:31 AM
Subject: The power of praise–1 Thessalonians 5:18

"Give thanks in all circumstances, for this is God's will for you in Christ Jesus." *1 Thessalonians 5:18* NIV

Today's passage is a rather well-known passage. Many of you may have read it before or may even have it memorized. Well, today I'm going to ask you to dissect this verse with me. I'm going to ask that you put it under a microscope and see what you discover. I want us to look at two little words: "in" and "all."

A couple of years ago my best friend gave me a book to read, *The Power of Praise.* I don't remember the author's name, but I remember the lesson within its covers as it explains how we are to give thanks in *all* circumstances. Praising God in literally all things is quite a powerful tool and weapon in this war we're fighting. My question to you today is have you really grasped what it means to give thanks in all circumstances? Or have you failed to notice the word "all"? I often ignore the word "all" and instead put the word "good" or "pleasing" in there. But His word quite blatantly states *all* circumstances.

Yeah. So what? Well, because "all" is a pretty large-scale word meaning *everything,* giving thanks in all circumstances would mean saying thanks in things like a friend's cancer, a child's injury or illness, a marriage gone bad, a stressful day, a lost job, a low point in your faith, your weaknesses, the skeletons in your closet, your bad grade, etc. WHAT?! Yes, even in those things we are to give *thanks.* Hard? Heck yeah!! But hear me out on this.

When we give thanks, even in the worst of circumstances, not only are we doing God's will (for giving thanks in ALL circumstances is God's will for us in Christ Jesus), but we're also protecting our hearts. There's a reason the Lord gave this as a command. Satan loves to take our circumstances and try to deceive us. He comes to steal, kill, and destroy (John 10:10) and takes every opportunity to steal our minds, kill our faith, and destroy our intimacy with Jesus Christ. Therefore, when we go through the deep waters of life He's going to put thoughts of an unloving, distrustful, unsympathetic God at the doorstep of our heart so that if we give the slightest inch, these thoughts will race in and quickly take root in our heart. And oh how Satan loves to use our "bad" circumstances to blind us to the Lord's love, grace, and provision! By giving thanks, we're guarding our hearts and minds from Satan's deceptive schemes.

Yeah, but what do I thank Him for? I'm not thankful for my friend's cancer or for my awful situation? No, I'm not either. But we can be thankful for how God's working and going to work in and through the circumstances at hand. Huh? Be thankful *in* all circumstances. Maybe that means during all circumstances. I don't know, but Psalm 121:3 reminds us that He who watches over us will not slumber, which means He's *always* watching over us (AKA, in Jessica-terminology, always at work). Therefore, even amidst our darkest moments and toughest situations we are guaranteed that the Lord is at work for we don't have a heavenly Father who hides in the foxholes. Rather, He's on the frontlines of battle every day. So if nothing else you can give thanks *in* all circumstances for how the Lord is working: how you are going to see His love and grace through this, or experience His strength, healing, and provision. You may not see it now, but because of your faith in Jesus Christ you know He's working all things for your good (Romans 8:28). Again, there's the word "all." It doesn't say *some* things or *good* things. No. It says that *in all things* God works for the good of those who love Him. Do I believe all "bad" circumstances come from the Lord? No. But do I believe that in all circumstances He can work out good from them? My answer would be a resounding YES! I've experienced it one too many times to say no, even though I still struggle with giving thanks in all circumstances. I know in my heart of hearts that Jesus is at work and for that I can honestly be thankful.

Today I encourage you to give thanks in all of your circumstances. If you can't say thanks for a circumstance, that's okay. You can still say thanks *in* a circumstance. You can say thanks for how God is working for most assuredly He is! In doing so, you are acknowledging that God is bigger than the situation. He is more powerful than what's happening. And most importantly, you are acknowledging that He is sovereign and that you trust Him to bring good out of even the worst of circumstances. This is key, for it will help to release your mind from Satan's deceiving schemes. That doesn't mean your friend will be healed or your weaknesses will immediately become strengths, but it does mean that some good will come of it. You will experience the Lord somehow in the circumstance—in fact, because of it. And for the opportunity to experience God, you can be truly thankful.

Don't let Satan get his tentacles into your heart and burn you. Give thanks and watch the power of praise go to work in your life and in your circumstances. The power of praise often releases the power of God. It may not change the circumstance, but it will change your attitude in and towards your situation. So give thanks in all circumstances for this is God's will for you in Christ Jesus, and remember that your circumstances just might also be God's will for you in Christ Jesus as well. Have a blessed day of thanks!

In His love and grace,

<>< Jessica

Prayer Requests? Praises?

From: Hisword2day
To: Your heart
Sent: Thursday, August 21, 2003 3:03 PM
Subject: Because of You - Galatians 1:24

"And they praised God because of me." *Galatians 1:24* **NIV**

I want you to do something for me today. Just prior to this verse, Paul is writing about how he was unknown to the churches of Judea. All they knew about him was that "the man who formerly persecuted us is now preaching the faith he once tried to destroy." Then, our verse for the day: "and they praised God because of me." This could mean they praised God for the conversion of Paul's heart and life. It could mean they praised God for how He used Paul. Or it could mean they praised God for something else we're unaware of, but whatever it was it was related to Paul. My task for you today is to ask yourself whether or not you believe Paul's statement above applies to your life. Do you believe people are praising God because of you?

If you answered no, then why not? I think that a lot of us feel like this verse doesn't or couldn't apply to our lives for a variety of reasons, but I want to remind you today that it does. The way you invest your life into others, the love you share with them, and the light you spread are all reasons for people to praise God because of you. Some of them might be praising Him for the blessing you are in their lives, while others might be praising Him for the work He's done in and through your life. Still others might come to know Jesus through you. Or it might just be the small act of kindness you showed a stranger today that causes someone to praise the Lord. (You never know when and how you might be blessing people or answering their prayers through something you say or do!) Whatever the case may be, you are being used and people can praise God because of you!

As I close I want to remind you that you bring God's kingdom glory by living out this thing called your life. Yes, we definitely can cause people to turn away from Jesus and we need to be extremely cautious about doing so! However, just realize that you don't have to do something extremely special, or you don't have to be in ministry for the Lord to work through you and for people to praise God because of you. *You are extremely special!* Therefore, just by being you you're doing something extraordinary! Furthermore, if you're a Christian then your life is ministry—don't forget that. So even though you may not feel like this verse can apply to your life right now, I pray that the Lord would help you to see that it can and it does. Allow Him to use you and He will in ways you have never dreamed of!

You are precious and honored in His sight and He uses those He loves. *He so deeply loves you.* Indeed, people are praising God because of you. *I* praise God because of you . . .

By His grace,

<>< Jessica

Prayer requests? Praises?

From: Hisword2day
To: Your heart
Sent: Monday, August 25, 2003 8:46 AM
Subject: God's flock under your care–1 Peter 5:2–3

"Be shepherds of God's flock that is under your care, serving as overseers—not because you must, but because you are willing, as God wants you to be; not greedy for money, but eager to serve; not lording it over those entrusted to you, but being examples to the flock." 1 Peter 5:2–3 NIV

When you read this verse did you think it could apply to you? Well, it most certainly does! See, the Lord gives us platforms throughout our lives. Your platforms might include your job, your role as a parent or sibling, your friendships, your position as a member on a sports team, your part as a member of a band, your role as a student, your position on a committee, your role as the leader of a group, etc. From each of these platforms, God is going to shine His light off of you for all those around you to see . . . for your flock to see.

You may not realize it, but there's a flock of people around you that need an example; they need to be shepherded. God has put people in your life for you to be a "shepherd" to. He's given you qualities and positions to serve the flock He's entrusted to you. This is big! Entrusted, according to Webster, means *to transfer or commit with confidence*; to charge with trust or responsibility***. Wow! So God has committed your gifts, qualities, characteristics, and most importantly people to you with *confidence!* He knows you can do great things with what He's entrusted to you! He's charged you with this responsibility. *He trusts you.* Pretty exciting if you ask me!

However, if you're like me, you too often disregard what's been entrusted to you. You forget about your responsibility or you don't even recognize it (so me!). You fail to recognize your flock. But friends, every aspect of your life is significant. Wherever you are and whatever you're doing, God's flock is under your care. So serve whomever, or whatever that may be as overseers, not because you must, but because you are willing, as God wants you to be. Not greedy for money, or dishonest gain, but eager to serve. Not lording it over those entrusted to you—don't put on airs or act high and mighty for the Lord quickly humbles the proud—but being an example to the flocks that He has entrusted to you . . . that he has committed to you *with confidence.*

Today I just encourage you to ask the Lord to reveal to you your flocks. To shepherd means to guide and guard and so as a shepherd guide and guard those who the Lord has put under your care as He, the Shepherd, would guide and guard you. Whatever you do, don't discharge the trust that's been given to you, but as Paul writes to Timothy, "Guard what has been entrusted to you" for Satan is quick to come kill, steal, and destroy (John 10:10). And get excited because you have been chosen for this position!!! The Lord of Lords has handpicked you and has confidence in the person He made you to be. He trusts His power, strength, wisdom, and love that He's placed in your heart. You don't shepherd alone . . . He always fights your fights with you. Have a blessed day being examples for Jesus Christ!

Because of His love,

<>< Jessica

Prayer requests? Praises?

*Merriam-Webster Online Dictionary

**The New American Webster Handy College Dictionary

From: Hisword2day
To: Your heart
Sent: Tuesday, August 26, 2003 7:58 AM
Subject: Discharging trust–1 Corinthians 9:16–17

"Yet when I preach the gospel, I cannot boast, for I am compelled to preach. Woe to me if I do not preach the gospel! If I preach voluntarily, I have a reward; if not voluntarily, I am simply discharging the trust committed to me." *1 Corinthians 9:16–17* **NIV**

These words of Paul have always been special to me. They've always touched and challenged me. Paul was called to preach . . . that was his job, the task the Lord had given him. Here Paul is telling how he's offering his preaching for free, even though he has the right to receive compensation for his preaching. And I just love what he says here, that when he preaches the gospel he cannot boast, for he is *compelled* to preach. Can you imagine hearing Paul preach the gospel? What a sermon that would be! Talk about powerful! Whew! But Paul knew that what he preached did not come from himself, but from the Lord and that it was the Lord's love that controlled him and compelled him to preach when, where and what he preached. Then, I love Paul's next remark, "Woe to me if I do not preach the gospel!" It's like he's saying, "Yikes! If I don't preach, ooooh I'm in for it!" For he realized that if he did what he was called to do voluntarily, he had a reward; and if not voluntarily he was simply discharging the trust committed to him.

Simply discharging the trust committed to him. That is a powerful statement and certainly one to ponder! What could it mean and why, Jessica, are you zeroing in on that phrase? Well, because I want you to ask yourself if you've ever discharged the trust committed to you. (I have!) *I want you to realize that, just like Paul, you have been entrusted with certain things and callings. You too have a role to play.* God may not have called you to preach, but He's blessed you with qualities, characteristics, roles, and positions, and as a believer in Christ, you become a reflection of Christ through all of these. Because of that, I think it would be safe to say that He truly has transferred and committed these qualities and responsibilities to you *with confidence.* Therefore, don't discharge the trust committed to you, rather let the Lord's love control you and then *let that love compel you to be who you were created to be and do far greater things than you could imagine!* That might mean He's called you to teach, or play a sport, or be a friend, or be a sister, wife, brother, or husband, or lead a committee, class, or group. Maybe He's called you to be a student. There are a million things the Lord can call you to do and be and it's not just "spiritual" things. *Remember nothing in your life is insignificant, and everything in your life has more than surface value . . . there's always more eternal meaning than we often realize.*

The Lord called Paul to be a preacher. He entrusted this position to Paul. The Lord has called you to be you; He has entrusted your calling(s) to you. And I just pray that you would realize what the Lord compels you to do and be, whatever it is, and that you would do it voluntarily, willingly. For then you shall receive a reward far greater than the riches or glory this world could ever offer! (Can you imagine getting the blue ribbon pinned on you from Jesus? Nifty thought, if you ask me!)

May you be blessed as you allow His love to control and compel you and may you not discharge the trust committed to you by your heavenly Father. Have a great day!

Controlled by His love,

<>< Jessica

Prayer Requests? Praises?

From: Hisword2day
To: Your heart
Sent: Wednesday, August 27, 2003 7:37 AM
Subject: Quieted by His love–Zephaniah 3:17

"The Lord your God is with you, he is mighty to save. He will take great delight in you, he will quiet you with his love, he will rejoice over you with singing." *Zephaniah 3:17* **NIV**

Oh what a blessing this verse has been to me! A very dear friend of mine shared it with me and I just had to share it with you! How very encouraging it is to read these words! Contemplate this verse for a moment. It's just awesome! He is with you and is mighty to save. Wherever you are, whatever you're experiencing the Lord is with you. And when needed, He will rescue you! He will take *delight* in you . . . wow! In other words, He is greatly pleased, has a high degree of satisfaction in you. He is thrilled with pleasure in you! An incredible thought!

Here's the one that just melted my heart: *He will quiet you with His love.* Oh what sweet words! Ever watched an upset child try to explain to a parent why he or she is so upset? Ever seen a child crying so hard and grasping for breath that words won't come out, that it's just a jumbled mess? Ever been that child before God crying out over your confusion, hurt, sadness, frustration, fear, agitation, hopelessness, loneliness, madness, distress, anxiety . . . and on and on? I have been that upset child standing before my Father. I have been a jumbled mess. Yet just as a parent soothes and eventually quiets the upset child with love, so our Father soothes and quiets us with His love. He listens to us and wipes away our tears and fears with a handkerchief of love.

And don't forget, He rejoices over you with singing!! What a fun thought! You truly are the Lord's delight and He wants to rejoice over you, even if you don't want to rejoice over yourself. You are His dearly beloved! Remember that today. And cling to the fact that He is with you. The Lord your God is with you and will never leave you. Trust Him and believe Him to be mighty to save. Allow Him to quiet you with His unfailing love. And listen to hear Him rejoicing over you . . . He will serenade you all day long! May God's word bring you joy, blessings, and peace today!

Quieted by His love,

<>< Jessica

Prayer Requests? Praises?

P.S. I have a prayer request . . . I'm having foot surgery tomorrow at 9:30 A.M. Please just pray for the surgery to run smoothly, for my surgeon's hands, and for a quick and painless recovery. Thanks! I'll let you know how it goes tomorrow . . .

From: Hisword2day
To: Your heart
Sent: Friday, August 29, 2003 7:33 AM
Subject: Surgery update

Well, the surgery went well! Thank you for your prayers! There were no complications and God put two wonderful nurses in charge of me in the recovery room. It truly was a divine appointment . . . both had hearts of gold for the Lord and were heavily involved in international mission work! They shared their experiences and stories with me . . . I mean they were HUGE encouragements and blessings! God is so good! Anyway, just wanted to thank you for your prayers! God did keep me safe and I know He was holding my right hand the entire time! Because my IV was in my right arm I kind of pretended that my IV was God's hand. ☺ Have a great day and thanks!

From: Hisword2day
To: Your heart
Sent: Tuesday, September 02, 2003 8:20 AM
Subject: The hope of glory–Colossians 1:27

"To them [the saints] God has chosen to make known among the Gentiles the glorious riches of this mystery, which is Christ in you, the hope of glory." *Colossians 1:27* **NIV**

I just loved the wording of this verse! The glorious riches of this mystery—Christ in you, the hope of glory. Have you every thought about the fact that you have a wellspring of glorious riches bubbling up inside of you? That Christ is in you? That the hope of glory dwells within your being?

If you're like me, you don't think of yourself as a wellspring of glorious riches, nor do you feel the hope of glory. Sometime situations seem beyond hope of anything glorious coming out of them. And many times you don't feel Christ in you. Yet, if you have accepted Jesus, accepted His atoning sacrifice for you on the cross and His resurrection, then indeed Christ is in you *at all times* and there is the hope of glory dwelling within your heart, despite yourself or your circumstances.

Christ is *in* you. And because God has made known to you the glorious riches of this mystery, you have become heir to these glorious riches. The hope of glory dwells within you for Christ has come and made His heart your home. And He's brought all of His belongings with Him . . . His mind, patience, kindness, gentleness, joy, peace, wisdom, knowledge, faithfulness, self-control, etc. As Christ renews and transforms your heart and mind, all of these attributes of Christ and more are becoming a wellspring of God's glorious riches welling up inside of you as you read! What an awesome thought!

My prayer for you today is that this would not be a mystery to you anymore. I pray that you would experience the glorious riches of Christ in you. I pray that you would realize that there is a hope of glory within you . . . you are a vessel of God's glory! And, as you face today's trials and tomorrow's tribulations remember that amidst them you have hope for glory because you have Christ. With Christ there is always a hope of glory—magnificence, wonder, and splendor—despite yourself and despite your circumstances for Christ is greater than your situation. He is greater than you. So let the wellspring of glorious riches—Christ in you—bubble over into others' lives through your words and deeds and cling to your hope of glory.

In His love and grace,

<>< Jessica

Prayer requests? Praises?

From: Hisword2day
To: Your heart
Sent: Tuesday, September 09, 2003 10:12 AM
Subject: Go take possession–Deuteronomy 1:20–21

" . . . You have reached the hill country of the Amorites, which the Lord our God is giving us. See, the Lord your God has given you the land. Go up and take possession of it as the Lord, the God of your fathers, told you. Do not be afraid; do not be discouraged." *Deuteronomy 1:20–21* **NIV**

Boy did this verse hit home with me today! Man! Please allow me to explain . . . in this verse we find Moses speaking to the Israelites about their next "move". They have traveled from Horeb (where they'd been staying) and have arrived at Kadesh Barnea, which was apparently the hill country of the Amorites, a people who could easily smash the Israelites with their power, strength, and resources. So not only were they in a new and strange territory, they were well aware that the Amorites could squash them. Just a little intimidating don't ya think?

Yet look at what God tells them to do. First, He instructs Moses to inform the Israelites that God is giving them this land—actually that He's given it to them. Isn't it rather interesting that the past tense is used here? Hmmm. Might signify that the Lord had gone before them and had already given it to them—aka He knew what the outcome would be if they had to fight for the land. And because He'd *given* the land to them, God told them to go take possession of it.

Wait a second. Did you catch that? *Go take possession of it.* That signifies taking action. God gave them the land and told them it was theirs. All they needed to do was go take possession of it. In order to receive their blessing, they had to go claim it. Well, something the Lord really convicted me of through this is that God often calls us to take action. He tells us to go take possession of certain "territory" He's given us. Your territory might be a person, place, or thing. God might be telling you to move, go do something new and different, make a new friend, etc. Whatever your territory is, God will often call you to take action . . . to go claim it. It will be nothing but a blessing and He wants to bless you, but He might call you to go take possession of that blessing.

On a personal note, I often hesitate to take action. I just think God's going to spoon feed blessings and territories to me . . . and well, He's not. He does indeed call us to take action . . . to go take possession of "territories". For me, Paris is one of these territories. God has definitely called me to go there. Yet I've felt very much like the Israelites—I know the territory will be new and different. I know I will be far outnumbered and Young Life's ministry could easily be squashed over there. But in God's very special way He has told me, "See the Lord your God has *given* you this land. Go take possession of it. Go claim it for Me! Do NOT be afraid and do NOT be discouraged." So as scary, unnerving, and discouraging as this territory seems, I must remember that God has given it to me. Past tense. He's already been here and wouldn't call me to go somewhere He hasn't already been. He's not going to send me into a battle alone. He will fight for me before my very eyes. He will do the work He needs to do in, through, and with me. And oh how thankful I am that HE will!

Now that is just one small example in my life, but I want you to know that this concept applies to your life. God will call you, and might be calling you to a "territory" that is new, strange, and even overwhelming. But remember, the Lord your God is going before you. He will fight for you as He has always done. He will give you what He's already prepared to give you. So trust Him today. Have faith that He will come through. NOTHING is too hard for our God. He is the Lord Almighty and He knows the plans He has for you and they are not to harm you, but to bless you. So ask God to reveal your "territories" to you and then go claim them, whatever, wherever that may be. Go be His witness and remember that His Holy Spirit will teach you in that very hour what you are to say and do (Luke 12:12). He *will* fight for you. He has gone before you and He knows the outcome. He has claimed the "territory". Do you trust Him? Then take action and receive a blessing in doing so. Go take possession in, by, and through the Lord your God. Don't be afraid . . . *do not be discouraged.*

By His strength and grace,

<>< Jessica

Prayer requests? Praises?

From: Hisword2day
To: Your heart
Sent: Monday, September 15, 2003 1:28 PM
Subject: Hypochondria of the heart–Philippians 4:8

"Finally, brothers, whatever is true, whatever is noble, whatever is right, whatever is pure, whatever is lovely, whatever is admirable—if anything is excellent or praiseworthy—think about such things." *Philippians 4:8* **NIV**

I've been in Mississippi and Alabama for the last week and half visiting family and friends and have had such a delightful time! I was blessed with amazing company and wonderful conversations, one of which inspired today's topic—hypochondria of the heart. You might be thinking, "What in the world are you talking about, Jessica?!" Well, please allow me to explain how the Lord struck me with a comment my friend made.

Mark was sitting across the table from me at Waffle House discussing all the world's problems (ha ha) and commented that a particular news channel was the "hypochondriac news station of America" because it seems to only report on all the bad stuff going on—*never* the good. It focuses on what could be wrong, what will go wrong, what has been going wrong, etc. It's just depressing to watch! As Mark said that I was convicted of how much this news channel mirrors the conversation of my heart.

By definition, hypochondria means "extreme depression of mind or spirits often centered on imaginary physical ailments."* A hypochondriac is "one who is morbidly anxious about his or her health or suffers imagined illnesses."** It can't be fun to suffer from this condition! However, if you're like me you do . . . Only it's not necessarily about physical health . . . it's about your life, your heart, your relationship with the Lord, who you are, etc. Rather than focusing on whatever is true, noble, right, pure, lovely and admirable, you focus on everything wrong or bad that is, could be, will be, or has been going on and become bogged down with the ailments (real or imagined) of life. You never notice any good in your life. At times you honestly don't feel like there is any. But friend, the Lord does not want you to suffer from hypochondria of the heart and soul. He does not desire that you have extreme depression of mind or that you have spirits centered on the bad, the wrong, and/or the ailments of your life. He came so that you could have an abundant life. He wants you to rejoice in the day He has made . . . not simply survive it!

Yeah, but then why is this happening in my life or why do I feel this particular way? Ever feel that way? Like you can't help but dwell on bad stuff because so much bad is going on? Well, let me encourage you, we've all been there! The Bible never said we wouldn't have bad days or experiences. In fact it warns that indeed we can expect bad, hard, and trying times! The Bible also *doesn't* say that we shouldn't acknowledge the bad, the wrong, or the "ailments" in our lives. Instead, we must recognize these things and face them. But there's a fine line between facing and dealing vs. dwelling. When we *dwell* on those "bad" things alone, they begin to consume us, and we become entangled in thoughts that weigh us down hindering us from running in the path of His commands. Furthermore, we begin to make them worse than they really are, thus allowing such thoughts to become a foothold for Satan to come in and steal our thoughts away from the Lord. We begin to not be able to see any good although there is an abundance of excellent and praiseworthy things in our lives! The floodgates of heaven have opened up and poured down so many blessings and so many wonderful things that we can't even begin to count them! Yet, hypochondria of the heart and soul hinders our ability to recognize those things that are true, noble, right, pure, lovely, and admirable. It hinders our ability to see the Lord's presence in our lives.

Today I challenge you to not only consider what's going array in your life, but to also consider and dwell on anything excellent or praiseworthy. Think about such things today. By doing so I'll bet that your seemingly camouflaged blessings will begin to become a bit clearer and you will become increasingly aware of the things in and around you that are true, noble, right, pure, lovely, admirable, excellent and praiseworthy.

Try not to have hypochondria of the heart. The Lord *knows* the plans He has for you and they are plans to prosper you and give you a hope and a future! So fear not and be not dismayed for the Lord your God is with you *wherever* you go. May you be blessed through and through with wonderful thoughts of Jesus' unfailing love towards you . . .

In His gracious love,
<>< Jessica

Prayer requests? Praises?

*Merriam-Webster Online Dictionary
**Oxford Reference Online

From: Hisword2day

To: Your heart

Sent: Tuesday, September 16, 2003 12:59 PM

Subject: God thinking out loud–Deuteronomy 5:29

"Oh, that their hearts would be inclined to fear me and keep all my commands always, so that it might go well with them and their children forever!" *Deuteronomy 5:29* NIV

As I read these precious words that fell from the Lord's lips, I was touched! I guess the wording of this passage just really struck me for it was as if this verse catches God thinking out loud. And I can just hear Him saying these words with a longing and yearning in His voice, with the deepest sincerity. "*Oh* that their hearts would be inclined to fear me! *Oh* that their hearts would be inclined to keep all my commands always so that it might go well with them and their children forever." Do you sense a hint of desperation in there? I do! This of course is just my interpretation and how God spoke to me through this passage, but I can sense God's passion and His furious love for us in this comment. He yearns for us to be inclined to fear Him, and I don't think He means the dreaded, being-afraid-of fear. I don't know the text in the original language but I strongly feel that in this case the Lord is referring to a fear that means honoring Him and ordering our lives in accordance with His will out of *reverence* for Him. Having this type of fear towards Him will help us yield to His commands and will, which in turn will only reap blessings after blessings in our lives and the lives of those that come after us.

Before I close, I want you to apply this verse to yourself because it very much does apply to you. "Oh that your heart would be inclined to fear me. (That you would revere me and trust me.) Oh that you would keep all my commands always so that it might go well with you and your children forever."

Now personalize it even more and put your own name in there. "Oh that Jessica's heart would be inclined to fear me. Oh that she would keep all my commands always so that it might go well with her and her children forever." Well, bless my heart!! Oh that He would be that personal! And He is! So, friend, remember that God longs to be gracious to *you* and He rises to show *you* compassion each and every morning. Isaiah 30:18 reminds us of that. Know in your heart that the Lord your God desperately desires you. He passionately loves you. And He abundantly blesses you. Incline your hearts to fearing Him today so that you might keep all of His commands. In doing so, you and a thousand generations to come will forever be blessed (Deuteronomy 5:10).

Have a blessed day pursuing the One who so furiously pursues you.

In Jesus' love and grace,

<>< Jessica

Prayer requests? Praises?

From: Hisword2day
To: Your heart
Sent: Wednesday, September 17, 2003 8:11 AM
Subject: Acknowledging God–Deuteronomy 4:39

"Acknowledge and take to heart this day that the Lord is God in heaven above and on the earth below. There is no other." *Deuteronomy 4:39* **NIV**

Boy howdy do I need to do this today! Truly, the Lord *is* God in heaven and on this little green planet we call Earth. *There is no other.* He alone is all we need. He alone is above all things. He alone is God. Oh how I need to acknowledge this today! How I need to admit, confess that He is the Lord in the heavens, on the earth, and *in my life.* How I need to take this to heart this day and surrender.

If you find yourself in the same shoes as me, then my prayer for you today is that you would indeed acknowledge and take to heart that the Lord is God in heaven above and on the earth below. Admit that He alone is God. Confess that He is above all things, even your circumstances. Recognize Him as the Lord *your* God. Pray that you would see the Lord for who He is, not for who you try to make Him to be, or not be. Let Him not be your crutch today, but allow Him to be your backbone. And I pray that in doing so you and I would both come to take to heart this day that truly, there is no other. Nothing and no one even compares! Oh how I pray we see that as a reality today!

As I close I leave you with three questions . . . do your words and deeds reflect that you have acknowledged and taken to heart that the Lord is God in heaven above and on the earth below? Do they reflect that He is the Lord over and below your life? Do you believe that there is no other? Acknowledge and take heart this day . . .

Grace, peace, love and joy,

<>< Jessica

Prayer requests? Praises?

From: Hisword2day
To: Your heart
Sent: Monday, September 22, 2003 3:50 PM
Subject: Paraphrasing David–Psalm 8:3,9

"When I consider thy heavens, the work of thy fingers, the moon and the stars, which thou hast ordained . . . O Lord our Lord, how excellent is thy name in all the earth!" *Psalm 8:3,9* **KJV**

Do you ever stop to contemplate creation? Have you ever simply found yourself captured by the radiance of the Lord's glory bursting forth before you? Do you ever take a moment to consider the works of His fingers?

I bet if we would all take a few brief moments each day to marvel at His works we too would echo David's praise here . . . O Lord, our Lord how excellent, how majestic is your name in all the earth! For truly, the earth is FULL of His unfailing love and presence!

Well, Louis Pasteur is one man who more than considered the works of the Lord's fingers and did indeed come to a conclusion similar to David's as he is quoted as having once said, "The more I study nature, the more I am amazed at the Creator." Sounds like Mr. Pasteur paraphrased David! ☺ However, for us to understand the gravity of what Pasteur said, we must understand that he was not your ordinary person speaking. He was one of the world's greatest scientists and understood nature and the intricacy of life more than most of us ever will even begin to fathom! The following are just a few things he is accredited with: He discovered that diseases are spread by bacteria and although bacteria live almost everywhere, their spread can be controlled. He disproved spontaneous generation, a theory that life could come from things that are not alive, such as dirt, thus proving that living things can only come from living things. He is responsible for the process of pasteurization, which by the way is a discovery that is responsible for saving the French wine industry in 1864. And all of us can thank Louis for the method of vaccinations—a discovery that has probably saved most of our lives in some form or fashion. So you can see that Pasteur truly had considered, quite thoroughly, the works of the God's fingers . . . and as a result he could echo the cry of David's heart as his studies and discoveries caused him to grow more in awe of the Creator. Pasteur understood how majestic God's name is in *all* the earth and came up with quite a nifty paraphrase of David, if you ask me!

Now, more than likely, you and I will never have the depths of this man's knowledge or understanding of this particular aspect of the Lord's creation. However, this is not to say that you and I can't be studiers of the Lord's works, and that we can't consider His great works and stand in awe of our Creator. We too can paraphrase David! Need I remind you that His radiance bursts forth with the dawning of every morning and the closing of every day? These displays of His mighty works are commonly known as sunrise and sunset. I'm telling you, and so is David, the heavens truly do declare His glory! Yet how rarely we consider/take note of His work . . . not just in the world around us, but in our own lives.

Today I encourage you to take just a few moments to consider the heavens, the work of His fingers, the moon and the stars, which He has ordained and may you begin to see how excellent is His name in all the earth! Take a few moments to reflect on the fact that it's not just the moon and the stars that have been ordained . . . it's your very own life that the Lord your God has ordained. How simply wonderful! I pray that you are able to recognize His work in your own life. However, if you can't seem to feel His presence or see His works then look to the heavens for there you will see His glory declared and His presence revealed! For what God is there in heaven or on earth who can do the works He does? Oh how I pray that as you do so you too would echo the cry of David's heart! That the more you study His works in yourself and the world around you—in the heavens and on the earth, the more you are *amazed* at your Creator.

Be captured by His radiant glory today even if just momentarily . . . and may you discover your own paraphrase of David!

In His love and graces,

<>< Jessica

Prayer requests? Praises?

From: Hisword2day
To: Your heart
Sent: Tuesday, September 23, 2003 8:54 AM
Subject: His compassions never fail–Lamentations 3:21–23

"Yet this I call to mind and therefore I have hope: Because of the LORD's great love we are not consumed, for his compassions never fail. They are new every morning; great is your faithfulness." *Lamentations 3:21–23* NIV

This morning New Braunfels, Texas witnessed a stunning sunrise! It truly was an example of the Lord's radiance bursting forth all over the sky! It was just incredible! Worth rising to see that's for sure! I was so touched by its beauty as it reminded me of His faithfulness. For as surely as the sun rises every morning, so the Lord rises to meet us every single morning. And to think that He rises to meet me every morning . . . that's just amazing! Furthermore, as each morning dawns, He renews His compassions and His faithfulness to us under the blanket of His great love! Incredible! A friend of mine wrote a song that really put this into perspective for me. He writes how Jesus stands at the foot of your bed, patiently waiting. His mercies are new every morning and when you open up your eyes and give a yawn, He greets you with a smile. Oh what a precious thought! So get excited for the Lord just can't wait to travel this journey called Today with you! What great blessings He has in store for you!

Now, I know that life will throw you some curve balls, and when it does, cling to these words in Lamentations . . . because of the Lord's great love we are not consumed. Your troubles will not consume you; your hardships will not overwhelm you. Oh yes, it may seem like they will at the time, but remember that the Lord who can create such marvelous wonders as a captivating sunrise is also the Lord over your life and He is more than able to handle what's going on in your life. He is more than able to sustain you. If He can create the heavens and the earth and all that is in them than just imagine what He can do in your very own life! So know that because of the Lord's great love, you will **not** be consumed, for His compassions—His care, concern, empathy, and kindness—they never fail. Never. They truly are new every morning and as consistently as the sun rises each morning so consistent and great is His faithfulness in your life.

May you call to mind the reminders of the Lord's compassions and faithfulness and may this give you hope as you go throughout your day. May you rise each morning to meet Him and may you greet Him with a smile.

With the love of Christ,

<>< Jessica

Prayer requests? Praises?

From: Hisword2day
To: Your heart
Sent: Thursday, September 25, 2003 8:59 AM
Subject: Better to trust the Lord–Psalm 118:8

"It is better to trust in the Lord than to put confidence in man."
Psalm 118:8 **KJV**

A friend of mine sent me an e-mail which included this verse and wow did it hit the bull's eye of my heart! I have really been struggling with doing this . . . trusting the Lord over man . . . over myself. Of course it's not so easy for me to admit that and if you'd talked to me my words might have deceived you that indeed I was trusting in the Lord and not myself. However, my anxious thoughts and actions would reveal otherwise and that is something the Lord has been faithful to reveal to me.

See, I'm a fairly independent person, but when it comes to God, that's the last thing I need to be. In fact, I need to be just the opposite— DEPENDENT. As most of you know, if it continues to be the Lord's will I am going to serve with Young Life in Paris, France. Because Young Life is a non-profit organization, I am required to raise my financial support, which is what I find myself smack dab in the middle of doing. Now, it *truly* has been such a blessed experience and part of the ministry, but it's also one of the most trying as well. Sometimes I just want to scream! And I all too often let myself get overwhelmed with it because, as the Lord has been so gracious to show me, I am placing my confidence in things other than Him, which well, then of course I'd get overwhelmed. Should I expect anything else? So through this experience, among others, the Lord has been getting my attention, and for that I am truly thankful. I need to learn some trust! He's had to slam some doors shut in my face to say, "JESSICA . . . it's not about you. It's not about what you write, what you say, or what you do. It's about ME! You're not going to get this done. I AM! Don't you know it is better to trust in ME than to put confidence in what you can do? Well, if you truly trust Me then don't fret and let My Spirit work! Trust in Me, take refuge in Me rather than in yourself."

Again, this experience is just one of *many* through which the Lord has been revealing that my confidence and trust have not been placed in Him. And when I stop to think about that I know how absurd that is! I mean my goodness, should I trust in me who would lose her head if it were not attached, or trust in the Lord Almighty, Creator of the heavens and the earth, the One who knit me together in my mother's womb, and the One who knows me better than I even know myself? Hmmm. Tough decision! I can't remember someone's name five minutes after I meet him/her and yet God knows all of the millions of stars' names! I think I'd rather trust in Him . . . and yet I still struggle with letting go and doing that. Furthermore, it's not like He hasn't proved Himself to me AMPLE times before . . . I know that it's well worth my while to trust in Him and Him alone. I have countless stories from my very own life that would reveal He is faithful and He is trustworthy. Basically, I've decided I'm an Israelite . . . constantly forgetting all that the Lord has done before my very eyes and oooh how that must frustrate the Lord. But how thankful I am that He is patient and *slow to anger!* Were He not, I would definitely have His anger burning against me daily!

Today I encourage you to look in your own life and see where you're placing your trust. Don't trust your words alone for, if you're like me, they might deceive you. I've found that often times my words say what I want to be like, how I want to feel, but my actions and inner thoughts reveal the true state of my heart. Remember that the Lord, *your* God is faithful. He is trustworthy. Look into your own life to see reminders of that. Be careful not to forget all that He's done for you (easier said than done, I know!) But y'all, it really is better to trust in the Lord and take refuge in Him than to put your confidence in yourself, this world, or the ways of man. God is bigger than you, this world, and any circumstance! His ways are better and His thoughts are higher. May you rest in His presence today and delight in His unfailing love!

By His grace,

<>< Jessica

Prayer requests? Praises?

From: Hisword2day
To: Your heart
Sent: Tuesday, September 30, 2003 12:33 PM
Subject: Display cases–1 Timothy 1:12–17

"I thank Christ Jesus our Lord, who has given me strength, that he considered me faithful, appointing me to his service. Even though I was once a blasphemer and a persecutor and a violent man, I was shown mercy because I acted in ignorance and unbelief. The grace of our Lord was poured out on me abundantly, along with the faith and love that are in Christ Jesus. Here is a trustworthy saying that deserves full acceptance: Christ Jesus came into the world to save sinners—of whom I am the worst. But for that very reason I was shown mercy so that in me, the worst of sinners, Christ Jesus might display his unlimited patience as an example for those who would believe on him and receive eternal life. Now to the King eternal, immortal, invisible, the only God, be honor and glory for ever and ever. Amen." *1 Timothy 1:12–17* **NIV**

AWESOME passage! This has to be one of my very favorite passages in the entire Bible because I could seriously be the one writing these words! I read these words and am just humbled quite literally to tears. For who am *I* that He would consider *me* faithful, appointing *me* to His service?! My words and actions, my life have so often blasphemed and persecuted His holy name, but despite that, I was shown mercy because I acted in ignorance and unbelief—the latter probably being the truest. And yet the grace of our Lord was quite literally poured out on me *abundantly* (for where sin abounds, grace abounds even more), along with the faith and love that are in Christ Jesus. Wow! That He would shower me with His love and grace like that! Sometimes I have to wonder why!

Oh, but there's a reason. *Well, why?* I love what Paul determines: to display His unlimited patience as an example for those who would believe on Him and receive eternal life.

Hmmm. Have you ever thought of that? Have you ever thought of yourself as a display case for the Lord? Really, have you? Well, I want us to contemplate this for a moment because if we do, I think we'll discover that indeed the Lord does make our heart and our lives display cases.

Display means to reveal, expose, show, exhibit, make manifest, etc. Now think about a display case. Stores quite frequently use display cases to reveal, show, and exhibit the merchandise they carry. *Okay, you ask, so how does that apply to me?* Friend, He has taken your heart and your life and because of the abundance of His love, grace, and mercy that has been poured into and on you, you yourself have become a display case for Christ. You have become an example to others. (Really, you have!) Through you, through your life and your circumstances, and through your past He is able to display His love, joy, peace, patience, kindness, goodness, faithfulness, gentleness, self-control (aka the fruits of the Spirit) in astounding, vivid ways. As with Paul, it might be because of the past you've come from, the sins you've committed that Christ can reveal His unlimited patience, love, and grace to another. That's definitely been a big one for me! That may not be the case for you, but somehow, you will or have been an example to others because of the transformation others see you undergo as a result of meeting Christ. For as one considered faithful and as one appointed to His service, Christ exhibits His attributes through you. He makes Himself manifest in and through your life. He exposes this world to His *abundant* love and grace, through *you.* For you, my friend, are a display case for Christ.

So take a moment today to thank Christ Jesus your Lord, who has given you strength, that He considered you faithful, appointing you to His service. Remember that even though we don't deserve it, Christ loves you *so much* that He has abundantly poured out onto you His love, grace, mercy, and faith so that you might be saved. Because He's done that, He can now use you, your life, and circumstances to be a display case for the entire world to see His love, grace, patience, and power. You just never know how Christ is going to use you or your circumstance, but rest assured He can!

I encourage you to let Christ use you today. Allow Him to display Himself in and through you. May your life and your heart be an exhibition of the Lord's love and grace. Now to the King eternal, immortal, invisible, the only God, be honor and glory through our lives!

A display case for Christ Jesus,

<>< Jessica

Prayer requests? Praises?

From: Hisword2day
To: Your heart
Sent: Thursday, October 02, 2003 12:46 PM
Subject: The voice of His word–Psalm 103:20

"Bless the Lord, you His angels, who excel in strength, who do His word, heeding the voice of His word." *Psalm 103:20* NKJV

Heeding the voice of His word . . . wow! Ever want to know His will? Ever want to know His thoughts? Ever want to hear God's voice?

I do! I so long to know God in the deepest ways . . . to have such an intimate relationship that I would know Him better and better, that I would be not merely a reader of His word, but a doer, that I would know and walk in His will, that I could better understand His thoughts, and that I would be able to recognize His voice. His voice seems to come to us in all different ways, (different tones and accents, if you will), so how do we know it's Him? Well, how does what we hear stand up to Scripture? If it stands up to the Word there's a better chance it's God's voice for as this verse reminds us Scripture is one of God's voices . . . it is the voice of His word.

What an incredible thought! The voice of His word . . . I want you to try something. Today pick a passage, any passage, and read it not as we usually do, monotone, but read it with passion and emotion. Picture God saying His word to you. What voice would He use? Really, try it. It's fun and can really touch your heart when you read it as it might be said to you.

Okay, one last parting thought . . . How are you doing at heeding the voice of God's word? Are you giving attention to, observing, considering, and taking careful notice of His word? Or are you even acknowledging it? The voice of God's word speaks to all who are willing to listen. If you turn on a stereo, music will sound. Similarly, if you open, "turn on" God's word, the voice of His word will come forth. You will be inspired by God through His word. The Lord your God will teach, rebuke, correct, and train you through His word so that you may be thoroughly equipped for every good work.

God's voice, His gentle whisper, can be heard in the voice of His word. I pray that you will seek the Lord in His word. I pray that as you seek Him

He would fill you with the knowledge of His will in all wisdom and spiritual understanding that you may walk worthy of the Lord, fully pleasing Him, being fruitful in every good work, and increasing in the knowledge of God. A good place to start in knowing God's will, His thoughts, and simply knowing God is in and through His word. So get to know God. Go get equipped. Open His word today and heed its voice. *Do* His word. You will be incredibly blessed by doing so, and you will also be blessing the Lord, your God. Yes, you can bless God. Go be a blessing . . .

In Jesus Christ, my Lord,

<>< Jessica

Prayer requests? Praises?

From: Hisword2day
To: Your heart
Sent: Monday, October 06, 2003 11:50 AM
Subject: A perverse heart–Psalm 101:3–4

"I will set nothing wicked before my eyes; I hate the work of those who fall away; it shall not cling to me. A perverse heart shall depart from me; I will not know wickedness." *Psalm 101:3–4* **NKJV**

Again, what a great passage from one of David's psalms! Reading this passage last night I became a bit curious as to what exactly perverse meant and how it would apply in this passage. So I did a little research on the word . . . it's always fun for me to do that and gives me a new, different perspective on ways verses can apply to me. As I was researching, I *quickly* came to realize that these words of David—a perverse heart shall depart from me–need to become a very regular prayer for my own heart. Maybe you will discover the same . . .

So what does a perverse heart look like? Well, I am unaware of the meaning of the word as it was used in the original text of this Psalm, but Webster defines *perverse* as turned away from what is right or good: corrupt; improper, incorrect: contrary to the evidence or the direction of the judge on a point of law, as in a *perverse* verdict; obstinate in opposing what is right, reasonable, or accepted. Synonyms for perverse include such words as headstrong, self-willed, stiff-necked, stubborn, unyielding.*

Applying this to the heart . . . yikes! I don't know about you, but I don't want a self-willed heart! I don't want a heart that has turned away from what is right and good . . . that has turned away from God. I don't want an obstinate heart. I don't want a heart that is contrary to the Judge— God; I want the opposite, a similar, parallel heart to God. And yet when I put the mirror up to my own heart I realize that I so very often have a perverse heart . . . a headstrong, self-willed, stiff-necked, stubborn, unyielding heart.

Can you relate? Have any of those words ever described your heart? Do they describe your heart right now?

Well, if you're like me and answered "yes" to any of these questions, I want to remind you that you can pray that a perverse heart would depart from you and that a God-willed, pliable, yielding heart would be given to you. That it would not be contrary to God but would instead be aligned with His will, His leading, and His heart. Remember that the Lord your God has unlimited patience with you (1 Timothy 1:16). (That is so comforting to me!) So when or if you ever find your heart condemning you, or when or if you ever find yourself having a perverse heart, set your heart at rest in His presence for God is greater than our hearts (1 John 3:20).

God has recently been showing me just how self-willed and unyielding my heart has been towards Him so this verse was really powerful to me. However, I think we could all benefit from praying this verse for our hearts . . . if for no other reason than to guard our hearts from becoming perverse. Therefore, I urge you to make this a prayer for your own heart, today. Take it one day at a time. Pray that a perverse heart would depart from you and then wait in anticipation to see how the Lord your God blesses this prayer of yours!

May you delight in the blessings that shall pour forth from having a God-willed, pliable, yielding heart! Let His love and grace embrace you . . . let Him change your heart today!

Praying for your perfection,

<>< Jessica

Prayer requests? Praises?

*Merriam-Webster Online Dictionary

From: Hisword2day
To: Your heart
Sent: Wednesday, October 08, 2003 10:49 AM
Subject: Believing and trusting the Lord–Romans 4:18–21

"Against all hope, Abraham in hope believed and so became the father of many nations, just as it had been said to him, 'So shall your offspring be.' Without weakening in his faith, he faced the fact that his body was as good as dead—since he was about a hundred years old—and that Sarah's womb was also dead. Yet he did not waver through unbelief regarding the promise of God, but was strengthened in his faith and gave glory to God, being fully persuaded that God had power to do what he had promised." *Romans 4:18–21* **NIV**

Sometimes things happen to *test* your faith and trust in God, sometimes things happen to *strengthen* your faith and trust in God, and other times things happen in your life to help *strengthen other people's faith.* Abraham's story is one that fits all of these descriptions. In Genesis, we can read about how God informs Abram (Abraham), who has yet to have a child and is in his late 90s at the time, that he is going to have a child (Genesis 15:4). Sarah, his wife, was not much younger and, I mean, who'd ever heard of people in their nineties having kids? Yeah right! Impossible! Seemingly so, but as the Lord tells Abraham and Sarah, *nothing* is too hard for the Lord (Genesis 18:14). God simply tells them that He will return to them at the appointed time the following year and Sarah will have a son.

Here's what gets me . . . when God tells Abram that he's going to have a child, even though all the odds are stacked against him, or as Paul writes, "his body was as good as dead as was Sarah's womb," "Abram believed the Lord." (Genesis 15:6) Sure enough he recognized the situation, that it was seemingly impossible. Yet against all hope, Abraham *in hope* believed God, despite his circumstances. He did not waver through unbelief regarding the promise God made to him. Rather He was strengthened in his faith and gave glory to God for he was fully persuaded . . . he was *convinced* that God had power to do what He had promised. He believed God. He trusted the Lord. And therefore, Abraham saw God's promise come true . . . he did have a child, Isaac, and his descendants were as numerous as the stars! Indeed, God had the power to do what He'd promised!

How does this apply to you? Friend, faith-testing moments will come your way . . . the Bible promises us that! There will be moments when it seems as though what God has promised can't possibly happen—it goes against all logic and human capabilities. Your resources and abilities will be exhausted. You will be able to do nothing. Situations will seem against all hope. You may even question God. Maybe He didn't promise this or that. Maybe you misunderstood Him. Maybe He's not in this. But friends, life doesn't go as we would always like it to. Even still, Abraham's story can be such a testimony to you. ANYTHING is possible if you believe! God never goes back on His promises!

However, remember, *timing is everything.* God told Abraham and Sarah that He would return to them at the *appointed* time. And Paul reminds us in 2 Peter 3:8–9 that God is not slack or slow concerning His promises, but that God's timetable looks a little differently than ours . . . one day is as 1000 years and 1000 years as one day. God's timing may not be your timing, but *God does not make blank promises.* What He promises, He comes through on. Ask God and seek His heart on what His specific promises are to you. They will look different than His specific promises to me, although there are some promises He makes to us all . . . He will never leave us nor forsake us. He will be with us always. He will fight our fights for us, etc.

As I close, I want to remind you that your faith-testing moments might happen to strengthen your faith and trust. They might happen to teach you to simply believe God. And they might happen to be a testimony to others . . . for others to see God's power and faithfulness through you, your life and/or circumstance. We never know exactly how God's working, but we can rest assured that God works good out of everything for those who are called according to His purposes (Romans 8:28). Claim that promise today. Remember that He has not forgotten His promise . . . He is not slow. He just works on a different timetable. Believe God. Trust Him like Abraham did. Recognize your circumstances and face the reality of them, but try to not be discouraged or to let your faith be weakened. Rather allow your faith to be strengthened. (Easier said than done, I know!) I pray that one day I would read the story of your life and read the words written about Abram . . . that you believed the Lord.

Remember who the Lord your God is and that nothing is impossible for Him. *Nothing.*

May you be strengthened in your faith and give glory to God, being fully persuaded that God has power to do what He has promised.

In Christ's love,

<>< Jessica

Prayer requests? Praises?

From: Hisword2day
To: Your heart
Sent: Friday, October 10, 2003 11:21 AM
Subject: REJOICE! Psalm 105:1–5

"Oh give thanks to the Lord! Call upon His name; Make known His deeds among the peoples! Sing to Him, sing psalms to Him; Talk of all His wondrous works! Glory in His holy name; Let the hearts of those rejoice who seek the Lord! Seek the Lord and His strength; seek His face evermore! Remember His marvelous works which He has done, His wonders, and the judgments of His mouth . . ." *Psalm 105:1–5 NKJV*

Okay, I have so little time to write as I should be leaving for work right now, and I hope to be able to share more in depth with you later, but the Lord has totally rocked my world today in just the most amazing ways and my heart is truly singing praises to Him for the marvelous works He alone has done! God's been teaching me a lot about "Ask and you shall receive" and not just about asking for physical, material items, but just about anything. Ask for perseverance, ask for joy, ask for peace etc. . . . and you shall receive! Again, I'll share more later . . . I will make known His deeds to you when I have more time, but for now I just want to encourage you to let your hearts rejoice! Sing praises of thanksgiving for the marvelous works He has done and will do! We often miss His wonders for we take for granted all that He has done (this is easy to do), but remember that you are surrounded by the radiance of His glory today. You are surrounded by His marvelous works! I mean, this is the day that the Lord has made . . . it is a wonder in and of itself! Today is nothing short of a miracle, for it is by the Lord's hand that the sun rose, the tides came in, the winds blow, the rains come, the earth turns, the birds chirp, and we arose from our sleep today. We are living and breathing—that alone is a miracle!

So my friends let your hearts rejoice!!! Let us rejoice and be glad in this day! Give thanks to the Lord your God for all of His wondrous works, in nature, in your very own lives, and within your own heart. Share with others what He's been doing, how you've seen that which He has done. Oh how it blesses me to hear what the Lord is doing in someone else's life! It encourages me to hear how He works and it reminds me of His marvelous works . . . His wonders. May you seek His face evermore today and be delighted in the ways you find Him!

Have an absolutely brilliant day calling upon His name! Glory in His holy name!

Rejoicing,

<>< Jessica

Prayer requests? Praises?

From: Hisword2day
To: Your heart
Sent: Tuesday, October 14, 2003 2:05 PM
Subject: It's a great day to be alive–Psalm 118:24

"This is the day the Lord has made; let us rejoice and be glad in it." *Psalm 118:24* **NIV**

I heard a song on the radio today that I've heard numerous times before, but I guess this time I actually *listened* to the words and wow, what a great message! It's a country song, so for any country music fans you might have heard this. For those of you who never listen to country music, it's a great song to listen to if you ever get a chance. The chorus includes a line that goes something like this: "It's a great day to be alive, the sun's still shining when I close my eyes . . ."

It's a great day to be alive . . . wow! What a great thought! It truly is a great day to be alive . . . for this is the day that the Lord has made. The marvelous works of His hands and His invisible attributes are being made clear to us this very day. We are getting a front row seat to the display of His glory! We are watching miracles happen today! It's easy to overlook everyday miracles, but we realized Friday, today is *nothing* short of a miracle. Remember that it is by His mighty hand that you are living and breathing and that life is existing—today.

I encourage you to not merely survive today. Don't simply endure the day and continue on just to remain existing. Even if it is just a rotten day for you I encourage you to muster up some strength and ask the Lord to grant you the ability to be glad in this very day, to find the hidden blessings in store for you, and to rejoice in this day . . . for today is the day that the Lord has made. Does that hit anyone else as hard as it does me? He *made* today—He fashioned it, completed it, prepared it, formed it, created it, and invented it! He made today, and it is a unique masterpiece in and of itself! Oh that He would share it with us! Wow! Let's thank Him that we are alive today for truly, it is a great day to be alive! Let's rejoice in the day that the Lord has made and be glad in it!

May the Lord be with your spirit today as you rejoice in your Maker. Be glad in your King . . .

Excited just to be alive,

<>< Jessica

Prayer requests? Praises?

From: Hisword2day
To: Your heart
Sent: Thursday, October 16, 2003 2:33 PM
Subject: The broken toaster–Psalm 51:10

"Create in me a pure heart, O God, and renew a steadfast spirit within me." *Psalm 51:10* **NIV**

Oh what a great verse! Last week we talked about praying that a perverse (self-willed, incorrect) heart would depart from us (Psalm 101:4). Well, does anyone else agree that Psalm 51:10 would be a great follow-up prayer?! They just seem to go hand in hand! Take a perverse heart away, protect me from it and grant me a pure heart! ☺

Again, when I rediscovered this verse I did a little word research and was blown away by what I discovered! In the past couple of weeks Jesus and I have been working on me grasping the fact that apart from Him I can do nothing (John 15:5). Namely, I cannot change myself. I alone cannot grow in my relationship with Him. I cannot even breathe by myself . . . I mean it is by His hand that oxygen is supplied! Yet trying to grasp the fact that I cannot change myself has been a bittersweet lesson for me to learn during this particular season of my life. I so desperately desire to know my Jesus better, but I find that I am all too often what Paul describes in Romans 7:15—that which I despise—and do not understand my actions! Nevertheless, I set out to try and fix myself and change my heart. My intentions are wonderful and the fact that I desire Him more must make God smile. However, as my friend Lauren so graciously reminded me, I cannot change myself. As she put it, "A broken toaster can't fix itself." Although I have a bit more ability and free will than a toaster, I still cannot fix myself. When she brought this to my attention it was like a light went on! The trumpets were resounding; the choir was singing "HALLELUJAH!" (Come on—picture it with me.) ☺ Wow . . . I can't change myself! I can't fix myself. *I simply can't.* But God can. Let repeat that again. *God can.*

Really, let that sink in for a second. *God can. He is able.*

No matter what mess you've made of yourself, your life, or situation, God is more than able. After all, He created you; therefore, He can change you. And as my little word research helped me discover, to create means to bring into existence, to make, fashion, invent, establish, form, build, construct, or bring about through a course of action or behavior, to produce through imaginative skill. He brought you into existence. He made you and fashioned you. He invented you! He established you. He formed you. He built you one cell at a time. He constructed you, your personality, and your character. And truly, He produced you with such imaginative skill! I mean there is not another you on this planet! For Him to have made each one of us so different is absolutely incredible! And isn't that just an amazing, mind boggling thought to ponder: the Lord your God has *created* you?!

Now how does all this apply to the verse? "Create in me a pure heart and renew a steadfast spirit within me." He can create a pure heart in you. He can bring a pure heart into existence within your being. He can make, fashion, form, invent, and generate a pure heart within in you. However, remember that more than likely it won't poof into existence. Rather it will be brought about gradually. It will be built and constructed within you through a process . . . through a course of action or behavior. Just as building/constructing a home is a process, building, constructing, creating a pure heart and renewing a steadfast spirit is a process. But get excited, for the Creator, who has such imaginative skill, is in charge! And your pure heart will truly be *established* in you with His imaginative skill!

Today I encourage you to let Him change you. Let Him create a pure heart in you. Don't be me. Don't be the broken toaster trying to fix itself. It's not a fun process I can assure you! Seek Jesus first and ask Him to help you. Beseech Him to create a pure heart and renew a steadfast spirit within you. Oh my goodness it's amazing . . . when we ask . . . we really do receive!

Lord, I pray for my friends today. Please, Jesus, take away and protect them from a perverse heart and create in them a pure heart, O God. By your great and wonderful power and imaginative skill, fashion and establish, build and construct a pure, unadulterated heart in each one of them. May their hearts and minds be Yours today. Bless them today as you renew a steadfast spirit within them. All for Your glory Christ Jesus . . . all for You.

Praying for your perfection,

<>< Jessica

Prayer requests? Praises?

From: Hisword2day
To: Your heart
Sent: Tuesday, October 21, 2003 2:31 PM
Subject: The beat of a different drummer–John 7:3–4, 8–10

"Jesus' brothers said to him, 'You ought to leave here and go to Judea, so that your disciples may see the miracles you do. No one who wants to become a public figure acts in secret. Since you are doing these things, show yourself to the world . . . ' [Then Jesus said] ' . . . I am not yet going up to this Feast, because for me the right time has not yet come.' Having said this, he stayed in Galilee. However, after his brothers had left for the Feast, he went also, not publicly but in secret." *John 7:3–4, 8–10* **NIV**

It's interesting to me, to read how Jesus acts in the scriptures. He often does things that I don't understand. I'll read passages in scripture that leave me a little dumbfounded. I'm left asking, "Why would you say __ __?" "Why would you do ____?" Scripture tells us that Jesus' disciples and His own brothers felt much the same way at times. In this passage from John, Jesus' brothers were trying to persuade Him to go up to Judea where the Feast of the Tabernacles was soon to be held. There would be quite a crowd there, and they wanted Him to go there to make a public display of Himself—to prove Himself, not only to the people of Judea, but to themselves for they, his own brothers, did not yet believe in Him (John 7:5). Jesus knew they didn't believe in Him. He knew there would be tons of people there. He knew He had the power to do miraculous wonders. Yet He also knew the right time had not come to make a public spectacle of Himself. That would soon come. (Again, we see timing is crucial.) When Jesus did go, He went not publicly, but in secret. Not the way this world would tell someone to make their entrance.

Ya know what this passage reminded me of? Jesus isn't of this world. *He doesn't always work in the ways of this world.* His clock runs on a different schedule than ours. With the Lord, One day is like 1000 years and 1000 years is like one day. People wanting to become known, as Jesus' brothers remind us, don't act in secret, rather they act very publicly—the world's way. Yet Jesus doesn't always act like we think He should—in ways we would.

Simply put, Jesus marches to the beat of a different drummer. (Something I know I need to be reminded of frequently!) He marches only to the beat that is in accordance with God's will. His timing is not always our timing. His ways are not our ways, nor are His thoughts our thoughts. Therefore, sometimes we may not understand why He acts the ways He does. We may be confused or dumbfounded by the way He acts. Certain events and circumstances and the timing of certain things in our lives may confuse us. You might find yourself asking, "Jesus, why don't you make your presence known without a shadow of a doubt?" "Why now?" "Why not now?" "Why this?" But remember, His ways and His thoughts are higher than ours. They are better. More than that, His ways are perfect and eternal (Habakkuk 3:6).

Remember that the Lord may or may not be doing something because the right time has not yet come. And/or He may be acting very differently than you hoped for, wanted, or would have expected. But as this passage can remind us, that's typical! He marches to the beat of a different drummer. His thoughts may not be your thoughts, but His thoughts are loving and faithful. His ways may not be your ways, but His ways are perfect and eternal. His timing may not be your timing, but we are not always to understand the time and dates the Father has set by His authority. How reassuring it is though to know that the times and dates *are* set by His authority! We are to live by faith . . . so do just that today for living by faith is a Fantastic Adventure In Trusting Him (F.A.I.T.H.)

May the grace and peace of our Lord Jesus Christ be with you as you seek to march to the beat of Jesus' drummer.

In His unfailing love,

<>< Jessica

Prayer Requests? Praises?

From: Hisword2day
To: Your heart
Sent: Friday, October 24, 2003 7:50 AM
Subject: The Lord is near–Philippians 4:5

" . . . The Lord is near." *Philippians 4:5* **NIV**

I did something I'm proud of yesterday. I did something completely illogical. I took time for myself.

That may sound like a no-brainer for some of you. "We all need to do that from time to time." Right. We do. But this is the girl who misread the memo stating we have 24 hours in a day and thought it read 42 hours. I am on the go *constantly.* I really don't know where my time goes, and it doesn't help that I'm downright rotten at time management. "To-do" lists help, but I still have no concept of time and how to utilize it. This is definitely one of my weaknesses, but for that I shall boast for in that weakness, somehow, the Lord's power is perfected . . . it is definitely magnified! I mean when I accomplish anything (actually do my list of "to-dos"), arrive somewhere on time (meaning only running 5 minutes late and not 10) it's *nothing* short of a miracle!

Therefore, when I was given the morning/early afternoon off at work yesterday I thought, *YES! TIME! I can go do this. I can go do that. I'll . . . Oh my goodness, Jessica. You are never going to get all of that done. And then there's this too. Don't forget that.* It wasn't long before anxious thoughts set in and I became overwhelmed. Now, one of the few things I've learned about myself is that if my heart is filled with anxious thoughts and is not at rest in His presence, even amidst a busy schedule, I'm useless. My emotions escalate, and I accomplish nothing . . . nada, zilch, rien. At times like these my heart just isn't right. And that's where I was . . . broken, with no strength, and no peace . . . broken.

About this time is when I felt the tug on my heart. "Cast your burdens on Me and I will sustain you. If you will just cry for help, if you will just let me, I will let you know that I am here." The Lord was nudging me to just go be still. I hesitated. I contemplated all I could potentially get done during my long break. *You've got this time to accomplish things. Don't waste it! Go and do! Don't stop!* was the thought resonating in my mind. I hesitated some more and put on my exercise clothes. *Pilates . . . that'll relieve some stress,* I thought. But somewhere down deep I heard a faint whisper say, "Nope. Pilates won't do. I just need you to be still, my child. Come away with me and rest in my presence for a moment. *Please.* I missed meeting with you this morning. Let's make up for it. I promise you, it will be well worth your time."

That did it. I finally surrendered. I knew Pilates couldn't fix me; only Jesus could. I was desperate for Jesus. I needed to let Him quiet me with His love. The sea of emotions I had been swimming in as I worked through the support-raising process of doing international missions had engulfed me and I needed to confess these feelings to Him. He already knew them; I just needed to surrender them. I needed to turn them over to the Lord. Let go.

So today I stopped. I put down my mile-long "to-do" list, turned off my phone, closed my e-mail, put on some comfortable clothes, grabbed my Bible, journal, and a pen and I went to a quiet place. I disconnected. (I STRONGLY suggest doing this sometime . . . it's fantastic not being able to be reached for a few moments!) In the world's eyes, this was completely illogical. I wasn't "maximizing my time." But really, I was. God was calling me to stop. He was calling me to be still. He was longing to be gracious to me. And when the Creator of the universe and the keeper of time tells you to stop, it's a good idea to listen. I don't usually because the volume of my life is so loud, but today, I *actually* listened to this gentle whisper. I stopped. I was illogical. I marched to the beat of a different drummer. I was still. I listened. I watched the deer study me, curious to see if I was going to feed them. I prayed. I wrote. I drained my heart out before God—something I haven't really done in quite some time.

Then, after just resting in His presence, I opened my Bible to nowhere in particular. I just asked God to speak to me. "Tell me what my soul is longing to hear." And this is what He said, "I AM NEAR."

"Then you will call and the Lord will answer; you will cry for help and He will say, 'Here I am.'" (Isaiah 58:9).

"I am near." Oh what blessed, precious words! "I am near." That is *exactly* what I needed to hear, what my soul had been desperately trying to grasp hold of. I could feel the warmth of His embrace as if He were drawing near just to whisper these words in my ear, "My Princess, my beloved child, I am near. You have drawn near to me and I have drawn even nearer to you. Rest your heart in my presence for my precious child, I am near. I have come to heal the brokenhearted and to bind up your wounds." He was there in that moment. He was with me in that quiet place. He was near.

Friend, I want you to know. No, I want you to experience, that God is near. Dwell on this thought for a moment. What does it mean to you? Your Lord and Savior, your Creator, your heavenly Father is near. He is close. He is in your vicinity. He is in close proximity to you. He is near. To me, in that moment, it meant that indeed He was an ever-present help in trouble. He does sustain me when I cast my burdens on Him. He will establish peace within me. He guards my heart and mind in Christ Jesus. He listens. He listens to *me*, a mere human who messes up every single day of her life, and yet He listens to me. He comforts me. But mostly, it meant that *He loves me.*

Jesus loves you, this I know. The Lord is near! May the thoughts of reassurance and peace flood your heart and mind as you too feel the warmth of His embrace.

Drawing near,

<>< Jessica

Prayer requests? Praises?

From: Hisword2day
To: Your heart
Sent: Monday, October 27, 2003 12:30 PM
Subject: The Spirit prays–Romans 8:26–27

"In the same way, the Spirit helps us in our weakness. We do not know what we ought to pray for, but the Spirit hmself intercedes for us with groans that words cannot express. And h who searches our hearts knows the mind of the Spirit, because the Spirit intercedes for the saints in accordance with God's will." *Romans 8:26–27* **NIV**

Do you ever feel like you just don't know what you need to pray for whether it be for yourself or someone else? You recognize that you need to pray. You even want to, but you go to do so and you draw a blank. You're speechless. You stand before the throne of your heavenly Father and can barely whisper a prayer. Words don't seem to be coming. You don't know exactly what you're feeling or experiencing and therefore, you don't really know what in the world to pray for, or even where to begin! Ever wandered down this path?

I've found myself walking this path a *lot* lately. There's so much I know I need to pray for, so much I want to pray for, and yet I go to do so and I'm blank. It doesn't help that I'm on a roller coaster of emotions and walking through some blazing hot refining fires. So not only do I feel overwhelmed and as though I'm not in touch with my heart, I also don't feel like I'm in touch with God's heart and His good and perfect will. Therefore, I don't know what I ought to pray or where to begin.

Well, when/if you find yourself walking in my footsteps not knowing God's will or what to pray (and I'm sure you will some time or another) than let Paul's words reassure you. *The Spirit helps you in your weakness.* (Oh thank you, Lord!)You may not know what you ought to pray for, but the Spirit Himself intercedes for you with groans that words cannot express. The Holy Spirit searches your heart and then prays or expresses for you on a level only God, Jesus, and the Holy Spirit can understand. Our small vocabulary can't encompass these "groans," nor can our finite minds comprehend them!

And although you may not fully understand God's will, the Holy Spirit does and He prays it over, through, and for your life. He prays in accordance—that is in agreement, harmony and unity—with God's will. Now that is some kind of reassuring for me! Can you just imagine how powerful and effective the Holy Spirit's prayers are for you!? "The prayer of a righteous man is powerful and effective" (James 5:16), and wouldn't you agree that the Holy Spirit embodies the definition of righteous? Exciting stuff!

So today I encourage us to let the Holy Spirit, who is in perfect unity and communication with Jesus and God, help us who are not in perfect unity and communication with Jesus and God (or ourselves for that matter!) to communicate with them. Know and believe that He helps you in your weaknesses. When you can barely whisper a prayer, ask the Holy Spirit to intercede for you and then know that He is praying for you, praying God's good and perfect will over, for, and through your life. Let Him show you what that will is and slowly but surely you'll begin to pray it over and for your own life as the Spirit leads.

Rest in the assurance of His love for you and delight in the fact that He has searched your heart. He knows how to pray for you in a way you simply cannot pray for yourself. God prays for you.

Praying for your perfection,

<>< Jessica

Prayer requests? Praises?

From: Hisword2day
To: Your heart
Sent: Tuesday, October 28, 2003 12:35 PM
Subject: What have you entrusted?–2 Timothy 1:12

"That is why I am suffering as I am. Yet I am not ashamed, because I know whom I have believed, and am convinced that he is able to guard what I have entrusted to him for that day." *2 Timothy 1:12* **NIV**

Bound and chained like a common criminal, Paul was thrown into a cold dungeon under the watchful, spiteful eye of Nero. At the time this verse was written, Nero was fiercely persecuting Christians and trying to stop the spread of their teachings, hence why Paul was imprisoned. As scripture reminds us, Paul is a herald, an apostle, and a teacher of the gospel and we know Paul well enough to know that the threat of persecution doesn't shut his mouth! I imagine Paul was openly spreading the gospel during that time and therefore, that is why he writes "that is why I am suffering as I am." He was doing exactly what God called him to do, and yes, that did lead to imprisonment.

Despite this, Paul was not ashamed of who he was or what he was doing. He was not ashamed to share Christ even when imprisonment and death were staring him in the eye. He was not ashamed, hindered, or intimidated to the point of not sharing because he knew in whom he believed. He had experienced and become so well acquainted with Jesus that he wasn't ashamed. Rather, he was convinced, he was certain that Jesus was able to guard what Paul had entrusted to Him and therefore, let nothing stand in his way.

Entrust: to commit to another with confidence*; to charge with trust or responsibility**

What was it Paul had entrusted to the one in whom he believed? Paul's writings confirm that he had entrusted everything to Jesus. Not just some things, but *everything:* his heart, mind, body, soul, time, and experiences. He committed his very life to Jesus . . . *with confidence.* "Yet I am not ashamed, because I know whom I have believed, and am convinced that He is able to guard what I have entrusted to Him for that day."

He had fully entrusted himself, his time, and his ways to Jesus. And he was convinced, persuaded, certain, assured, and confident that Jesus was able to guard what Paul had entrusted to Him for that day. Paul trusted Jesus on a daily basis. He was convinced that Jesus could guard, protect, care for, and shield all that he had entrusted to Him *one day at a time.*

Yet Paul also realized that this momentary journey on earth was not his final destination. So if death came his way, he knew to whom he had entrusted his heart and life and was convinced of where he would go. For he knew Jesus would guard him on Judgment Day. He was convinced (and rightly so) that Jesus would vouch for him on Judgment Day and say, "Not guilty. He's mine, Father. He was one of our good and faithful servants." Therefore, when imprisonment came, even when death came, Paul was fully assured, for he knew in whom he had believed and he was convinced that Jesus was able.

My question to you today is: what have you entrusted to Jesus? I mean really entrusted to Him, committed with confidence, and charged with trust and responsibility. Your heart? Your life? Okay, we may say, "Yeah." Let's go even further . . . How about your kids? Your spouse? Your singleness? Your relationships (friendships or dating)? Your financial situation? Your difficult circumstances? Your problems? Your decisions? Your exam? Your job? Your day?

Have you entrusted that stuff to Him? And are you convinced that He is able to guard what you have entrusted to Him?

I would like to think that I've entrusted those things to Jesus, but if I'm being really honest, maybe I haven't. And why I haven't is beyond me! I know He is more than able to guard ANYTHING that I entrust to Him, but maybe I am not convinced yet. (Although I have *every* reason to be!) Or maybe I just have a hard time letting go because I like to feel like I have to have some sort of control. However, I know deep down that the more out of control I am and the more in control He is, the more in control my life is, no matter how out of control it may appear. (Did that make any sense?) ☺

Today I just want to encourage you to look within your heart and ask the Lord to help you see what you have really entrusted to Him, and what you need to entrust to Him. Friend, He is able to guard whatever you commit to Him. He will protect, shield and take care of you, your heart, your life, your loved ones, and your circumstances. He is more than able, for is anything too hard for the Lord? (Genesis 18:14).

Don't be ashamed of Jesus . . . don't be ashamed of what you may be going through because of your faith in Him. May you be convinced of who He is and that He is able to guard that which you have entrusted to Him. Go ahead. Commit yourself, your heart, and your life to Jesus with confidence. Trust Him *today.*

His,

<>< Jessica

Prayer requests? Praises?

*Merriam-Webster Online Dictionary

**The New American Webster Handy College Dictionary

From: Hisword2day
To: Your heart
Sent: Thursday, October 30, 2003 1:08 PM
Subject: Miracles do happen–Genesis 18:14

"Is anything too hard for the Lord?" God - *Genesis 18:14*

I spoke with a walking, living, breathing miracle today. Daniel is his name, and Daniel is a miracle. Daniel's story will remind you that indeed nothing is too hard for the Lord.

Several weeks ago Daniel and his friends were out on 6th Street, a street in Austin famous for its night life, and got a ride home with a stranger. (Note: *never* take a ride from a stranger.) The stranger had other plans than to take them home. LONG story short, Daniel and his friends were all severely beaten, all hospitalized, Daniel being the worst. His friends were released, after X-rays, bandages, and surgeries, but Daniel was put in ICU. He was clinging to life by a thread. Eleven blows had been dealt to his head and as a result, his brain was swelling quite severely. His eye sockets had been shattered along with his cheek bone. To the police, he was dead. With a 30% chance of survival (and that being generous), the police went ahead and filed his case as a homicide.

The doctors and nurses said that if he survived it would literally be a miracle. IF that were to happen, it wouldn't be an easy life for him. He would be in the hospital for weeks, rehab for months, might possibly have 40% of his vision to his left eye, would not have much of his memory, would have to relearn how to speak, read, and write, might forget who his parents were, and his personality would be different. He basically wouldn't be the same Daniel and would struggle the rest of his life.

His situation was grim, seemingly hopeless. There was nothing we could *do* for Daniel. Doctors and nurses would do their best to take care of him, but at the state he was in it was truly up to the Lord to save Daniel's life. Prayer was our biggest and only weapon. (It always is anyway.) So pray, pray, pray we did. Daniel had a multitude of people praying for him, and over him. Hands were laid on him, and scripture was claimed over his life.

And wow did God prove that prayers are powerful and effective! Wow, did He proved that *nothing* is too hard for Him! Today I saw Daniel. And I not only saw him, I *talked* with Daniel. I held a normal, intelligent conversation with a guy who a month ago medically should have been dead. I'd seen this guy lying on his death bed! And here I was *talking* with him. He recognized me, knew who I was, even remembered that I'm moving overseas. I couldn't help but be utterly astounded!

As for his recovery: his vision is currently at 92%, not 40%. Therapy? Not needed. He went in on Monday to his first therapy session and they sent him home the next day. They told him he didn't need it. They even asked him, "Are you sure you received a head injury?" As for memory, he remembered his social security number, his driver's license number, and his cell phone number, and he even remembered the pass code to receive his voice mail. He can even remember several of the events leading up to what happened to him. And his personality? Exactly the same.

Miracles do happen. Daniel is a miracle.

Isn't that just the neatest story?! I think it's absolutely amazing!!! From death to life! Quite literally! As I was walking away from seeing him, I was saying "What god is there in heaven or on earth who can do the deeds and mighty works you do?" God's answer was simple. He said, "Jessica is *anything* too hard for me? Remember his story. *Nothing, nothing, nothing* is too hard for me."

So friends, I just want to remind you too, nothing is too hard for the Lord. He can heal the wounded, and save the dying. He can mend a relationship and provide a friend. He can meet all your needs, financially and emotionally. He can part oceans and save a nation. He can raise the dead. He can set captives free. He can restore. He can guard and protect. He can do immeasurably more than we could ever even imagine! He has no limit! *Nothing is too hard for Him!*

Earlier we talked about entrusting things to the Lord. Really believing in this verse will help you entrust more to Him. Nothing is too hard for the Lord your God. Your life or certain areas of your life may seem in the same shape as Daniel was . . . beaten up beyond repair, on a "death bed." Well, let Daniel's story remind you that the Lord is able to heal and restore. He can save. He is able.

I feel like I must remind you though, just because nothing is too hard for the Lord doesn't mean He does everything He's able to do in all situations. We do not know the mind, dates, or times the Lord has set in His authority and therefore some things may not go as *we* planned.

However, know that His plans are perfect (despite how imperfect they may seem), and know that He is *more than able* to do anything. Just look outside at the canvas of this world and may that be a reminder of His mighty ability. Think of Daniel's story and may you be comforted in knowing that as impossible as something may seem, nothing is too hard, difficult, or troublesome for the Lord.

I pray you are blown away at what the Lord is able to do! Stand in awe of the Lord Almighty, for miracles do happen.

Amazed,

<>< Jessica

Prayer requests? Praises?

From: Hisword2day
To: Your heart
Sent: Monday, November 03, 2003 3:05 PM
Subject: Not to us, but to the Lord be glory–Psalm 115:1

"Not to us, O LORD, not to us but to your name be the glory because of your love and faithfulness." *Psalm 115:1* **NIV**

Oh how my heart cries out this prayer for you and for me!

Lord don't let me be glorified, may you be glorified in and through me. To your name be the glory and honor because of your love and faithfulness. It is because of you and for you that we are here, Father. Let us never forget that! By your mighty hands the earth was formed. In your great love you breathed life into my friends, into me, and into all of creation. And because of your faithfulness, we are still here . . . serving you.

Lord Jesus, I am *nothing* without you! I shudder to think of where I would be without your love and faithfulness! I'd still be stuck in that miry pit, in that slimy pit of the muck and mud of my own doing. But Lord Jesus, you lifted me out. You set me free and set my feet on the rock of your love. It is by faith I have gained access into this firm place of your grace in which I now stand. Help me stand firm here!

Jesus, I thank you. With all that I have and with all that I am, I thank you for loving me despite how unlovable I can be. Thank you for being faithful even when I am faithless! How great is your faithfulness?! Thank you! Because of your love and faithfulness, I surrender. I want to be a vessel for your glory. I want to be a reflection of your glory . . . let me deflect your love and faithfulness into this world. But Lord, let it not be because of what you do, but may it be because of who you are that I magnify your name. You are the Lord of Lords, the King of Kings, the Lord Almighty, the Lord of Hosts, the Sovereign One, the Savior of the world . . . and you are the Lord my God. How precious that thought is to me, Lord!

Be our King and help us to be your faithful servants. Make our lives display cases for you. And Father I beg you, not to me O Lord, not to us, but to your name be the glory, because of your unfailing love and faithfulness.

May all the glory, honor and praise be yours! How worthy you are! I love you, my Father, my Savior, and my Friend. I love you.

AMEN

From: Hisword2day
To: Your heart
Sent: Tuesday, November 04, 2003 1:17 PM
Subject: Pen or Pencil?–Proverbs 27:1

"Do not boast about tomorrow for you do not know what a day may bring forth." *Proverbs 27:1* NIV

AH! The story of my life! I've said numerous times before that this is my theme verse because I've learned, the hard way, that this verse is such a reality! We don't know what a day is going to bring forth! "Many are the plans in a man's heart, but it is the Lord's purpose that prevails" (Proverbs 19:21). I often make plans; God often changes them.

Anyway, this past spring my friend Brad and I were catching up. He was explaining to me that his life was completely up in the air. Things were in total disarray. Nothing was going as he'd planned. Simply put, he was going through a lot and learning the truth of Proverbs 19:21 and 27:1.

However, despite his somewhat aggravating and stressful times, Brad had a great attitude. He'd gotten over the frustration of "things not going as planned" and had just started laughing at his situation. He said something to me that day which has stuck with me ever since. "Jess, I can tell you this, I've learned one thing: If you want to make God laugh, make plans."

If you want to make God laugh, make plans.

WOW! I busted out laughing because AMEN to that! Oh my goodness! How true is that?! That being the case, I REALLY make God laugh! So many times it seems that as soon as I make plans for something . . . big or small, WHAM! God throws me a curve ball. DETOUR Jessica! He changes my plans. Yes, *my* plans, because His plans don't always coincide with my plans so He has to make some abrupt changes in *my* rigid schedule in order for it to align with His. Now, I know in my heart of hearts that His ways are perfect (2 Samuel 22:31), and that I want His plans over mine, but oooh, you wouldn't know that by the way I react sometimes! I get downright flustered, aggravated, frustrated, annoyed, and sometimes just ticked off! How dare He, right?! As if God needs our permission to change our plans! Ha!

Well, Jesus and I have been working on this attitude. After all, my time is His time, so we're working on me, letting Him make changes in my schedule with a better attitude. See, I've been handing God my schedule and asking for His approval, which has resulted in Him laughing . . . a lot . . . I've been writing my schedule in ink, not pencil. Let me explain.

I work as a receptionist at a salon and make appointments all day long. However, appointments often need to be rescheduled because unexpected events occur . . . a plane is delayed, last-minute trips come up, a car breaks down, a meeting is rescheduled causing a conflict with an appointment, traffic is horrible, kids are sick, the person scheduled to come in is sick, a doctor they've been waiting to see can only fit them in during the time slot they had scheduled for their hair appointment, etc, etc, etc. Long story short, people's plans change, often times beyond their control. Now, can you imagine what the appointment book would look like if it were written in pen? It'd be one book of scratched out mess! So it's either scratch out, go broke buying White-out, or write in pencil. Knowing that indeed we do not know what a day is going to bring forth, we're prepared and opt for scheduling in pencil.

Yet me, I've been writing in ink. My life's "appointment book" has not been so prepared for the unexpected. Instead of realizing that my time is God's time and I do not know what a day is going to bring forth— things are going to happen beyond my control—I've been getting frustrated and stressed when things don't go as planned. As a result, God's been telling me, "Jess, honey, we need to work on this. My child, you don't know what a day brings forth, but I do. Yes, make plans. Go ahead! Just make them in pencil. Let's not make your life a scratched out mess. Allow me to make the necessary changes so that no matter what plans you make, my plans will prevail. If you write in pencil (make plans lightly) you'll be able to enjoy me and these changes more. My darling, I know the plans I have for you. Trust them. Trust me."

So today I ask you: is your life's "appointment book" written in pen or pencil? Do you recognize His sovereignty and perfect plan? Or do you simply look to Him for approval of your plans? I pray that each of us would learn to write in pencil, to let God change and rearrange. So yes, make plans. But make plans lightly with the awareness that God has the right and the ability to change them. There will be some bumps in your road and some detours to be taken in this journey of life, but remember that it is the Lord who directs your steps.

Give Him your pencil and eraser today. Let Him add to, take away, and make the necessary changes. Let Him rearrange. We are not God and, therefore, do not know what a day brings forth. We have many plans, but it is the Lord's purpose, His will that will prevail. No, His ways are not our ways; but He has declared that He knows the plans HE has for us and they are plans for good, not harm. They are plans for a future and a hope.

Jesus, let us not be a hindrance to you and your plans. Rather, do with our time and do with us as you please, for we are your servants.

May you be blessed abundantly as the Lord directs your steps.

Making God laugh,

<>< Jessica ☺

Prayer requests? Praises?

From: Hisword2day
To: Your heart
Sent: Thursday, November 06, 2003 1:29 PM
Subject: Carry a lighter load–Matthew 7:13–14

"Enter through the narrow gate. For wide is the gate and broad is the road that leads to destruction, and many enter through it. But small is the gate and narrow the road that leads to life and only a few find it." *Matthew 7:13–14* **NIV**

I am a busybody. I am *constantly* on the go and my nature is to multi-task. I may be on the phone, but I'll be cleaning up around my desk at the same time. I may be at work, but I will also bring some other things to work on.

Simply put, my plate is always full. Usually too full. I just try to do too much. Like I said in a previous e-mail, I misread the memo about there being only 24 hours in the day and instead I try to cram 42 hours worth of stuff into a 24-hour day. Not good! So God and I have been working on this issue. Yes, I need to manage my time and yes I do have a full plate. Having a full plate is not necessarily a bad thing, but I have got to learn how to handle this load. I have also got to learn to try not to bear more than I can handle. I've got to learn my limits and recognize when enough is enough.

Well, this past Saturday God provided me with a great visual lesson! I was coming home from work and had to bring a lot of stuff home with me in my car. As I said above, I often take some stuff with me to work on while I am at work, so this day I had my little handy dandy file folder, my bag of "stuff," my purse, two boxes of leftovers, a coffee mug, and my Nalgene water bottle . . . oh yeah, and my tennis shoes.

Now our garage space is limited. When I pull in, I have just enough room for my door to open and for my purse and me to snuggly slide through. It's a narrow space. However, do you think this multitasker was going to make more than one trip to and from the car? Heck no! I tried to pile *all* of my junk into my arms and fit it through that narrow space. It had to be a funny sight! I have the smallest hands known to mankind and yet there I was trying to carry this gigantic load! God simply had to be laughing down at me, saying, "My child, carry a lighter load so you can fit through this narrow space easier!"

As you can imagine . . . disaster happened! The leftovers slipped, I dropped my coffee mug, the shoes went in opposite directions, and my file folder almost busted open, which would have REALLY left me with a mess. (Fortunately my car caught it.) I was simply trying to carry too much stuff through a tiny little space. I was trying to carry more than I could handle.

As the chaos unfolded, I looked up at my mom who was observing my futile efforts, and laughed, "Mom, this is my life! This is what my life looks like!" She, of all people, knows that it's true! She knows that this scene resembles my life to a tee. So she giggled, came to my rescue, and responded, "You just try to do too much." She's right. I do.

So let me ask you: does this scene resemble your life? Is your plate too full? Do you try to do too much? Do you too try to walk down this narrow road of life with too much to carry?

Brothers and sisters, you're not alone! I've been there . . . I'm wearing those shoes as we speak! We've *all* been there. Life can be extremely busy. This is to be expected. God blesses us with so many things! Tests, papers, deadlines, jobs, families, friends, activities, sports, Bible studies, on and on and on. (Don't forget those are blessings . . . if you weren't blessed with the opportunity to go to school, you wouldn't have to worry about tests and papers. If you weren't blessed with a job, you wouldn't have the opportunity to complain about it or work hard to meet a deadline. If you weren't blessed with family and friends you wouldn't have this "problem" of juggling time with all of them. And if you weren't blessed with certain abilities and opportunities you wouldn't have to worry about making it to practice on time or straining in training.) Let's focus on blessing management rather than stress management. We've got to recognize our blessings, but we've also got to learn our limits and how to manage our blessings.

Okay, back from that aside . . . ☺

"Enter through the narrow gate. For wide is the gate and broad is the road that leads to destruction, and many enter through it. But small is the gate and narrow the road that leads to life and only a few find it."

We're called to enter through that narrow gate. As scriptures tell us, Jesus is the gate and once you've entered that gate you're traveling down a narrow road, which is a beautiful and wonderful thing! It's not intended to be restrictive, but rather freeing! Remember, God wants to give you an abundant life! (John 10:10). He wants you to enjoy life to the fullest! He came so that your joy and your life can be complete!

(John 15:11). However that doesn't mean taking every opportunity that comes your way and piling your plate with more than you can handle. It doesn't mean stressing yourself out trying to do it all. You and I both know that doing these things doesn't make our joy complete . . . instead they strip it from us! We look like I did on Saturday! A disaster!

So if you are in a relationship with Christ and are traveling this narrow road, remember you're no longer on the broad road . . . you aren't on a road to destruction. And you weren't meant to do it all. You simply can't! You don't have that much time (contrary to my belief, there's not 42 hours in a day). ☺ Nor do you alone have the ability to handle it all (Apart from Christ you can do nothing - John 15:5).

Remember, God has already chosen the good works you were intended to do (Ephesians 2:10). As my friend Ben says, "Choose your battles wisely." Ask God to show you what battles He's chosen for you to fight, what load you are to bear this month, this week, this day, this hour! And remember, whatever battles you face, no matter how great they may seem, the Lord your God is going with you to fight for you (Exodus 14:14, Deuteronomy 20:1–4).

So my friends, yes, you have a lot to bear in this life. This just means that God trusts you with *a lot!* Because of that, He's going to give you the strength and ability to handle it. But know that He's also given you the ability to discern what you simply can and cannot handle. If you're overwhelmed, if you're plate seems too full, and if you're carrying too much, ask the Lord to reveal to you what you need to take off your plate or how to manage your blessings better. Ask and you shall receive. Seek and you shall find.

And never forget that *you have a helper.* When life's load seems to be too much to handle, too much for you to bear, and too large for you to fit down this narrow road, then let your Helper come to your rescue. Just as my mom came to my rescue and helped me bear my load, so your Father will come help you bear your load. He wants you to give Him your burdens. He wants to help (Matthew 11:28). LET HIM! Let Him show you your limits and then ask Him to help you live within them! Can't you hear Him saying, "Carry a lighter load so you can fit through this narrow space easier"? That may mean taking some things completely off your plate. It may not, but either way He'll help you discern.

As you give Him your burdens and let Him help you carry your overbearing loads, as you and God choose and fight your battles, may you delight and find pure joy in traveling with as light a load as is possible down this narrow road leading to the abundant life for which you were intended!!

Traveling lighter,

<>< Jessica

Prayer requests? Praises?

From: Hisword2day
To: Your heart
Sent: Friday, November 07, 2003 11:01 AM
Subject: Best or rest?–Exodus 23:19

"Bring the best of the firstfruits of your soil to the house of the Lord your God." *Exodus 23:19* **NIV**

The topic of firstfruits has come up several times in the scripture I've been reading lately. As a result, the Lord's been teaching me a little history and has been giving me a deeper understanding of this principle.

God called His people to offer to Him the firstfruits of their harvest. As our scripture for today tells us, they were not to offer their leftovers. They were to bring the *best* of their harvest to the Lord. They were to offer their *finest* to the Lord (Numbers 18:12). These offerings of firstfruits were a way for God's people to acknowledge that the harvest and all of its blessings came from God and wholly belonged to Him. It was a way for them to say thanks . . . and also a way for them to help themselves not forget from whom their blessings came.

Friend, the principle of firstfruits still applies to you today.

I realize that most of you are not farmers or ranchers and don't produce a literal harvest. However, you still have a "harvest." Your life. Your gifts and abilities. Your resources. Your time. You. You in and of yourself are a "harvest" as God has abundantly blessed you. **And friend, the Lord your God deserves your best, not your rest.** He deserves more than your leftovers.

As God's people, we are still to offer our finest to Him. After all, it is still from His hands that our life, our gifts, our abilities, and our blessings come and these belong wholly to Him. By offering Him our best we are saying thanks and acknowledging where our blessings come from so that we don't forget and don't become conceited in thinking that it is from our hands, from our doing that our blessings pour forth.

Are you giving Him your best? Or your rest? Are you acknowledging that all you've been blessed with has come from the Lord? Are you showing Him that your "harvest" wholly belongs to Him?

I haven't been! I've been giving Him my rest, my leftovers, and oh how He deserves so much more! Recently, God has taken His eraser and has gone to work on my schedule to help me give Him my best—we're still working on that task. I'm a work in progress. ☺ I'll explain that one more on Monday, but in the meantime I encourage you to seek the Lord's heart to see if there is an area in your life and in your heart where you are not giving Him your firstfruits.

The concept of giving your firstfruits really is essential! Saying thanks and acknowledging God is extremely important! Not only to protect you, but for God to continue to bless you (Read Deuteronomy 8:10–20). The Lord your God *longs* to be gracious to you. He wants to open up the floodgates of heaven upon you and to pour out so many blessings that you can't count them! He does not request your firstfruits to deprive you, but to bless you. He wants your best to give you your rest.

And *never ever* forget, He's given you His best. Jesus.

Bring the best of you before your God and may you be richly blessed and truly humbled by bringing the best of the firstfruits of your harvest to the house of the Lord your God.

Because of His Best,

<>< Jessica

Prayer requests? Praises?

From: Hisword2day
To: Your heart
Sent: Monday, November 10, 2003 3:33 PM
Subject: Sweet tea–Proverbs 13:19

"A longing fulfilled is sweet to the soul . . ." *Proverbs 13:19* NIV

My mom makes *great* sweet tea. I've tried my best to imitate it and have failed miserably every time! Well, two weekends ago I watched her make it and discovered her secret. You may know this trick: she puts the sweetener in the pitcher first and *then* pours the tea. Therefore, the tea is sweetened and flavored as she pours. And mmmm is it good!

Well, my life needs to mirror this method. Put the sweetener in first, then pour.

What in the world am I talking about? I am a morning person. That's when I'm at my best; therefore, in order for me to give God the firstfruits of my day and me means I need to spend my solitude time in the mornings. It's when I'm least preoccupied with the day and can more fully give Him all of me. Furthermore, it just starts my day off right. It sets the tone for the day.

Well, have you ever realized that our *deepest* longing is for the Lord? Often times we feel there is something missing in our lives. And there is. Sometimes we desire certain things, and they are GOD GIVEN desires. Remember, He gives us desires, otherwise His word would not tell us He will give us the desires of our heart (Psalm 37:4). However, all too often we misinterpret our longing for something else, when what is really missing, what we are truly longing for is intimacy with our Father . . . a deep, deepening relationship with Jesus, time with the Lord our God, fellowship with Him. He's the sweetener to our heart, mind, body and soul, and when this longing for Him is met, it is *so* sweet to the soul. When it's not, we miss out on something.

So I learned a valuable lesson through Mom teaching me how to make the perfect sweet tea. God showed me that I needed to make it a priority to start my days off with Him because A) I am giving Him the firstfruits of me and the firstfruits of my day and B) He wants to bless me.

See, when I start my day off with Him I'm putting the sweetener in first. And my life is very much like making sweet tea. Put the sweetener in first, then pour the tea and it's sweetened and flavored as it's poured. Well, by putting Jesus—the sweetener to my soul—in first, then as the day is poured into me my day is sweetened and flavored by the time I've had with Him.

Now you may be different. The firstfruits of you and your time might not be in the mornings and that's okay! We are all made different and we should delight in those differences. You are fearfully and wonderfully made, my friend! However, I think starting your day off with Jesus is essential for everyone so that indeed it is Him who will sweeten and flavor your heart, mind, body and soul as your day and its experiences are poured into you. I'm not suggesting that you spend your solitude time with Him in the mornings. That may not work for you. But I am suggesting that you start your day off with some sort of time with Him. Maybe that's just a quick prayer surrendering the day, your heart and mind to Him for the day.

I think we'd all be amazed if we took just five minutes in prayer every morning before we even stepped out of the bed just to be in His presence. He is your deepest desire and He sticks to His word (Numbers 23:19, 2 Peter 3:9), therefore, your time with Him *will* be sweet to your soul.

Today I encourage you to seek the Lord's heart and to ask Him to reveal to you how you can give Him the firstfruits of you. That may mean, as it did for me, rearranging your schedule, or letting God erase something. Furthermore, I encourage you to seek the Lord on how your heart and soul's deepest desire can be fulfilled. I pray that you see and experience that the longing of your soul is Jesus and that this longing for Him is fulfilled today. May you discover anew just how sweet it is to be in the presence of your King! Make sweet tea out of your life . . . put the sweetener in first and let Him flavor your day as life's experiences are poured into you!

Sweetened by His love and grace,

<>< Jessica ☺

Prayer requests? Praises?

From: Hisword2day
To: Your heart
Sent: Wednesday, November 12, 2003 11:59 AM
Subject: Let your light shine–Matthew 5:16

"Let your light so shine before others that they may see your good works and glorify your Father in heaven." _Matthew 5:16_ NKJV

My friend Lisa wrote me an e-mail yesterday in which she described a unique experience she recently had with the Lord. One that brought this verse to life.

"Tonight as I was driving home from class I was driving through a lot of fog and I have never really driven through fog and it was very hard to see the road and things in front of me, but if I kept my eyes on the car's lights that were nearby I could see just enough to get me through, until at last I got home safely. With the lights of other cars driving by I could see clearer and farther than with only my lights. Through this I heard God saying, 'Keep your lights on and look for the lights ahead . . . the road may be unclear but soon you will be home.'"

Lisa went on to explain how the Lord showed her that this situation mirrors life. _"We may not always know what is going to happen next, but we must keep our light shining, even through the presence of sin we must continue to hope for the best and know that soon we will be home with our Lord and Savior Jesus Christ. And he will help us in our journeys with the light of those around us!"_

I had a similar experience to Lisa's this summer. I was driving in a torrential downpour and literally couldn't see the road or much more than 20 feet ahead. All I could see and all that was guiding me were the taillights of the car in front of me. This car kept me on the road and got me safely to my destination. I was so thankful for those lights! Had they not been there, I might not have made it home. So I agree! The lights of those around me greatly helped me!

We know that when we hit fog and rain, the lights better be on! They guide us, keep people from crashing into each other, and the lights of others help us to stay on the road and help lead others to their destination. So we keep our lights on for multiple purposes!

Well, friends, do you realize that this principle applies to our journey down the Road of Life?

Jesus tells us that in this world we will have trouble (John 16:33). Therefore, we can expect to come upon foggy patches of confusion, pain, fear, sin, and frustration. We can expect the torrential downpours we encounter to leave us in a state similar to the one I was in that day in the storm . . . scared, bewildered, not sure where the road is, and unaware of what lies ahead.

However, as the Lord told Lisa, we must keep our light shining amidst our fogs and storms. God's word tells us that He will never leave us nor forsake us. Plus, we are assured that what He promises He fulfills (Numbers 23:19), so we know that there will always be *just enough* light, enough of Christ to get us through those rough spots. It may be *just enough* as Lisa had just enough light to get her through the next small part of her journey until she was at last safely home, but know and believe that you will have enough. His word tells us that He guides us always (Isaiah 58:11) so indeed, no matter how stormy and dense the fog may seem, you will have Christ's light to guide you through this dark world until at last you are home with Him in heaven.

Therefore, keep your eyes focused on Christ's light as you travel this road of life. As the car lights in front of Lisa helped to guide and direct her on the roads, the Lord, who goes before you (Deuteronomy 31:8) will be there to shine His lights to guide and direct you. (Never forget that His word is a lamp unto your feet and a light for your path. Turn it on each day! Especially in those hard times! Open up His word and discover the riches within!)

Furthermore, the Lord will send others along the road to help keep you on the road that leads to life. There will be others that come in front of you who will guide and direct you down the dark, foggy, stormy times in your life. As Lisa said, the Lord will indeed help you along this journey by the light of others . . . and aren't you thankful for those people who have so let their light shine? They help you to see clearer and farther than you can alone.

This is all the more reason for you to let *your* light shine. Because, friend, *you* might be that person to someone else, right this very moment. How devastating that would be if you turned your lights off! For you never know when someone is behind you and the Lord is using your light to help guide and direct that person . . . to keep that person on the road that leads to life. You may be the one who Christ sent to be the lights to help lead someone home—into a relationship with Him. Or you may be the one who Christ sends to help someone travel through his or her stormy, foggy patches . . . to help him or her see clearer and farther down his or her path.

So don't let your light be hindered, don't turn it off! Let your light *shine!* Let Christ beam His light through you. He will help guide and direct you, but He may also be using your light to bring others to praise and glorify Him. You may be leading someone home . . . pointing someone to Christ as you travel through your storms . . . so in everything, LET YOUR LIGHT SHINE!

Shining because of Christ,

<>< Jessica

Prayer requests? Praises?

From: Hisword2day
To: Your heart
Sent: Friday, November 14, 2003 11:08 AM
Subject: Peace is a noun–John 14:27

"Peace I leave with you; my peace I give you. I do not give to you as the world gives. Do not let your hearts be troubled and do not be afraid." *John 14:27* **NIV**

I've read this verse countless times. It's one I've hidden in my heart. Yet God opened my heart to a detail I'd never noticed before and it really stood out to me: *Peace I leave with you; My peace I give you.*

Peace is a noun, not an adjective.

Christ does not say we are going to have peace*ful* lives. In fact, He tells us in John 16:33 that in this world we will have trouble. Paul recounts his experiences with trials and tribulations and warns us that turmoil will swirl around us throughout our lives. So we can expect life to not be so peaceful at times. Yet that doesn't mean we won't or can't have lives full of peace.

See, peace, in this passage and when described as a fruit of the Spirit in Galatians 5:22, is a noun . . . it's an entity, an "object," a state of being. *It's a gift from God,* which is why we can have peace when life isn't so peaceful. Seems like an oxymoron, but it's just how Christ works. His ways far surpass our comprehension! He doesn't depend on this world and His ways are not of this world. So it would only be in conjunction with His character that His peace is not related to your life's circumstances. It's related to Him; totally and utterly dependent on Him and independent of this world.

Therefore, we must recognize that His peace is not an adjective, but a noun. For if we were to mistake what Christ was saying here and replace peace for an adjective, we would get a totally different picture and find that Jesus is going back on His word, which we know He never does! What He promises, He fulfills! (Numbers 23:19) And **because He's promised us peace, peace we will have**, yet not as the world gives, not always as you'd expect, but as He gives. Jesus is NOT saying that we will have peaceful lives with no troubles or problems; in fact, He tells us to expect trouble (John 16:33). Therefore, peace is not an adjective describing what your life will look like. Peace is a noun, an entity in and of itself; it is His gift, a lasting legacy given to us. See, the adjective peaceful does not equate to "full of peace". You can have a peaceful life and not be full of peace. Or you can have a life full of peace and never have a peaceful day in your life.

My friend, remember that peace has been given to you. Christ's peace! Receive it anew each and every day so that you do not let your heart become troubled by your circumstances. Don't be afraid. Jesus is with you always, whether it be on life's mountaintops or in the depths of despair and where He goes, His peace goes with Him. Know that your peace is unrelated to *you* and *your situation* and that it's totally dependent on God. He's the most dependable person you know. Therefore, when times aren't so peaceful, when they do get rough (and they will) seek, fall back, and rely on Him and allow His peace to resonate in your heart and mind for the peace He gives is permanent and constant in a world that isn't.

You have been given peace. Will you choose to pursue this peace and live a life filled with peace? Will you allow Him to fill you with His peace? I pray that each of you would and that the peace of God, which transcends all understanding, would guard your heart and mind in Christ Jesus.

Given His peace,

<>< Jessica

Prayer requests? Praises?

From: Hisword2day
To: Your heart
Sent: Monday, November 17, 2003 2:33 PM
Subject: God is faithful and loving–Psalm 145:13

" . . . The Lord is faithful to all his promises and loving toward all he has made." *Psalm 145:13* **NIV**

What an encouraging verse! The Lord has really just been flooding me with verses and reminders that He is a God who fulfills His promises. When He speaks, He acts! And how awesome that we serve one who is so faithful!

Friend, I pray that you remember that you are God's creation. You are His treasured possession, the apple of His eye, the song of His heart. You are His masterpiece. And in accordance with scripture, that means that He loves you. All that He does is meant to be an expression of His love for you. The cross is the **best** example and display of His unfailing love for and towards you . . . it says in a way that words could never express, *"I LOVE YOU! With all that I am and with all that I have, I love you and I will do whatever it takes to keep my promises . . . to express the depths of my unfailing love towards you!"* So whenever you see a cross may it always serve as a reminder that He is faithful to keep all of His promises and that He loves all He has made. May it remind you that He loves you, that you are His masterpiece, that you are fearfully and wonderfully made, that you are the apple of His eye, and that you are His treasured possession!

Friend, let this sink in: God sealed His covenant to us through Christ's blood on the cross, and if He was willing to face the cross, He meant serious business! He definitely said, "I **will** be faithful. I **will** keep my promises!" I mean for Him to send His *only* begotten Son, to leave His throne in heaven to walk in the valleys of this earth, and then die a criminal's death so that you and I might be able to dance in the courts of the Lord forever is nearly unbelievable! Oh how incomprehensible His love is towards us!

Today my friend, I just wanted to send this verse to you as a reminder that the Lord *your* God is faithful to *all* of His promises. Not just some of them, but *all* of them. How and when He acts will be different for each one of us, but you can be sure that He will act in His perfect timing . .

. He will protect, sustain, strengthen, bless, pursue, guard, meet with, delight in, and love you. (And those are just the tip of the iceberg!) *He has promised to be your God and that He will be.*

I pray that this day you will know, experience, and then delight in the fact that your Father in Heaven, your Savior, and your Friend is faithful to what He promises and loves all He has made. Will you be faithful and loving towards Him?

In His unfailing love and grace,

<>< Jessica

Prayer requests? Praises?

From: Hisword2day
To: Your heart
Sent: Thursday, November 20, 2003 9:30 AM
Subject: Know and rely on God's love–1 John 4:15–16

"If anyone acknowledges that Jesus is the Son of God, God lives in him and he in God. And so we know and rely on the love God has for us." *1 John 4:15–16* **NIV**

Do you know and rely on God's love?

Now before you answer, let's look at what this question is really asking. "Rely" means to be dependent, and to have confidence based on experience. So in other words we must ask ourselves, "Am I *dependent* on God's love? Do I trust God's love? Am I confident in God's love based on experience? (What have been your experiences with the Lord's love?)

As I've been wading through these questions myself, I've discovered that indeed *sometimes* I am dependent on God's love. *Sometimes* I wholeheartedly trust it. *Sometimes* I know that He is faithful. *Sometimes* I've experienced His unfailing love and have tons of confidence in it and in Him!

Sometimes.

Why? Why is it that I only sometimes rely on His love?

This question is one that has plagued my heart and mind for quite some time now. To help me discover why, the Lord told me a couple things. With all the love in His heart, He said, "Jessica, you often don't *allow yourself* to experience my love. My love is constant and unchanging. I am the same yesterday, today, and forever. I expressed my love best on the cross. There Christ displayed the depth and power of my love. But my child, you have not allowed the cross to be sufficient for you. (OUCH!) As a result, you have limited your ability to experience my love. The more you experience my love, the more you know it. The more you know my love, the more you trust it. The more you trust it and are completely dependent on it, the more confidence you gain in my love based on your experiences. The more confidence you have in my love, the more you will rely on my love . . . the more you will rely on me. So my precious, let me be your God. Let Jesus' cross be sufficient for you. Let yourself experience my love for you! And then let my love be your guide. I'm not going to harm you. I could never do that! I love you! So you can trust my love. You can trust me . . . wholeheartedly."

Today I ask you . . . how are you doing when it comes to relying on God's love? Do you trust it? Wholeheartedly and consistently? Or just sometimes? Do you know His love . . . have you experienced it? Or are you hindering your ability to experience Christ's love? If so, what is it that's hindering you from knowing and relying on His love? Is the cross sufficient for you?

These are some questions on which we must get brutally honest with ourselves if we want to know, experience, trust, and rely on God's love . . . and if we ever intend to live the lives we were meant to live. I really challenge you to seek the answers out in your heart. Be honest with yourself. Pray that if you are not relying on His love, that He would show you how you can begin to do so more and more. How I pray that we would begin to truly grasp how deep is the love of Christ! It is a love that prompts Him to be a God that fulfills His promises. It is a love that prompts Him to be a God that cares so deeply, loves so passionately, and pursues so furiously. It is a love that makes Him be *your* God. It is a love that took Him to the cross. And if you know Christ, if His Spirit has been nestled in your heart, you have every reason under the sun (and Son) to know, rely, trust, experience, and be dependent on God's unfailing love for you!

Go ahead; let His love be your guide. Let Him love you today . . . He *so* desperately desires to do so! May you know that God's love is steady and unchanging. He will *never* fail you. Trust Him. Trust that because of His love for you He will never leave you nor forsake you. He will never take you down a path in life that He has not already traveled. He will never lead you into a battle He's not going with you to fight. He will always meet your needs. He will always be the Lord *your* God. And know, know, know . . . that the cross is sufficient . . . His love is sufficient. Know and rely on God's love.

By and through the love and grace of Jesus Christ,

<>< Jessica

Prayer Requests? Praises?

From: Hisword2day
To: Your heart
Sent: Friday, November 21, 2003 7:19 PM
Subject: A lesson from the deer–Psalm 13:5–6

"But I trust in your unfailing love; my heart rejoices in your salvation. I will sing to the Lord, for he has been good to me." *Psalm 13:5–6 NIV*

Since moving to New Braunfels, my family and I have taken great delight in feeding the deer in our neighborhood. We can throw corn over our back deck and watch them eat and interact with each other. It's quite amusing, and one of our favorite things to do. We love it! Recently, we've had a crew that enjoys being fed in our *front* yard. They've figured out our schedules and when we arrive home, they are there waiting. And if we take too long inside, one trusting and confident doe and her two fawns will walk right on up to the house as if to say, "Ah hum . . . we're here and WE'RE HUNGRY! Please come feed us!"

Now most of the deer are not this bold. In fact, the majority of them are really skittish around us. They'll get close, but they wouldn't dare get *too* close. Even though we've never harmed one of them, nor would we ever do so, they're still not too sure of us. They're a bit leery and jump or dash away whenever we get in too close of a proximity to them. They love the food we throw out, but they're still a little uncertain of our intentions. Simply put: they don't trust us.

However, our confident little doe is different. She's figured out that it's okay to get close. That we're not going to harm her, but rather bless her. She wasn't born with this knowledge, but she's learned it. We've desperately tried to get the deer to eat out of our hands. We'll stand there with our hands outstretched, yet none have taken us up on our offer. But this little doe decided to one day. She took a leap of faith and got close, real close. She ate out of our hands. After waiting twelve years for one to do this, we were slightly thrilled! She must have been too because now she approaches us without any reservations, knowing we're going to be good to her. Her experiences proved to her that she *can* trust us. There's no need for her to be leery of us or to jump back when we draw near to her. She can get close, real close.

Watching these deer interact with me is like watching us interact with

God. There He stands with His hands outstretched, desperately yearning for us to draw near. Yet most of us are a bit leery, unsure, skittish. Like the deer, we'll get close to Him, but don't dare get *too* close. Even though He's never harmed us, nor would He *ever* do so, and even though He's been nothing but good to us, we're still not too sure of Him. We're a bit doubtful and jump or dash away whenever the Lord draws too near for our comfort. We love the blessings He lavishly hands out, but are still a little uncertain of His intentions. Simply put: we don't trust Him.

However, there are those who are not like this. These people have figured out that it's okay to get close; that the Lord is not going to harm them, but rather bless them. This knowledge is not something they were born with, rather it has been learned. To gain this trust, these people had to take God up on His offer. They had to go up to His outstretched hand, which meant getting real close. It meant taking a leap of faith and drawing near to Him. It meant trusting Him even if they were a little scared to do so. In trusting Him and taking this leap of faith they learned they don't need to be leery of the Lord. Taking that leap of faith gave them the experience, which in turn gave them the confidence, to trust in the Lord and to continue to approach Him. They now know that they can get close, real close. This type of willingness to draw near to God absolutely thrills Him!

So which are you? Do you trust in Him and in His unfailing love and therefore draw near? Do you approach Him? Or are you leery, a bit unsure, and skittish when you draw near or sense Him drawing near?

I pray that you trust the Lord. I pray that you draw near, for when you draw near to God, He will draw near to you (James 4:8). Remember that to rely on, to trust God's love means you have confidence in Him based on experience. Are you letting yourself experience His love and therefore trust in it? If you happen to be the skittish deer at this moment in your relationship with Jesus, I pray that you will take that leap of faith. I pray that you will let go and trust. He is ever so trustworthy! He has been so good to you . . . and He will continue to be good to you because of His unfailing love towards you. You are His beloved, His creation, His masterpiece, His treasured possession, coheir to His kingdom, the apple of His eye. You are His and His word reminds us that He will never leave you nor forsake you. So you can trust His intentions for He longs to be gracious to you (Isaiah 30:18).

Today, I encourage you to approach Him. Draw near to Him. Trust Him.

Let go of whatever reservations you have towards the Lord and trust in His unfailing love for, my friend, He has been good to you. May you see and experience His goodness to you and then may that lead you to trust in the Lord your God. Trust in His *unfailing* love.

Don't be skittish. Get close. Get *real* close.

Drawing near,

<>< Jessica

Prayer requests? Praises?

From: Hisword2day
To: Your heart
Sent: Tuesday, November 25, 2003 11:06 AM
Subject: You are so richly blessed–Psalm 107:1

"Give thanks to the Lord, for he is good; his love endures forever."
Psalm 107:1 **NIV**

As Thanksgiving is rapidly approaching, I want to encourage you to start thinking about the *countless* ways the Lord has lavishly bestowed blessings upon you, your family, and your life. Many of you don't have to think long and hard about this for you have seen the abundance of His love and grace in every aspect of your life! Yet, many of you may have experienced a lot of rough times this past year. You may have felt like you've walked through a series of deep, dark valleys or a vast desert. Or you may have felt abandoned by the Lord your God in more ways than one. However, you were not abandoned for, God promises to never leave you nor forsake you (Deuteronomy 31:6), and the Lord is faithful to all His promises (Psalm 145:13). And you did not walk through your valleys and deserts alone this year, for, from the mouth of Jesus Himself, "I am with you always, to the very end of the age" (Matthew 28:20).

The fact that He is a loving and faithful God, that He has and never will abandon you, that His grace is sufficient for you . . . that He will be with you when you walk through the valleys, deserts, storms, and fires of life (Isaiah 43:2) . . . that He is good . . . and the fact that He gives so freely of Himself, His love and His grace to you and me . . . these blessings *alone* are reason enough for us to offer endless praises to the Lord our God!!! But today I want to share something with you that my friend Judy sent to me. I pray that it will remind you that you have so, so, so much to be thankful for. I pray that it will remind you that indeed, you are so richly blessed.

If you woke up this morning with more health than illness, you are more blessed than the million who won't survive the week.

If you have never experienced the danger of battle, the loneliness of imprisonment, the agony of torture, or the pangs of starvation, you are ahead of *20 million people* around the world.

If you attend a church meeting without fear of harassment, arrest, torture, or death, you are more blessed than almost 3 *billion people* in the world.

If you have food in your refrigerator, clothes on your back, a roof over your head, and a place to sleep, *you are richer than 75% of this world.*

If you have money in the bank, in your wallet, and spare change in a dish some place, *you are among the top 8% of the world's wealthy.* (Shocking huh?!)

If your parents are still married and alive, you are very rare, especially in the USA.

If you hold up your head with a smile on your face and are truly thankful, you are blessed because the majority can, but most do not.

If you can hold someone's hand, hug them, or even touch them on the shoulder, you are blessed because you can offer God's healing touch.

If you can read this message, you are more blessed than over 2 billion people in the world that cannot read anything at all.

Beloved, you are so blessed in ways you may never know! The Lord has been gracious to you this year. Every morning He has risen and shown you compassion; He has renewed His compassions to you. He has blessed you with every spiritual blessing. He has given you such an abundant life filled with the abundance of His love and grace. The Lord your God has been *your* God . . . He has protected you, sustained you, provided for you, helped you, redeemed you, encouraged you, carried you, delighted in you, rejoiced over you, laughed with you, and most importantly, He has loved you. He has indeed been faithful and good to you. His love endures forever! And for all that and most importantly for who He is, give thanks . . . give *lots* of thanks.

May you start each day with a prayer of thanksgiving . . . not just in the season of Thanksgiving, but every single day of your life. Our lives need to be one long season of thanksgiving for we are so richly blessed.

Blessed beyond belief,

<>< Jessica

Prayer requests? Praises?

From: Hisword2day
To: Your heart
Sent: Wednesday, November 26, 2003 10:38 AM
Subject: Be a blessing to God–Deuteronomy 8:10

(Below are the same two verses, but from different versions. Read them both carefully. There are some slight differences, but I think they are well worth noting.)

"When you have eaten and are satisfied, praise the Lord your God for the good land he has given you." *Deuteronomy 8:10* **NIV**

"When you have eaten and are full, then you shall bless the Lord your God for the good land which He has given you." *Deuteronomy 8:10* **NKJV**

Scripture tells us that we are to praise the Lord for lots of reasons. First and foremost, we are to give thanks in everything for this is the will of God in Christ Jesus (1 Thessalonians 5:18). That alone is enough reason . . . it's God's will! However, Scripture also outlines some other reasons why praising God and giving thanks to Him is a good thing to do. Doing so helps us to not forget the Lord our God, for it is through Him and by Him that we have and can do all things (Deuteronomy 8:10–20). Praising God with thanksgiving also helps to guard and protect our hearts and minds in Christ Jesus (Philippians 4:6–7). And of course, praising the Lord should just be an overflow of our hearts for He is good (Psalm 107:1).

Have you ever wondered how you could ever return a favor to God? How you could ever repay Him for His goodness, love, kindness, grace, provision, and blessings? How you could ever bless the Lord for the rich blessings He has given you? Well, you must realize that you will never be able to repay Him, but that you can bless Him. Yes, you and I can bless the Lord our God.

Reread the passages. Did you catch the differences? The first passage says: *When you have eaten and are satisfied,* **praise** *the Lord your God . . .* the second passages says: *When you have eaten and are full,* **bless** *the Lord your God . . .*

Praising the Lord blesses the Lord. Wow! It is crazy how simple that is! Your praise and thanksgiving not only help you, but they also bless God! Amazing! And isn't He more than deserving of *at least* your praise and thanks? After all, it is the Lord your God who has blessed you with everything under the sun—your life, your friends, your family, your job, your possessions, your health, your home, your abilities, your opportunities . . . and on and on.

So today, tomorrow, and always, I encourage you to stay in the will of God. Guard your heart and mind in Christ. Let the overflow of your heart be praise. Return to God what He so rightly deserves: offer up a sacrifice of thanks. Don't just expect blessings *from* Him; be a blessing *to* Him. Praise Him for He is so good!

Happy Thanksgiving!

Blessing the Lord my God,

<>< Jessica

Prayer requests? Praises?

From: Hisword2day
To: Your heart
Sent: Tuesday, December 02, 2003 12:03 AM
Subject: He appears faithfully–Hosea 6:3

"Let us acknowledge the Lord; let us press on to acknowledge him. As surely as the sun rises, he will appear; he will come to us like the winter rains, like the spring rains that water the earth." *Hosea 6:3* **NIV**

As I pondered all of the many things that I was thankful for this Thanksgiving weekend, I was humbly reminded of one of the biggest blessings in my life: God's faithfulness and consistency. Today I want to tell you how God yet again revealed to me His faithfulness and how He also provided me with a vivid picture of how I treat Him.

I'm currently working with the high school Sunday School class at my church. These kids have been a tremendous blessing to me in countless ways! God has used this experience to teach me so much and to help prepare me for what He will have me doing in Paris.

However, I don't always see it as a blessing to be able to serve these kids. In fact, I have *many* moments when I battle with a bad attitude . . . when I get very discouraged. I often feel like I am the teacher in the cartoon *Charlie Brown* to the kids . . . wa wa wa wa wa wa. Their actions seem to say, "I could really care less about what you have to say and I don't want to be here." Many of them are only at class out of obligation . . . Mommy and Daddy make them come, etc. They love to distract the conversation from the lesson. And I sometimes flat out feel like it wouldn't matter to them if I showed up at all. "Why go?" I sometimes ask myself. "It's not like I'm helping them or really doing anything. I'm not teaching them anything. I'm just showing up and just filling a space in the room." What a bad attitude!!! Yet how patient the Lord is with me! Praise be to Him!

Well, this past Sunday I was REALLY battling these feelings. Self-pity and selfishness rose high on my emotional chart that day! Despite this, I went to Sunday School anyway. A little grudgingly, but I felt God's nudge on my heart that I needed to be there. I was soon to find out that it wasn't so much for the students that I was going, rather it was for me. God needed to teach me a humbling, startling lesson . . . He'd been trying to help me see this lesson for quite some time, but it wasn't until I reached this very discouraged spot that I finally sought God and was able to learn the lesson being taught through some wise words of a very dear friend.

First of all, God had one of the students remind me that indeed I was where God wanted me to be. Through her the Lord said, "Jess, you are doing as I told you to and I am using you. Remember to walk in obedience and don't get so caught up in the fruits of your labor. That's up to me. I just need you to be obedient. But here's an encouragement for your discouraged heart." This student said words to me that I will never forget! Words that humbled me to tears!

However, the biggest lesson of the day was brought to my attention as I was talking to my friend about how God had encouraged me through this student. As I explained my feelings from earlier in the morning and then how the Lord had humbled me and encouraged me, my friend reminded that this picture of the Sunday School class is a picture of how I interact with the Lord. See, I am very much the distracted, disinterested teenager in my relationship with Jesus. My actions seem to say, "I could really care less about what you have to say and I don't want to be here in this moment learning about you." I often show up—go before the Lord—out of obligation, not because it's the desire of my heart to be in His presence. And I have this tendency to get distracted from whatever lesson God is trying to teach me.

Now can you imagine how that must make the Lord feel?! After all He's done and then for me to act like that!? Yet despite how lackadaisical and disinterested I may be towards Him at times, He *consistently* shows up on the scene of my life. He's with me always (Matthew 28:20). He goes with me wherever I go (Joshua 1:9). He even goes before me (Deuteronomy 31:8). He rises to show me compassion (Isaiah 30:18). He renews His compassions every single morning (Lamentations. 3:23). When I awake, I am still with Him for He's standing at the foot of my bed, anxiously waiting for me with His outstretched hand (Psalm 139:18). Simply put: He is wildly in love with me and will be faithful and consistent for, as surely as the sun rises, He appears. (Wow! His love and faithfulness are so incomprehensible and unfathomable to me!)

Today I challenge you to ask yourself if the Sunday School scene I described paints a portrait of your relationship with Jesus. Are you the disinterested teenager at times? If so, may you be humbled by the fact that out of His great love for you, He still shows up. No matter how much your words or deeds may tell Him He's not wanted, He still appears. (With a much better attitude than I had going to Sunday School that day might I add!) What determination and zeal He must have for us! Therefore, let us press on to acknowledge Him. Let us acknowledge His consistency and faithfulness. And let us bless Him and say thank you. Thank Him for being as consistent and faithful as the sun rising each morning. Thank Him for appearing each day of your life. Thank Him for who He is and that He would set His love and affections on *you*. How the Lord your God delights in you!

May you delight in being in the presence of your Lord and King as you press on to acknowledge Him! How I pray that you and I would appear before Jesus today with excitement, joy, and humility . . . may we strive to appear before Jesus as consistently and faithfully as He appears on the scenes of our lives.

Pressing on,

<>< Jessica

Prayer requests? Praises?

From: Hisword2day
To: Your heart
Sent: Wednesday, December 03, 2003 11:59 AM
Subject: Time–2 Peter 3:8

"But, beloved, do not forget this one thing, that with the Lord one day is as a thousand years and a thousand years as one day." *2 Peter 3:8* **NKJV**

The past few days I have been fighting a SERIOUS battle against time. I have too much to do and too little time in which to do it . . . and that inevitably makes this little heart a little anxious at times. (Does that sound familiar to anyone else?!) Well, yesterday evening, as I worked on one of my many tasks, I was rummaging through an old file and felt like I'd struck gold as it had all kinds of good information for my task at hand! The file was my study abroad program folder so it contained important documents and information, as well as some of my personal e-mails that Mom had apparently printed out. I took a quick stroll down "memory lane," reading about my experiences, adventures, and all that I had learned—all the blessings God had given me! And then I ran across an e-mail that was aimed at the bulls-eye of my heart. It zeroed in on what I have been struggling with the past few days. It was *exactly* what I needed to read last night. Funny how God works sometimes! Below is that e-mail and added in are a few thoughts and lessons I've learned since April 5, 2001.

One of the many things that the Lord has been showing me is how bound to the world's clock that I am . . . what a slave I am to the daily routines and ways of life. I have the mentality that I always must be maximizing my time. A mentality this world seems to teach us from day one . . . go, go, go, do, do, do. However, God prefers that we *be* rather than *do*. "*Be* still and know that I am God" (Psalm 46:10). And yet, how often it is that I allow myself to get so busy that I fail to simply *be* with Jesus and set my heart at rest in His presence. As a result, I'm sure I have missed out on countless opportunities to share or experience His love in some of the sweetest, simplest ways.

Furthermore, I find that I want to know what the plans are for tomorrow. I struggle with this Proverbs 27:1 "you-do-not-know-what-a-day-will-bring-forth" business because doggone it! I want to be able to have things in order so that I can plan accordingly (even though I've noticed that plans really seem to cramp my style). I catch myself wanting to scribble away on my life's appointment book . . . unfortunately, in pen.

But oh, in God's faithfulness to me He has just been shattering that part of my life! When I try to *make* things happen, put myself on some schedule that doesn't include Him or time with Him, when I try to put Him on some time regimen, He keeps reminding me, "Wait a minute, Jess! You cannot box me into this world's timeframe. It's just not gonna happen! I am not of this world, but my child, neither are you. Remember, Beloved, you are now a citizen in my kingdom and are, therefore, on MY timetable, which, as my word reminds you, is *not* like the world's. Yes, you must live in this world, and yes, you must live within the timetable of this world, but Dear One, with me one day is as a thousand years and a thousand years is as one day.

"Did you catch that? Jessica, pay close attention . . . *with* me. Not apart from me, but *with* me. You must do things with me to stay on my timetable. Therefore, don't push me out of your schedule; but rather let me be a part of your schedule and all that you have on your schedule. Stop trying to do things without me! Apart from me you can do nothing, but with me you can do *all* things. Yes, you can even accomplish the gazillion things you've got on your "to-do" list. Don't you know that if you just trust your time to me I will bless it? One day is as a thousand years . . . I'll help you maximize your time! ☺ Often times in some interesting ways; my ways. I love you, Jessica, and I want to take care of you . . . I want to meet you where you are. I want to help you. *I want to do things with you. I want you to do things with me.* I know the things that you have need of before you do and I am going to provide for you! Haven't I always? And Jessica, so many of your "worries" are things of this world and are a result of you trying to please this world. But you are not here to serve two masters. You are on earth for me. So what about your time with me? Can't you just be still even a few minutes a day and know that I am who I say I am? You will receive nothing short of a blessing if you just let me quiet you with my love. Relax in the knowledge that you are MY child and that I am YOUR Father, your Abba Father at that (Daddy) . . . know and rely on my love!"

OH MY GOODNESS! SO EXACTLY WHAT I NEEDED TO BE REMINDED OF LAST NIGHT! Now friend, I know deadlines are fast approaching and you've got a million and ten things going on, but God knows too. He really does. And He's really going to help you today. He alone knows what tomorrow brings, for He's been there before you, and

He's going to provide for you. He will provide the time, strength, energy, peace, and all that you need to accomplish all the good works He has prepared in advance for you to do today, tomorrow, and always.

So trust your time to God . . . make time with Him your priority each day. How I pray that you and I would set our hearts on Him and rest in His presence, that we would make time to simply be with Him, and that we would allow Him to help us remember that with the Lord a day is as a thousand years and a thousand years is as one day. How I pray that He would remind us again and again that He is not in as much of a hurry as we are and that He is going to abundantly bless *any* time we spend with Him! You have the time to spend with God today. You don't have the time to *not* spend time with Him. So don't push Him off your schedule, for you'll be shattered like me. Don't learn the hard way. Let my pain be your peace. ☺ You cannot do anything without the Lord, but *with* the Lord you can accomplish anything . . . you can do the impossible.

God knows the plans HE has for you. He has pondered all of your ways and He knows the times and dates of the events in your life for they have been set by His awesome authority. That means He knows how every last little detail fits into your life. Yes, that means He even knows how everything will fit into each 24-hour day. You can trust Him for His works are perfect, and all His ways are just. He is a faithful God who does no wrong (Deuteronomy 32:4); therefore, His timing is p-e-r-f-e-c-t! And . . . His timing will prevail over your timing for it is always the Lord's timing and purpose that will prevail! (Proverbs 19:21). So may you submit to following, *wherever* He may lead your time, and may your focus always be on Christ Jesus, not your schedules and deadlines; for when you seek first His Kingdom and love Him with all your heart, mind, body, and soul, all things will be added unto you . . . even time.

Because of Him,

<>< Jessica

Prayer requests? Praises?

From: Hisword2day
To: Your heart
Sent: Thursday, December 04, 2003 11:35 AM
Subject: Be at rest for the Lord has been good–Psalm 116:7–9

"Be at rest once more, O my soul, for the Lord has been good to you. For You, O Lord, have delivered my soul from death, my eyes from tears, my feet from stumbling, that I may walk before the Lord in the land of the living." *Psalm 116:7–9* **NIV**

My life has been spinning out of control for the past three days! Not in a bad way—I've just been battling with time, all the fun things I need to accomplish, and then of course the anxious thoughts that come with being overwhelmed. This time of year I always tend to have a lot on my plate. That's nothing new for me. A full, or rather double-booked schedule is not out of the ordinary for my life. However, recently I seem to be exceptionally busy and have allowed myself to get overwhelmed by the tasks at hand, and have forgotten the blessings at hand.

See, something God has really convicted me of is the truth behind Luke 12:48–49, *"From everyone who has been given much, much will be demanded; and from the one who had been entrusted with much, much more will be asked."* And I know this to be true . . . I just often fail to remember the blessing behind this truth. Therefore, I have been trying to remind myself that my overflowing schedule is simply a reminder of an overflow of blessings, that God has been so very good to me. He has showered so much of His love and grace upon me in so many different ways that I don't know how to handle it all! I've made it a conscious effort to bring to mind that God has given so very much to me; therefore, much will be demanded of me. And WOW! What a true honor it is for the Lord to have entrusted me with so much!

After writing to you yesterday, I went to God and said, "Okay, Jesus, it's you and me. We're doing this day *together.* I want to do everything with and for you. But, Lord, I'm gonna be honest with you. I know I'm letting things get to me a little too much today. And I don't want to! Hello! I need to rejoice in this day, not simply survive it! I want to delight in you and the abundance of blessings you have so graciously given me! So, Jesus, I'm asking you to humble me. Yes, I'm actually asking that . . . I know, I know. You've been waiting. Set my heart at rest once more,

Jesus. Remind me of Your goodness to me so that I don't drown in this sea of "AH! Look at what all I've got going on!?" Remind me of my blessings. Help me to not see things as burdens, but blessings. Really, Lord, humble me . . . set my heart straight today. Readjust my focus. And dear Jesus, help me with blessing management!" ☺

Well, the Lord definitely heard my voice. Within moments of my prayer, I was reminded of how tremendously blessed I am and just how truly "off" my focus had been. Simply put, Jesus humbled me *greatly.*

I received an e-mail from a friend of mine asking me to pray for a high school buddy of ours, Matt, who has been diagnosed with cancer and is about to undergo all kinds of tests and surgeries.

That knocked me to my knees in humility.

Here is a guy *my* age, 23 years old . . . so very, very young who is undergoing a battle far greater than I can comprehend. So if the *greatest* of my worries right now is a full schedule and a struggle with Blessing Management 101 then dear goodness! Be at rest once more, O my soul, for the Lord has indeed been good to me! A busy schedule means I am alive, healthy, and *able* to accomplish much. So much has been given to me! LIFE! In His great love, and in accordance with His perfect will, I am not entangled by the cords of something that could lead to death. My heart is not overcome with this sorrow and anguish. I am walking, *alive and well,* before the Lord in the land of the living. Oh my goodness, how blessed I am!!!!

So today I ask you to do two things. Please pray for Matthew I do not know what type of cancer he has, but pray for him please. James 5:15–16 says, ". . . . the prayer offered in faith will make the sick person well . . . pray for each other so that you may be healed." God can heal Matthew I know He is able. It doesn't mean it is in God's will to do so, but I know that He is able. Furthermore, your prayers can and will help Matt fight this battle with cancer on every level, for the prayer of the righteous is *powerful and effective* (James 5:16).

And the other thing I ask of you today is for you to go before the Lord your God. Seek His face today. Ask Him to restore to you the joy of your salvation. Ask Him to humble you . . . to remind you of His goodness to you. You are so blessed! Therefore, I strongly urge you to set your heart at rest in His presence today for it is there that He can quiet you with His love. It is there that He can put your soul at rest once more and that He can remind you of His goodness to you. It is in His presence that He can remind you of who He is, who you are *to* Him, and who you are *in*

Him. Therefore, go before Jesus right now, literally the moment you are reading these words and say, "Thank you, Lord, for you have been so good to me. Thank you for my life. Humble me today with reminders of your goodness. Help me not forget the abundance of your love, grace, and goodness to me. I bless your holy name."

My prayer for you today is that your heart and soul would be at rest once more, for the Lord has indeed been good to you. I pray that you and I might see life with a new perspective today and realize the blessings which the Lord has lavishly given us. May we see our "burdens" for what they truly are—reminders of His love, grace, and goodness. And may we take this day that we have been given in which we are able to walk before the Lord in the land of the living to bless, honor, and glorify the Lord your God.

Humbled and blessed by His goodness,

<>< Jessica

Prayer requests? Praises?

From: Hisword2day
To: Your heart
Sent: Monday, December 15, 2003 1:47 PM
Subject: Come let us adore Him–Matthew 2:11

"On coming to the house, they (the Magi) saw the child with his mother Mary, and they bowed down and worshiped him." *Matthew 2:11* **NIV**

During the Christmas season, we hear and sing songs, see decorations, and hear messages that remind us that we are celebrating the birth and life of our Lord and Savior Jesus Christ. One such song that the Lord seems to touch my heart with each year is "O Come Let Us Adore Him." As we sang this song in church yesterday, I was reminded of a lesson the Lord taught me last year.

First of all, I was reminded that this is what this season is about: adoring Christ Jesus . . . celebrating who He is and what He has done for us. It's not about the hustle and bustle of buying gifts, going to parties, sending cards, and baking goodies. It's about Jesus.

Then the Lord humbled my heart even more as He gently whispered these words into my heart, "Beloved, you don't need this season to adore me. You are invited to do this every day. Don't let worshiping and adoring Jesus be a seasonal thing; let it be a daily thing. Let it be your lifestyle."

Wow! Did I ever need to be reminded of that! As God's thoughts to me and the words of this song resonated within my heart, I was reminded of the Magi and how I need to follow their example of coming into Jesus' presence and then bowing down and worshiping Him . . . adoring Him. I was reminded that I need to walk in their footsteps, not just during the Christmas season, but *all* the days of my life! More than that, I *want* to! I *want* to bow down and worship my Lord and Savior, my precious Jesus. It is my heart's desire, for He is more than worthy! After all, Jesus descended from heaven (Ephesians 4:9). He left heaven (really contemplate that thought). He left his position at the right hand of God the Father to come to earth, to be born in a dirty stable, to be placed on a "throne" of wood and hay, and to live the life of a regular human being. He had no worldly crowns, powerful armies, or chests of gold to His name. And He did all of this out of His great love for us . . . He was sacrificed on a cross and then raised from the dead so that you and I might have an abundant life of knowing the Lord in a personal and intimate way. Oh He is so worthy of our praise!

Therefore, as you enjoy the festivities of this glorious season and make preparations for the celebration of Jesus' birthday, how I pray that Jesus would always be at the forefront of your heart and mind. For He is the only reason we are celebrating anything this time of year. And how I pray that because of who Christ is, you and I would be prompted to walk in the footsteps of the Magi. So come let us adore Him, not just during this season, but all the days of our lives . . . for He alone is worthy.

Because of Jesus,

<>< Jessica

Prayer requests? Praises?

From: Hisword2day
To: Your heart
Sent: Wednesday, December 17, 2003 12:41
Subject: A lesson in worship from the Magi–Matthew 2:11

"On coming to the house, they saw the child with his mother Mary, and they bowed down and worshiped him. Then they opened their treasures and presented him with gifts of gold, and of incense, and of myrrh." *Matthew 2:11* **NIV**

As we prepare for the Christmas celebration, I am always drawn back to the Christmas story as told in the gospels of Matthew and Luke. It fascinates me! And it seems that each time I read about the Lord's birth God reveals new and wonderful things to me about Himself and always brings lessons and truths I can apply to my own life and walk. So for the rest of this week we're going to be looking at this passage. Some of this may be a review from last year, but we're going to go a little deeper this time. Just a head's up. Now on we go to have another lesson from the Magi . . .

I found that when and how the Magi worshiped Christ is quite significant. See, when the Magi arrived, Christ had yet to do anything. Yes, of course, we mustn't forget that He had left heaven (Ephesians 4:9), (which is HUGE) but at the time of the Magi's arrival Jesus had yet to perform any miracles. He had not restored sight to the blind, had not raised the dead, nor had He cast out demons or fed the 5000. He had yet to speak a word, much less a prophecy. He had endured no hardships, had not surrendered to the cross, and had yet to be resurrected. He had no works to His human life to illicit the gifts and worship of the Magi. Therefore, the Magi's worship and bringing of gifts was not based on what Jesus had *done* for them, rather it was based on who He was.

Wow! Can you take a lesson from them on that one or what?! I sure could! Our worship of the Lord and bringing of gifts (of all kinds) should not be totally dependent on *what He does,* although He is most worthy of praise for all He has done for us. Instead, He deserves gifts of worship, adoration, and praise simply because of *who He is.* After all, He is the Wonderful Counselor, Mighty God, the Everlasting Father, Prince of Peace (Isaiah 9:6), the Lamb of God, Immanuel, God with us . . . He is Christ Jesus, our Lord and Savior, our friend. How worthy of praise He is!

Today I encourage you to heed this lesson from the Magi: Bow down and worship Him not only for what He has done for you, but also in reaction to who He is and who He is to you. Who Christ is determines what He has done and what He will continue to do in your life. Who Christ is brought Him down from heaven to walk on this earth and led Him to the cross 2000 years ago. Therefore, bring Him the richest treasure you can find . . . bring Him your heart and set it at rest in His glorious presence.

May you have a blessed day worshiping your precious Jesus. Oh how He loves you with an unfailing, passionate, and ceaseless love!

Because of who He is,

<>< Jessica

Prayer requests? Praises?

Isn't it so God that men from years ago can teach us lessons for life today? It is so God! Don't you just love Him?!

From: Hisword2day
To: Your heart
Sent: Thursday, December 18, 2003 10:37 AM
Subject: The gifts of the Magi–Matthew 2:11

"On coming to the house, they saw the child with his mother Mary, and they bowed down and worshiped him. Then they opened their treasures and presented him with gifts and of gold, incense, and of myrrh." *Matthew 2:11* **NIV**

I was a history major in college, which means I had to read lots of primary sources (original documents). In order to gain a better understanding of these documents, we were taught to look at who wrote them, to whom they were written, the circumstances surrounding what was written (aka "why"), and what exactly was written—paying close attention to what was included and excluded. Doing so can reveal a lot! Because this approach to reading has been engrained in my mind, I found it rather interesting that the author of Matthew found it important to include what gifts the Magi gave, but apparently found it irrelevant to include their names. Hmmm . . . seems to me there must be a reason! Time for a little research! Well, a little searching did indeed prove there is a reason! So today we're going to take a general look at the Magi's gifts and how they are significant to you and to me.

First of all, these men gave gifts that were rare, precious, and of great worth. They gave the best they had to give in honor of the one who they believed to be the King of Kings. We, too, should seek to give our best in honor of the one who we believe to be the King of Kings. What are you giving to the Lord that is rare, precious, and of great worth? Remember, it doesn't have to be something physical. One of the things God has been showing me is that one of my gifts to Him can be time . . . that's definitely a very rare and precious commodity in my life! ☺

Secondly, gold, frankincense, and myrrh could all be found in the region of the world from which the Magi came. Therefore, they gave gifts that were local to them. They didn't go searching elsewhere to find these rare, precious, and valuable gifts. This fact really caught my attention. See, you and I need to follow the Magi's example. We don't have to go searching in some foreign place (for example: trying to be someone we're not) to find gifts to give to the Lord; we are to give that which is "local" to us. We need to search within ourselves to present the Lord with the treasures from within our own country (our own heart and life). For, friend, hear me on this: *you have gifts that are rare, precious, and are of such great worth.* Your gifts may be different from others, but that's perfectly okay! Scripture tells us that we have different gifts according to the grace given us (Romans 12:6) and His grace to you is NOT without effect! (1 Corinthians 15:10). God made you who you are and gave you this "lot" in life for a reason. He has blessed you with different gifts, *just as He desires* (1 Corinthians 12:18). The gifts you have stored up within your heart and life are not available to all, which makes them all the more rare and all the more valuable! So give from within your heart and from what's available to you. Your gifts will most likely be different from those given by your neighbor, friends, and family, but I promise you, your gifts to the Lord, what you bring to Him to symbolize your love, respect, surrender, and adoration—whatever they may be—will be precious and of such great worth in His eyes.

And thirdly, the Magi's gifts were a part of their worship, just as the gifts we offer should be for us. When we give to the Lord in all of the various ways we can give, it is an act of worship! How amazing that it can be that simple!

Today I pray that you and I will take a little lesson from the Magi in giving to the Lord. Let's give Jesus things that are rare, precious, and of great worth for He is so worthy. May we not give Him a foreign gift; rather, may we give Him something local to us. Gifts from your heart, gifts of your heart are what He desires most.

And lastly, please let this truth resonate within your heart today and always: *you are so rare, precious, and of great worth to Jesus.* You were fearfully and wonderfully made just the way you are! You are a reflection of His love and grace in so many ways, and therefore, have so very much to offer this world . . . and so very much to offer the Lord! So, give from within yourself . . . give of yourself for in doing so you are offering up a holy and pleasing spiritual act of worship.

Have a blessed day as you joyfully give Him your all!

Because of Jesus,

<>< Jessica

Prayer requests? Praises?

From: Hisword2day
To: Your heart
Sent: Monday, December 22, 2003 4:33 PM
Subject: Highly favored–Luke 1:28–30

"The angel went to her and said, 'Greetings, you who are highly favored! The Lord is with you.' Mary was greatly troubled at his words and wondered what kind of greeting this might be. But the angel said to her, 'Do not be afraid, Mary, you have found favor with God.'" *Luke 1:28–30 NIV*

As I read this passage about Mary, I found that she and I have something in common! We're troubled by the Lord's voice and are often curious, confused, or bewildered by what His greeting might be, what He might be saying or wanting. Ever been there? When God speaks to you in His own personal way, have you too, been troubled? I'm guessing you have. So today I wanted to share with you something that else I learned from the Christmas story.

Let's recap: in this passage Gabriel has been sent to tell Mary that she has been chosen to bear the Messiah into this world. She's going to be His mother. (Wow!) Yet prior to even telling her and delving into all of the details of how this would all come about, Gabriel reminds her of something to which we should pay close attention. *"Greetings, you who are highly favored! The Lord is with you! Do not be afraid, Mary, you have found favor with God."* He seems to be reminding her that because she had found favor with God she was being called in this way. *Because* the Lord was with her she need not be afraid, no matter how absurd it may seem. She was highly favored by the Most High and the Most High apparently wanted her to be confident of that!

Well, my friend, countless times throughout your life God will speak to you in various ways. As His servant, He will also call you to bear Christ into this world. It may be different than how He called Mary to do so, but remember that God has blessed us each with unique and special ways of bringing Christ to life. Sometimes what God tells you and what He calls you to do may seem absurd and impossible, but nothing is impossible with God (Luke 1:37). Furthermore, when you hear God's voice (however it may come to you) and when He calls you to do or to be something, no matter how confusing or troubling it may seem at first, be ever so encouraged! For what that means is that *you* have found favor with God. Therefore, you need not be afraid because you are highly favored; you are being called to serve the Lord in certain ways! WOW!

May you go forth into your day with the knowledge that you are highly favored by the Lord your God. He absolutely delights in you! Do not be afraid . . . for remember, *you have found favor with God.* And if God is for you, who can be against you?

Have a blessed day preparing for Jesus' birthday!

By grace, highly favored,

<>< Jessica

Prayer requests? Praises?

From: Hisword2day
To: Your heart
Sent: Wednesday, December 24, 2003 7:10 PM
Subject: To us a Son is given–Isaiah 9:6

"For to us a child is born, to us a son is given, and the government will be on his shoulders. And he will be called Wonderful Counselor, Mighty God, Everlasting Father, Prince of Peace." *Isaiah 9:6* **NIV**

New Braunfels, Texas had an absolutely brilliant morning! The cool, crisp air was filled with the fragrant smells of winter and Christmas, and the sunrise . . . oh it was captivating! It was definitely a morning that vividly displayed the radiance of God's glory! I decided that since it was *such* a lovely morning I ought to be out in the midst of it, enjoying it. So I went for a little walk and talk with God. How wonderful and refreshing my time with Jesus was and oh how He spoke to my heart! Watching the sun rise above the horizon and grace this world with its light painted a beautiful picture for me of what we celebrate on Christmas . . . the Son of God rising above the horizon of this earth gracing the world and our lives with His light. For it was a little over 2000 years ago that Jesus graced this planet with His presence for the very first time. And what a blessing He has been to us ever since!

However you celebrate this glorious holiday, I pray that you will first and foremost remember Jesus as it is Him we are truly honoring and celebrating. For to us a child was born, to us a son was *given*. Jesus was *given* to you, my friend. Let that sink in. He is a gift from God and the most precious gift your heart could ever desire! How are you doing on accepting His gift? How are you doing on giving His gift to others?

May you and your family be filled with the love, joy, hope, and peace of Christ, and may your hearts rejoice in knowing that through Jesus, God gave you a Wonderful Counselor, Mighty God, Everlasting Father, and the Prince of Peace!

Merry Christmas from my heart to yours . . .

Because of Jesus,

<>< Jessica

Prayer requests? Praises?

From: Hisword2day
To: Your heart
Sent: Tuesday, December 30, 2003 8:32 AM
Subject: A prayer for you–Psalm 90:14

"Satisfy us in the morning with your unfailing love, that we may sing for joy and be glad all our days." *Psalm 90:14* **NIV**

Daddy, precious Jesus, I want to thank you today for my friends. How precious they are in your sight Lord! Remind them of that truth today . . . satisfy them this morning with your unfailing love. May the thought of your love and abundant grace flood their hearts with joy and help them to be glad all day long for great is your love for us! Help my friends to experience you in unique ways today. Open the eyes of their hearts so that they may see how deeply loved, honored, and cherished they are by you. Please meet their needs in every way and encourage them to find their satisfaction, strength, and joy in you. May their joy be complete today because of you! Thank you Jesus for your love. Thank you for who you are. Thank you for all you do and have done. Thank you for blessing me with my friends, Lord. How truly honored I feel to have them in my life! I love you and ask that you help us live lives worthy of you today. Starting with today God, I just pray that you would satisfy us with your unfailing love, that we may sing for joy and be glad all of our days. We love you, we need you, we bless you . . . In Jesus' name . . . AMEN!

Have a blessed day!

<>< Jessica

Prayer requests? Praises?

From: Hisword2day
To: Your heart
Sent: Monday, January 05, 2004 12:22 PM
Subject: Life is not a white elephant gift–Ecclesiastes 5:18–19

"Then I realized that it is good and proper for a man to eat and drink, and to find satisfaction in his toilsome labor under the sun during the few days of life God has given him—for this is his lot. Moreover, when God gives any man wealth and possessions, and enables him to enjoy them, to accept his lot and be happy in his work—this is a gift from God." *Ecclesiastes 5:18–19* **NIV**

HAPPY 2004!!! I hope everyone is off to a blessed start this New Year!! Isn't it a wonderful thought that five days ago we embarked on yet another journey with the Lord? What great plans He has in store for those of us who love Him! What an adventure in life, in faith, in love this year will provide! We should all be so excited for the Lord's agenda this year!

As excited as I am about this New Year, I know how easy it is for me to lose this excitement and zeal! I get bogged down with the hustle and bustle of life. I get discouraged with where I find myself emotionally, physically, spiritually, financially, etc. Simply put, I lose focus of the fact that the few days of life the Lord has given me here on this earth are nothing short of a blessing and gift! (Can you relate?) Yesterday as I was driving, God pressed a challenge on my heart to see my life and my circumstances—my lot—in a new light, His light, so that I might ever increasingly enjoy Him and the abundant blessing I call my "life." For, as this verse reminds us, to accept our lot and be happy with our work (which I like to think of as our life) truly is a gift from God.

The "white elephant" gift exchange is quite a popular activity at holiday events. The point is to bring a "gag" gift. Often times, a possession, unwanted by the owner but difficult to dispose of, becomes a gift. Other times, pointless, senseless, or useless gifts are given . . . all in good humor . . . and it is indeed rather amusing to watch people open these random, comical gifts!

I've been told that the idea behind this game originated from a 19th century King of Siam who would give an albino, Indian elephant to any courtier he found unpleasant, offensive, or disagreeable. One might think, "Oh how wonderful! A white elephant! How rare!" That might be true, but really it was a gift you didn't want for the upkeep of this animal was so extensive and expensive that it would ruin the owner, emotionally, physically, mentally, and financially. It was definitely a possession entailing great expense out of proportion to its value.*

Well, how many of us feel like God has given us a "white elephant" gift called "my life?" Do you feel like your life, or your circumstances are a burden, not a blessing? Do you feel like the upkeep of your life is so extensive and expensive (emotionally, physically, mentally, spiritually, and/or financially) that it's ruining you? Do you ever feel like you've found disfavor with God and that that's why you have the life you do or are in the situations you are in?

First of all, let me tell you, it's not an issue of you not finding favor in God's eyes. You are the apple of His eye! The firstfruit of His creation! He doesn't have plans to harm you, but rather to bless you (Jeremiah 29:11). Secondly, Jesus Himself warned us we were going to have troubles in this world (John 16:33). We will indeed face hardships, trials, and tribulations, but we never face them alone (Matthew 28:20, Deuteronomy 31:6–8). These hard times will not consume us

And thirdly, God never gave us life to be a burden. He gave us life as a gift, but not a "white elephant" gift. How can I say that with certainty? Because He sent Jesus, His one and only begotten Son, to earth so that we might have an abundant life, not a forsaken life (John 10:10). He came so that our joy might be complete, not depleted (John 15:11). Had God not meant for life to be a blessing and a gift, He wouldn't have gone to such extreme measures for our sake. Furthermore, as this verse in Ecclesiastes reminds us, it is good and proper to find satisfaction in our lot in life.

God's challenge to me, and to all of us, is to stop seeing life as a "white elephant" gift and to realize what a true gift it really is. He longs to be gracious to us and to show us compassion (Isaiah 30:18). Therefore, it wouldn't fit with His character if He wanted us to be miserable and to despise our lives. He gave us our lives for a reason and we each play a HUGE role in His kingdom *just where we are, just the way we are!!!* (1 Corinthians 15:10).

How I pray that today we would *accept* our lot. For the verse today seems to signify that when we finally accept our lot, we unlock the rich blessings within us and we begin to find satisfaction, contentment, happiness, and joy, which are all gifts from God. Therefore, my challenge to all of us for 2004 is to seek the Lord with all of our hearts and to enjoy life to the fullest day by day. Don't see life as a "white elephant" gift. Rather see it as a blessing and get excited! For no one has seen, heard, or can even conceive of the great things the Lord has in store for those who love Him!!!

May the Lord give you a spirit of wisdom and revelation so that you may know Him better and see Him more through your lot. May you realize that life is filled with so many blessings, but may you be keenly aware that blessings are not always tangible. In fact, many times they are the intangibles . . . love, grace, peace, joy, health, patience, family, friends, gratitude, contentment, and life itself. May you find satisfaction, joy, and contentment where you are and in what you experience. And may you always look for Jesus in everything.

Praying for your perfection,

<>< Jessica

Prayer requests? Praises?

*Merriam-Webster Online Dictionary

From: Hisword2day
To: Your heart
Sent: Tuesday, January 06, 2004 1:57 PM
Subject: Out of town

Just a quick note to let you know I will be at Young Life All-Staff Conference in Florida until Tuesday, January 13th, and will not have access to a computer to send e-mails. I should be able to check my e-mails with my cell phone, so you can still send prayer requests—I just won't be able to reply to them.

I need you to please keep me in your prayers this week as I meet, for the first time, the Young Life Paris team I will be working with. I also ask that you pray for God to soften my heart to Him.

Thank you so much for your prayers! Have a great week and remember to seek the Lord with all your heart!

In His unfailing love and grace,

<>< Jessica

From: Hisword2day
To: Your heart
Sent: Wednesday, January 14, 2004 4:16 PM
Subject: Thank you–Colossians 4:12

"Epaphras, who is one of you and a servant of Christ Jesus, sends greetings. He is always wrestling in prayer for you, that you may stand firm, in all the will of God, mature and fully assured." *Colossians 4:12* **NIV**

Prior to leaving for Young Life's All-Staff Conference, I wrote to you asking you to "pray for me as I was going to meet, for the first time, the team I will be working with in Paris." Well, they are just amazing and we are so very blessed . . . God has given our team such a sense of unity and love! We had a blast together! They are just incredible and I am so excited and blessed to be called to serve alongside them as we share Jesus with kids in Paris!

I also asked you to "pray for God to soften my heart to Him." Well, today I just want to say thank you. I had quite an overwhelming experience . . . wonderful, but one which is so hard to capture in words. I went into this week with my heart and mind swirling with emotions, doubts, and fatigue. Yet I walked away standing firm in God's will, fully assured of His love and grace (and calling), rejuvenated in heart, mind, body, and soul, and refreshed. All of this was made possible because of what happened inside of me this week. Something for which I will be forever grateful to you as it is something that has, and will, change my heart and life for eternity, I'm sure . . . I fell absolutely, head over heels, passionately *in love* with Jesus.

I don't know if this is the first time or one of many, but I can tell you this . . . I have never in my entire relationship with Jesus been so *in love* with Him as I am today. (OH He is so amazing!) Today I just want to thank you *from the bottom of my heart* for helping me to get to this point of surrender, this point of love. I would not be here if it weren't for you. See, you, my friend, have been Epaphras to me. You have been faithful at wrestling for me in prayer and for that I truly do thank you as it is so apparent that your prayers have been so very powerful and effective in my life! They have indeed softened my heart to Him and helped give me the spirit of wisdom and revelation so that I might know Christ better, love Him deeper, and be known by Him more intimately.

For all this and more . . . thank you. Thank you for helping to make this whole experience possible for me through your love, financial support, and mostly through your prayers. You truly have been Epaphras to me and because of you, I have grown in knowledge and understanding of who Jesus is to me, who I am to Him, and have become fully assured of who I am in Him so that I may stand firm in all of the will of God. Thank you, my friend. Thank you so very much for helping me to fall passionately in love with Jesus again!!!

How I desperately pray that you too will fall in love with Jesus as you grow in your knowledge and understanding of Jesus and how He loves *you*. He does . . . He loves you *so very, very much*.

By and through the love and grace of Jesus Christ,

<>< Jessica

Prayer requests? Praises?

From: Hisword2day
To: Your heart
Sent: Friday, January 16, 2004 2:04 PM
Subject: Embracing the cross–Matthew 16:24

"Then Jesus said to His disciples, 'If anyone desires to be My disciple, let him deny himself and take up his cross and follow Me.'"
Matthew 16:24 Amp.

At Young Life's All-Staff Conference, I was blessed with an incredible opportunity to watch Mel Gibson's movie *The Passion of the Christ.* Friends, GO SEE IT! Words cannot even begin to grasp the depth to which this movie pierced my heart, my mind, and my soul. It allows you to get a mere *glimpse* at the physical and emotional torture Jesus suffered. You can see His pain—the betrayal, the fierce lashings, His blood, sweat and tears. You feel His agony. But in His speech grace pours forth. In His eyes you see His love and His resolute fixation is on the joy set before Him. You watch His determination despite His desperation. You watch Jesus pouring out His life so that you might have life.

Simply put, the scenes of this movie have made Jesus and the cross, His love and His grace, more real to me than *ever* before.

One particular scene shows Jesus carrying His cross. He has been brutally beaten beyond recognition and drained of any physical strength. He stumbles and catches Himself on His cross, clinging to it as if it were life itself. He lingers there for a brief moment, and a man from the crowd yells out to Him, "Why . . . why do you embrace your cross?"*

Embrace . . . picture it . . . Jesus is *hugging* the cross. Squeezing it tightly. Holding on with what little might He has . . . He's *embracing* it. Embracing it as if He were accepting it.

As I watched this scene, my heart broke. My heart echoed the cry of the bystander . . ."Why, Jesus, do you embrace this cross? WHY?!" And His response to me was one I shall *never* forget. As the camera zoomed in on Jesus and I watched . . . as I saw Him hugging His cross . . . as I saw Him embracing it . . . almost as if He were cherishing the moment . . . He said to me, "Why, Jessica? You are the answer. I love you, my princess. *I embraced my cross so I could embrace you."*

My heart be still . . . tears, oh the tears! As I continue to see this scene in my head, I can't help but remember Jesus' words to me. *"So I could embrace you . . ."* Wow! That He would go through so much to bridge that gap between God and me so that He could embrace *me.*

It brings a whole new meaning to denying oneself and taking up your cross. Jesus did just that. For He was in very nature God, yet He did not consider equality with God something to be grasped. No, instead the King of Kings made Himself nothing, took on the very nature of a servant, came down from heaven (Ephesians 4:9) in human likeness, and humbled Himself to the point of death on a cross. He lost sight of the pain and suffering and for the joy set before Him endured the excruciating pain of crucifixion knowing that His momentary pain was achieving an eternal glory that far outweighed all His suffering.

This verse now speaks a bit more powerfully to me. I desperately want to deny myself. I want to disregard my life and my own interests. I want to conform to Jesus' example . . . I want to take up my cross (whatever that may mean) just as Jesus took up His. I want to cherish it and cling to it knowing that indeed the cross does bring life. I want to know Him so that others might know Him through me. I want to hug the cross . . . my cross. I want to accept my cross and embrace it as Jesus did for me, so that others might accept and embrace Him.

Well, I could go on and on. ☺ However for the sake of not writing a novel I will close. I pray today that you may know in your heart that Jesus loves you, deeply, passionately, furiously! He absolutely cherishes you! May you never forget the love that led Him to embrace His cross and endure such opposition so that He could embrace *you.* He did it for the joy that was set before Him . . . you. Feel His arms of love around you as He hugs you from heaven today.

Embracing the cross,

<>< Jessica

Prayer requests? Praises?

*The Passion of the Christ

From: Hisword2day
To: Your heart
Sent: Thursday, January 22, 2004
Subject: To know Christ–Philippians 3:10–11

"I want to know Christ and the power of his resurrection and the fellowship of sharing in his sufferings, becoming like him in his death, and so, somehow, to attain to the resurrection from the dead." *Philippians 3:10–11* NIV

Everywhere I turn the Lord seems to be teaching me about this concept . . . knowing Christ. It has been the topic of conversation with my friends, it has been in the scriptures I've read, it has been in the sermons I've heard, etc. I still have lots to learn, but it's been great learning and growing in this area! Praise Jesus! So today I wanted to ask you if you've ever thought about what an awesome privilege it is to know Christ? Really . . . have you ever thought about what this means?

According to Webster and the Amplified Bible, "to know" means to be acquainted with, to identify with, to have experience of, to be on familiar terms with, to perceive directly, to recognize the nature of, to be aware of the truth or factuality of: be convinced or certain of, to have a practical understanding of. Wow! To *know* Christ . . .

Do *you* want to *know* Christ? Do you want to become intimately acquainted and personally familiar with Him? Do you want to have experience of Him? Do you want to directly perceive Him and recognize His nature? Do you want to be keenly aware of Him?

If you answered "yes" then I must ask you, do you want to identify with Him? Do you want to have a practical understanding of Him?

I hope and pray we all answered "yes" again. However, we must realize that identifying with Him means sharing in similar experiences with Him. Being able to empathize with Him, not just sympathize. That entails sharing in the power of His resurrection (joys and triumphs), but also sharing in His sufferings. Identifying with the cross. It is by doing so that we gain a practical, personal understanding of Him, and can then begin to perceive the great depths of His love and grace!

Life provides *incredible* opportunities to get to know Jesus, to share in joys and sufferings. We don't always look at our life and its circumstances as such a blessing, but in reality every moment of our life, whether joy or pain, yields another chance to grow in our knowledge and understanding of Jesus.

Today I just want to encourage and challenge you . . . whatever you are experiencing, whether if be pleasure or pain, know that the Lord is with you (Matthew 28:20). He is your refuge and strength, an ever-present help (Psalm 46:1). He's walked alongside you through *everything* (Deuteronomy 31:6). Even more, He's walked in your shoes (Hebrews 4:15). No, His ways are not always your ways; they are much higher (Isaiah 55:8–9). His ways are eternal and perfect (Habakkuk 3:6). Furthermore, He knows every need before you even ask (Matthew 6:8). He doesn't change (Malachi 3:6), so He's going to continue to be your God—guarding, guiding, providing, refining, and loving you. Friend, **you can trust Him**.

And my challenge to you is this: **get to know Jesus**. You have been given many opportunities to "become more deeply and intimately acquainted with Him, perceiving, recognizing, and understanding the wonders of His Person more strongly and more clearly" (Philippians 3:10 Amp.) . . . so go deep. Get personal. Carpe Diem . . . seize the opportunities to get to know Him this very day. Pray that He will grant you a spirit of wisdom and revelation so that you may know Him better. Pray that He will grant you a perspective to see this day and your life's circumstances as precious moments to identify and get more familiar with Jesus.

And lastly, thank Him for such a privilege. Thank God that you have the *amazing* opportunity to get to know Jesus. For it is through His love and by His invitation under grace that you get to know the King of Kings, the Lord of Lords, the Mighty God, the Everlasting Father, the Ancient of Days, the Creator of the universe—the Creator of *you*—the Prince of Peace, Immanuel, the Alpha and Omega, the Great Physician, I AM, the Holy of Holies, your Rock eternal, the Most high, your Shepherd, your Provider, your Counselor, the Author and Perfecter of your faith, the Lamb of God, your Deliverer, Daystar, Guardian of your soul, your Comforter, your Advocate, your Sanctifier, your Savior.

May you be truly blessed as you get better acquainted with Jesus today.

Getting to know Christ,

<>< Jessica

Prayer requests? Praises?

From: Hisword2day
To: Your heart
Sent: Friday, January 23, 2004 3:30 PM
Subject: The Lord longs to be gracious to you–Isaiah 30:18

"Yet the Lord longs to be gracious to you; he rises to show you compassion. For the Lord is a God of justice. Blessed are all who wait for him." *Isaiah 30:18* **NIV**

This is one of my all-time favorite passages and today I just wanted to remind you of this truth as you head into your weekend. I pray that this week has been an exceptionally blessed week for you and that you've been able to experience Jesus in some personal, unique, and humbling ways.

My friend, remember, cherish this fact: the Lord your God, your Savior and Friend, longs to be gracious to you. (Yes, *you!*) He earnestly *seeks out* ways to show you His love. His eyes are ever upon you and they are looking for and expecting opportunities to come so that He can shower you with His mercy and grace and cradle you in His arms of love. He desires to show you loving-kindness in ways you can't imagine, for you, my dear friend, are the love of His heart, the apple of His eye, the first-fruit of His creation. You are His and *He simply wants to love you.*

This weekend I pray that this verse becomes so very real to you. I pray that Jesus helps you to feel His love and grace and how much He longs for you. May you see and experience His loving-kindness and be ever aware of His presence in every scene of your life. May you wait on Him. Expect, look for, and long for Him as He expects looks for, and longs for you. When you seek Him, you will surely find Him and in finding Him you will find His victory, His favor, His love, His peace, His joy, and His matchless, unbroken companionship (Isaiah 30:18 Amp.).

How I pray that the Lord will indeed be ever so gracious to you this weekend . . . may you find rest and peace in His unfailing love!

In His love and grace,

<>< Jessica

Prayer requests? Praises?

From: Hisword2day
To: Your heart
Sent: Monday, January 26, 2004 1:11 PM
Subject: A glimpse of God's grace–Romans 1:20

**"For since the creation of the world God's invisible quali-
ties—his eternal power and divine nature—have been clearly
seen, being understood from what has been made, so that
men are without excuse."** *Romans 1:20 NIV*

We had a rather nasty Saturday here in New Braunfels, Texas: overcast
and rainy. Just yucky. Yet somehow, God painted us a beautiful sunset
in one area of the sky. Dark, daunting clouds blanketed the sky, yet
there was one area that was radiant with beautiful colors. The clouds
had become objects to reflect the sun's light and, therefore, displayed
beauty in vibrant colors for all to see. The canvas of the sky, with all
of its clouds, had been painted with the Lord's beauty in quite a vivid
way!

For me, this sunset was more than just beauty; it was a portrait of my
life. It made one of God's invisible attributes, qualities, and blessings so
very clearly understood. This sunset was a glimpse of God's grace.

I often see God's grace in a sunset, but Saturday night it was exceptionally clear. The dark clouds had been there all day long. Yet when the
sun took a certain position in the sky, these dark, nasty clouds became
objects to reflect the sun's light, and the sun's reflection upon them
were what made the sunset so vibrant and beautiful. These clouds were
resplendent with light! It was truly a sight to behold . . . breathtaking!

And to me, that is just such a beautiful picture of grace! We all have
dark, nasty clouds in our lives (circumstances, sins, fears, pains, trials,
etc.) and many have been there "all day long"—a long time—but the
sky mirrors our lives. When Jesus, the Son, takes a certain position in
our lives and when His grace sets in amidst our clouds, these clouds
simply become objects from which the Son's light will be reflected. For
as the clouds in the sky help to make the sunset so beautiful, your life's
clouds will become beautiful accents in your life . . . they will be what
help make your life and your heart so vibrant . . . so beautiful . . . so
resplendent with the Light of the Lord. I'm a sunset nut and believe me,
no sunset in the world is as breathtaking as watching God's grace set
among your clouds!

So delight in His grace. Thank Jesus for His grace and for the beauty He can make out of your clouds. (Isn't He amazing!?) No matter how dark and daunting your clouds may seem right now, your life and your heart are so beautiful my friend. Remember the sunset and may it remind you that as the Son's grace sets in your life, your clouds will become objects to reflect His light and love. As a result, the canvas of your life, with all of its clouds, will be painted with the Lord's beauty in quite a vivid, vibrant, beautiful way!

Saturday I experienced grace through a sunset. Today may you experience another attribute of the Lord. Do as my friend Chad reminds me to do, "Look for Jesus," for He is all around you! The earth is FULL of His unfailing love! (Psalm 33:5). His invisible qualities are made clearly visible in what He has made. So seek Him and surely you will find Him! How I pray that you are richly blessed and encouraged as you see, hear, and experience the Lord's love, grace, mercy, peace, joy, and loving-kindness. Go get a glimpse of the Lord today.

In His love and grace,

<>< Jessica

Prayer requests? Praises?

From: Hisword2day
To: Your heart
Sent: Tuesday, January 27, 2004 1:30 PM
Subject: Jesus today–Luke 4:18 -19, 21

"The Spirit of the Lord is on me, because he has anointed me to preach good news to the poor. He has sent me to proclaim freedom for the prisoners and recovery of sight for the blind, to release the oppressed, to proclaim the year of the Lord's favor . . . Today this scripture is fulfilled in your hearing." *Luke 4:18–19, 21* **NIV**

We talked about this passage on Sunday at church. It was a wonderful sermon filled with much wisdom and spiritual truth. One of the words in this passage that Larry, my pastor, encouraged us to pay extra close attention to was *today*. He emphasized the importance of this word and wow was it powerful!

See, Jesus was reminding the crowd at the synagogue that the person mentioned in this reading was Himself. They were witnessing fulfillment of this verse before their very eyes . . . in the moment they heard those words escape Jesus' lips! He was basically saying to them, "Hey, I'm the One anointed to preach the good news, proclaim freedom, recover sight, release the oppressed, and proclaim the Lord's favor. I'm your man!"

And, as Larry reminded us, Jesus fulfills this scripture still today. This *very day* Jesus is preaching the good news to the poor . . . poor in spirit, poor in health, poor in wealth. (Can you hear Him speaking truth into your life?)

He is here *today* to proclaim freedom for the prisoners. If there seems to be something holding you or someone you know captive, if something—some feeling or circumstance is oppressing you—know that *today* Jesus is here to proclaim freedom, to release you. After all it is for freedom that Christ has set you free (Galatians 5:1) and He can indeed set you free from your chains so that you may praise His name (Psalm 142:7). Remember, His grace and His favor are sufficient for you, no matter how great the struggle or how tight your chains may seem. Claim freedom in your life *today* . . . you can do so with confidence because of Jesus! Then watch as He starts to work . . . and wait in anticipation for what does!

If you seem to be blinded, in some form or fashion, know that *today* Jesus can restore your sight—whether it be physical or spiritual. As Paul prays for his friends, so we should pray for ourselves and each other that the Lord will open the eyes of our hearts so that we may know Him better, that we may grow in wisdom and insight. Often times we seem blindsided by our circumstances and emotions . . . we can't see the Lord's hand or presence at all. But remember the warning on the side mirrors of your car . . . objects in mirror are closer than they appear . . . Jesus is closer than He often appears. Furthermore, often times when you can't see a car it's because it is so close that it's right beside you . . . in your blind spot. We may often find ourselves in similar situations with the Lord . . . He's so close that we can't see Him . . . He's in our blind spot. Yet remember, He has come today to help you see.

And *today,* as surely as the sun rose, Jesus appeared to proclaim His favor over you.

So *today* know that the Lord is the Lord *your* God. He is who He says He will be . . . yesterday, today, and tomorrow. He will be your Provider, Healer, Sustainer, the Prince of Peace, God with us, King of Kings, Lord of Lords, Mighty God, Everlasting Father, Alpha and Omega, the Great Physician, I AM, the Holy of Holies, your Rock eternal, the Most high, your Shepherd, Provider, Counselor, the Author and Perfecter of your faith, the Lamb of God, your Deliverer, Guardian of your soul, your Comforter, Advocate, Sanctifier, and your Savior. How very reassuring that thought is to me!

Trust Him . . . **today**. Know Him . . . **today**. Love Him . . . **today**. *For today* He loves you.

Through the love and grace of Jesus,

<>< Jessica

Prayer requests? Praises?

From: Hisword2day
To: Your heart
Sent: Wednesday, January 28, 2004 12:39 PM
Subject: In the same boat–Luke 8:22–25

"One day Jesus said to his disciples, 'Let's go over to the other side of the lake.' So they got into a boat and set out. As they sailed, he fell asleep. A squall came down on the lake, so that the boat was being swamped, and they were in great danger. The disciples went and woke him, saying 'Master! Master! We're going to drown!' He got up rebuked the wind and the raging waters; the storm subsided, and all was calm. 'Where is your faith?' he asked his disciples. In fear and amazement they asked on another, 'Who is this? He commands even the winds and the water, and they obey him.'" *Luke 8:22–25* **NIV**

I struggle with storms in my life. And when they come, oh buddy can I see myself in the disciples . . . running to Jesus in desperation and saying, "Oh my goodness, Lord! I'm swamped! HELP! I'm going to drown! This is going to consume me!" However, today as I read this passage, the Lord highlighted some little details in this story that I seemed to have previously missed and used them to remind me of some important truths we must cling to as we encounter the raging squalls of our own lives.

First of all, notice who suggested they go out into the waters: Jesus. It was HIS idea. And from what we know of the Lord He is all-knowing and He goes before us (Deuteronomy 31:8). Therefore, He *must have* known that the storm was awaiting them. Yet He still encouraged them to go. He knew He could handle the storm, that the winds and waters would obey Him. He knew the storm would not drown them. And He might have even thought it would be a good opportunity for them to bolster their faith and trust in Him.

Secondly, notice that Jesus was in the boat *with* them. He didn't tell them, "Okay, go to the other side of the lake. I'm just going to sit here. Bon voyage!" Nope. In typical Jesus fashion, He hopped right in there with them to make the journey alongside them. And because He was in the boat with them, look at what the disciples did: when troubles arose and when the winds began to blow and the storm began to rage, they called upon Him. They **went** to Him and beseeched Him for help. And look what He did . . . He saved them. He rebuked the raging winds and turbulent waters and calm was restored. The storm was always completely under **His** control.

Then look at how the disciples reacted. In fear and amazement they asked one another, "Who is this? Even the winds and the waters obey Him!" They were in awe. Complete awe. They saw Isaiah 58:9 come true right before their very eyes . . . they cried out to Him for help and oh did He ever say "Here I AM."

Well, my friend, when storms rage in your life (and you most definitely will encounter some turbulent storms) I encourage you to think of this passage and the disciples' experience for it teaches us so much.

Know that if Jesus has suggested an idea, if He has called you to do something or be somewhere, if He has put you into a certain situation, then remember He is all-knowing. He has gone before you and therefore, just as He knew what awaited the disciples, He knows what is awaiting you. He knows the storms you will face and He knows they will not consume you for He can handle them . . . they too will always be under His control. For just as the winds and waters of the disciples' squall were subject to the Lord, so the "winds" and "waters" of your squalls are subject to Him.

Furthermore, know that you are not alone. Jesus never calls you to go alone. He promised you that He would be **with** you always, to the ends of the earth (Matthew 28:20), that He would never leave you nor forsake you (Deuteronomy 31:6–8), and that He would be with you **wherever** you go (Josh. 1:9). Now we know that He is a man of His Word (quite literally) therefore, we do not need to be terrified. We do not need to be discouraged. Instead we must be strong and courageous for the Lord our God is in the same boat as us.

Remember, Jesus might allow certain storms to surround you so that your faith might be tested and grow, so that you might learn to rely on God (2 Corinthians 1:8–9), and so that you too may stand in fear and amazement at the Lord your God. You may react as the disciples did . . . with fear, doubt, confusion, etc. You may hear Jesus saying to you, "Where is your faith?" Or in my mind, "Why are you so terrified? Don't you trust me? Do you not see that I am in the same boat as you? I am here **with** you. I, the Lord your God am in control . . . not the winds and the rain, not your circumstances . . . these things must obey me. You are not subject to them; they are subject to me. Did you really believe that I would let you be consumed by this storm? I mean seriously!"

But, friend, because of the Lord's great love you will not be consumed (Lamentations. 3:22). Your storms *will* subside. Your circumstances *are* under His control and they *must* obey Him. Remember our three friends in the fire, Shadrach, Meshach, and Abednego and remember the disciples . . . they were not saved *from* experiencing their fires and storms, rather they were saved *in* them, amidst them. As Isaiah 43:2 came true for them so it will come true for you . . . when you pass through the waters, Jesus will be with you; and when you pass through the rivers, they will not sweep over you. When you walk through the fire you will not be burned. Your storms and fires are always under *His* control.

So go forth in your day with the knowledge that the Lord is with you; He is in the same boat as you . . . He is your shipmate! How exciting and encouraging to know that! The Lord your God can handle *any* circumstance, can subside *any* storm, and can calm *any* fear . . . whether it's emotional, spiritual, physical, or psychological. Nothing is too hard for the Lord your God (Genesis 18:14) and all things are subject to Him, are under His control, and must obey Him.

May you grow in faith and trust today as you grow in the knowledge of His love knowing that when storms come, calm will be returned . . . turn to Him today!

His shipmate and yours,

<>< Jessica

Prayer requests? Praises?

From: Hisword2day
To: Your heart
Sent: Tuesday, February 03, 2004 2:11 PM
Subject: As Jesus went–Luke 8:42–44

"As Jesus went, the people pressed together around Him almost suffocating Him. And a woman who had suffered from a flow of blood for 12 years and had spent all her living upon physicians, and could not be healed by anyone, came up behind Him and touched the fringe of His garment, and immediately her flow of blood ceased." *Luke 8:42–44* Amp.

Reading this passage I was struck by three simple words. "As Jesus went." See, it was as Jesus went that He healed this woman. He did not seek her out; she sought Him out. Furthermore, He was on His way to heal Jarius' daughter. He had another agenda. Yet *as He went* He healed this woman. He touched her life in a profound way . . . and He was just going about His business.

Well, my friend, I encourage you to look to Jesus' example and realize that often times as *you* go, God is going to touch people's lives through you. You may have a different agenda and be on your way (literally, or figuratively) to something else. However, as you go on your way, living your life, running your errands, studying for exams, toiling at work, simply doing what you do and being who you are, the Lord may cross your path with someone and somehow you may touch a life in a profound way.

So never feel as though you can't make an impact for the Lord where you are, doing what you're doing. Live a life worthy of the calling you've received because, as this verse reminds us, as we go about our business the Lord can heal, encourage, comfort, minister to, and bless someone's life through us.

Jesus felt power leave Him (8:46). Are you letting His power leave through you? I pray that you are! For when people encounter Jesus through you, as His power escapes you, hearts will be touched, lives will be changed, and wounds will be healed *wherever* you are, wherever you're headed.

Remain connected and committed to Jesus and go as Jesus went knowing that *as you go,* you too will marvel at how the Lord works in, around, and through you.

Because of Him,

<>< Jessica

Prayer requests? Praises?

From: Hisword2day
To: Your heart
Sent: Thursday, February 05, 2004 8:50 AM
Subject: Great is His love–Psalm 86:11–13

"Teach me your way, O Lord, and I will walk in your truth; give me an undivided heart, that I may fear Your name. I will praise You, O Lord my God, with all my heart; I will glorify your name forever. For great is your love toward me; you have delivered me from the depths of the grave." *Psalm 86:11–13* NIV

How precious this passage is to me! I have it taped to my bathroom mirror and see it on a daily basis. Doesn't mean I always read it, but it's always there. Well, last night as I read these words again for the millionth time, they seemed to captivate the attention of my heart. I was reminded that no matter what the circumstances may be in my life, I should and I need to want to praise the Lord my God, for oh how great is His love towards me! He has delivered me from the depths of the grave! So many times He has delivered me out of my circumstances, but then quite literally Jesus has delivered me from death and given me life . . . abundant life, eternal life. How my light and momentary troubles seemed to not be so troublesome when I was reminded of that! ☺

Furthermore, Psalm 84:10 reminds us that "better is *one* day in the Lord's courts than a thousand elsewhere." Well, my friend, may you never forget that by an invitation of grace sealed in love on a cross, you have been given the blessed opportunity to walk *all* the days of your life in His courts . . . not just one day, but *all* days. Wow! We can't even imagine! (1 Corinthians 2:9). How I pray that each of you have responded in acceptance to this invitation. And if you have, I pray that this verse is just the overflow of your heart.

As I close, just know that today I prayed this verse for you. I hope that you too will pray through it for yourself. May the Lord open your heart to Him teaching you His ways and may you walk continually in His truths. Give Him your undivided heart. After all, He gave you His. And may you revere Him and praise Him with *all* that you are, with *all* that you do, and with *all* of your heart. No matter what your circumstances may be today, may the cross be at the forefront of your mind and may you be reminded of *how great His love is towards you.*

Go dance in His courts today!
In His love and grace,
<>< Jessica
Prayer requests? Praises?

From: Hisword2day
To: Your heart
Sent: Tuesday, February 10, 2004 12:51 PM
Subject: 3 challenges for you–Psalm 119:56–58

"This has been my practice: I obey your precepts. You are my portion, O Lord; I have promised to obey your words. I have sought your face with all my heart; be gracious to me according to your promise." *Psalm 119:56–58* **NIV**

I pray that today this psalm would be the theme of your song to the Lord.

I pray that today, if it is not already your practice, that it would become your practice to obey the Lord's precepts—His teachings and guidelines—that you would promise to obey His words. Obedience always brings blessings. Furthermore, His word saves (James 1:21), and don't we all need saving from time to time! Boy howdy, I do!

Ask yourself this question: "Is the Lord my portion?" Portion is defined as an individual's part or share of something—a share received by gift or inheritance; dowry; enough food especially of one kind to serve one person at one meal; an individual's lot, fate, or fortune. Well . . . is the Lord your portion?

I pray that today you would find and feel from the depths of your heart that indeed, the Lord *is* your portion. He is enough, more than enough, for today and for always. He is the treasure that you give to others. He is your fortune. And may it always be at the forefront of your heart and mind that through Jesus' gift on the cross you have been qualified to share in the inheritance of the kingdom of light (Col. 1:12). Friend, the Lord is your portion.

I pray that today you would indeed seek the Lord's face with all of your heart. For when you seek Him with all your heart, you will find Him.

I pray that today you would ask the Lord to be gracious to you according to His promise. Remember that not one of all of the Lord's good promises to the house of Israel failed; *every single one* was fulfilled (Joshua 21:45). I mean, when the Lord speaks, He acts; when He promises, He fulfills! (Numbers 24:19). If the Lord is the same yesterday, today, and forever, why should we doubt that He would not keep

His own word? What the Lord promises with His mouth, He fulfills with His mighty hands (1 Kings 8:24).

Today I give you three challenges to make this psalm the theme of your song today:

1. Put His word into practice. Those who hear the word should be doers of the word (James 1:22). Therefore, promise to keep His word, and really do it. (Don't make an empty promise to God . . . that is DANGEROUS!) Obey Him one precept at a time. He'll give you the strength to keep this promise.

2. If you don't feel as though the Lord is your portion, ask Him to reveal to you that He is. Then live in such a way that shows it.

3. And lastly, truly seek out the Lord with all of your heart, mind, body, and soul today (however you may do that) and then watch and be utterly amazed at how gracious He is to you as He keeps His promises!

May you hear, receive, love, and obey God's word. May you hear, receive, love, and obey Jesus . . . what a gift of God's grace!

In His love, grace, hope, joy, and peace,

<>< Jessica

Prayer requests? Praises?

From: Hisword2day
To: Your heart
Sent: Thursday, February 12, 2004 1:12 PM
Subject: Where's Jesus?–Jeremiah 29:13

"Then you will seek Me, inquire for, and require Me [as a vital necessity] and find Me when you search for Me with all your heart." *Jeremiah 29:13* **Amp.**

Have you ever played "Where's Waldo?" It's a fun little game of trying to find an inconspicuous character, Waldo, amidst a scene of craziness! The pictures are usually loud, with distractions everywhere and a crazy assortment of characters doing all kinds of different activities. Some scenes make it fairly easy to find Waldo—you don't have to search too long to find him. In others he is more difficult to find and it usually takes longer to find him. In fact, it sometimes takes more than one try to find him. You may need to let the frustration die down and come back with a fresh perspective. Nevertheless, no matter how simple or chaotic the scene may be, Waldo's in every scene, therefore when you search for him, you will eventually find him.

Do you see the lesson I see?

Your life may often look like a scene from "Where's Waldo?" . . . loud, filled with distractions, full of craziness, and with chaos everywhere. Some of these scenes still allow us to find Jesus rather easily. But then there are some in which Jesus is extremely difficult to find . . . He's seemingly very well hidden or disguised. However, no matter how simple or chaotic the scene of your life may be, no matter how visible or how hidden Jesus may seem, Jesus is in *every* scene, therefore when you search for Him with all of your heart, you will surely find Him.

Yes, searching for Him requires something of us. How quickly we forget that we have an *interactive* relationship with Jesus. We get mad at the Lord and claim He's not there, that He's abandoned us, when really we just haven't looked for Him. We haven't sought Him. Therefore, when the chaos and distractions in our lives are temporarily hiding or disguising Jesus, remember that it may take more than one try to find Him, but as His word tells us (Deuteronomy 31:6, Matthew 28:20, Isaiah 43:2), He is in every scene of our lives and therefore, can always be found. How reassuring that is to me!

I encourage you today to seek Him, inquire of Him, require Him as a vital necessity with all your heart and surely you will find Him. Have a truly blessed day looking for and finding Jesus!

Seeking and finding,

<>< Jessica

Prayer requests? Praises?

From: Hisword2day
To: Your heart
Sent: Tuesday, February 17, 2004 7:48 AM
Subject: Prayer requests for Jess–Luke 12:11–12

"And when they bring you before the synagogues and the magistrates and the authorities, do not be anxious beforehand how you shall reply in defense or what you are to say. For the Holy Spirit will teach you in that very hour and moment what you ought to say." *Luke 12:11–12* Amp.

Today I'm writing you asking you to pray for me. I am going before the French Consulate this morning around 10:30–11:00 A.M. (Texas time) with all of my visa papers ready to process. I am supposed to go in for an interview, which is why that I ask you to pray this passage over me . . . for indeed I will be going before the authorities today and desperately need the Holy Spirit's protection, guidance, direction, and words. What a blessed reassurance this passage has been for me as I've prepared for this day! Thank you, Lord for your Holy Spirit!

For a quick update/reminder, the Lord has called me to go on staff with Young Life, a non-denominational, Christian outreach organization dedicated to introducing adolescents to Jesus Christ and helping them grow in their faith. If it continues to be the Lord's will, I will be serving in Paris, France. France is an enchanting country, intriguing and charming. Yet, you may be surprised to learn, as I was, that France, in particular, Paris, is one of the spiritually darkest places in the world. Over the years Christianity's presence there has dwindled drastically. Simply put, Paris is a very, very difficult place to do ministry. (I've heard it said that Paris, and other European cities, are considered to be "missionary graveyards.")

Not only will it be difficult being there (which I still count as a rich blessing), it is difficult *getting* there. Yet I count this as a blessing too, as I have had such amazing opportunities to watch the Lord work in quite literally some miraculous ways. Today I'm asking you to help me and pray for one such miracle to happen. ☺

The French government has really cracked down on the visas they issue. According to an article I recently read, the French government strongly desires to maintain the secular nature of the state, which makes getting a visa to work for a Christian organization an added challenge. Some missionaries in the past have had their visas denied so today I am asking for your special prayers as I will going into the same consulate that has previously denied visas on the grounds of religion.

By our world's view, this looks impossible and hopeless, but with the Lord ALL things are possible! Furthermore, we have hope because we have Jesus. And as the Lord has recently reminded me through His word, "Don't be seized with alarm or struck with fear; simply believe in Me as *able* to do this, Jessica." (Luke 8:50) And oh He is able!! NOTHING is too hard for the Lord our God! This doesn't mean I will for sure receive a visa, but I know that He is able to get one in my hands if He wants to. I don't doubt that in the least bit! Whatever is HIS good pleasure, whatever is HIS will, shall come to pass and I trust that HIS ways are absolutely perfect with blessings always waiting to happen!

So today I'm just asking that you pray for me as I go into the consulate's office. As I mentioned earlier, after handing in my papers, I will be interviewed to discuss why I want a visa, what I will be doing there, and for them to clarify any questions they might have regarding my reasons for going to France.

PRAYER REQUESTS:

PLEASE pray that they would not ask me any questions I will have a hard time answering truthfully, but if they do, pray that I would have faith and strength knowing that the Lord's promise in the passage above will be true—He will be with me and teach me in that *very moment* what I am to say.

Pray that I will have discernment regarding what the Holy Spirit is telling me to say. I'm going to be bold in my requests—please pray that the people I talk with will be friendly and that we will get along well. (The Lord tells us to make every request made known to Him.) ☺

Pray that the hearts of those to whom I will be speaking will be softened and pray for their salvation if they don't already know Jesus.

Pray for my protection, guidance, peace, courage, and words. And ultimately, pray for HIS WILL TO BE DONE.

Friend, I want to thank you that I can turn to you for prayer. What a joy it is for me to know that we are doing this together . . . and truly we are! I would **never** have the strength to be doing this without your prayers! You have helped and are helping my by your prayers . . . never ever doubt that! James 5:16 says, "The prayer of the righteous is POWER-FUL and EFFECTIVE!"

I also want to thank you that I can share with you my roller coaster of emotions, struggles, joys, fears, and victories! Today I'm excited and nervous at the same time. I feel as though I am going into a lion's den . . . but as we all know, from our Old Testament friends, the Lord can keep the lions' mouths shut and He will guard and protect! God has given me such great reassurance and strength through His word lately! It has been AMAZING! He's just been reminding me over, and over, and over again that He is our Rock, Shield, Fortress, Deliverer, Refuge, Strength, and Peace. That He prepares us for battle, arms us with strength, goes with us, guards us with His shield of victory, etc. etc. etc. (Read Psalm 17–18. These chapters have been my inspiration as I've been facing this!) I know that with your help I can advance against a troop . . . with God I can scale a wall (Ps. 18:29). I can face whatever is thrown at me today . . . whether it be a walk in the park or the most difficult time ever!

How blessed I feel to know that the Lord is on my side and if HE is for me, who can be against me, right? ☺ Thank you for guarding, protecting, and preparing me by your prayers today. Thank you, my dear friend. Thank you so much! How I pray that you too will know the promises within this passage. The Holy Spirit is with you and will teach you as you go.

Walking by faith and for His glory,

<>< Jessica

Prayer requests? Praises

From: Hisword2day
To: Your heart
Sent: Wednesday, February 18, 2004 10:12 PM
Subject: WOW, God! Thanks!

"WOW, God! Thanks!" were the words escaping my lips as I walked out of the consulate's office yesterday . . . what a day! **Thank you so much for your prayers**!!!!!!! I can't even begin to express in words just how powerful and effective they were!!!!!!!!!!!!!!!!!!!! It was quite a unique experience all together! I won't know if I get a visa for another couple of months, but today I am just thankful for how the Lord answered our prayers. He always does, but I tell you what, He quite literally answered the requests we put before Him yesterday! I mean just reread the e-mail I sent yesterday and then read this one and you will see that *literally* almost EVERY SINGLE request was answered as we'd requested!

Yesterday I wrote that, "I feel as though I am going into a lion's den . . . but as we know, from our Old Testament friends, the Lord can keep the lions' mouths shut and He will guard and protect!" Well, the "lion's mouth" was never even opened. I didn't have to even go in for an interview . . . bizarre! I had asked you to pray that I wouldn't have to answer any difficult questions and I didn't have to answer a single one! What a nice walk in the park! ☺

I'd asked you to pray for friendly encounters with people. Sure enough, the Lord gave me *extremely* friendly people working at the consulate and others requesting their visa who I *promise* were angels! It was as if they were waiting for me there or coming there to meet me . . . it was really an interesting day!

Furthermore, I walked in there with a peace that surpasses all understanding—it was a peace that can only come from the Holy Spirit!!! So thank you my friend for arming me with strength, sending a shield of protection over me, blessing me with peace, and praying God's will over me. THANK YOU SO MUCH FOR YOUR PRAYERS! How very, very powerful and effective your prayers were over me yesterday! I don't think I've ever been more bathed in prayer than I was yesterday! I'm humbled, honored, and SO VERY blessed to have such a wonderful cloud of witnesses surrounding me and helping me fight each daily battle! It is a blessing beyond what words can capture!

I wish I had more time to tell you what a unique experience it was . . . it truly was an amazing day . . . I'm still trying to sort through it all! I'll try to write more later this week, but know that your prayers were heard and answered . . . as they *always* are! Ask and keep on asking and you shall receive as Matthew and Luke remind us. We asked and kept on asking, and WOW did we receive! THANKS GOD! Please keep my visa in your prayers as it processes . . . pray that His perfect will be done!

Thank you friend! From the bottom of my heart, THANK YOU!

Overjoyed,

<>< Jessica

Prayer requests? PRAISES?

From: Hisword2day
To: Your heart
Sent: Friday, February 20, 2004 2:23 PM
Subject: He always listens–John 11:40–42

"Jesus said to her [Martha], 'Did I not tell you and promise you that if you would believe and rely on Me, you would see the glory of God?' So they took away the stone. And Jesus lifted up His eyes and said, 'Father I thank You that You have heard Me. Yes, I know You always hear and listen to Me . . . '" *John 11:40–42* Amp.

In this verse we find Jesus about to raise Lazarus from the dead. He has been dead four days, a fact of which Martha made sure Jesus was fully aware "Take away the stone," Jesus said. And Martha reminded him, "But Lord He's going to stink . . . and something awful! He's been dead four days!" To which Jesus replied the above verse, "Did I not tell you and *promise* you that if you would believe and rely on ME, you would see the glory of God?" They took away the stone and then Jesus went before His Father in prayers of thanks . . ."Father, I thank you that you have heard me. Yes, I know . . . you always hear and listen to me."

This passage holds a very, very special place in my heart for several reasons. First of all, when I was asking the Lord about direction on how to go before the French Consulate for my visa . . . with Young Life documents, or devising a scheme that would surely get me a visa with no problems, the Lord spoke to me through Luke 8:50, "Jessica," He said, "don't be struck with alarm or seized with fear. Just believe in me as able to do this." WOW! "Okay," I said, "I'm trusting you as able to do this instead of relying on some smart scheme of mine." So the first part of this passage really hits home on that note . . . I can almost hear Jesus saying, "Jessica, I don't know why you're so shocked things went as well as they did on Tuesday. Did I not tell you and *promise* you that if you would believe and rely on me that you would see the glory of God?" Boy howdy did we ever see it on Tuesday! (But don't we see it every day???)

And secondly this verse struck me because these were the words that escaped my mouth leaving the consulate . . ."WOW, God! Thanks! Thank you for hearing my prayer, our prayers!" To which the Lord replied, "Jessica, I always hear and listen to your prayers." And I was reminded of Jesus' words that were now my own, "Yes, I know, you always hear and listen to me."

Now the Lord happened to answer our prayers on Tuesday *as we'd asked.* I didn't have to answer any difficult questions. I encountered friendly people. A miracle did happen. I had peace (beyond comprehension!), courage, protection (like I've never felt before!) and guidance . . . etc. etc.

However, you and I both know and have experienced that the Lord doesn't always answer our prayers as we request—He doesn't always answer our prayers like we hope or think He will. It is in these moments that we must ask ourselves if we really believe that He does answer our prayers. Do you believe that He does? Regardless of **how** you answered, do you know that He always listens and hears you? Do you trust this promise? Okay, then do you really trust His ways over yours? Do you trust His thoughts over your own? Do you believe that His ways are perfect?

Friend, as the Lord reminded me on Tuesday, I want to remind you from the mouth of Jesus Himself, He *always* hears us. He *always* listens. And He *always* answers. It may not be like you think He will, but your prayers never fall on deaf ears. They are always heard. You are always listened to.

Today I just wanted you to be mindful of this truth. Regardless of how Tuesday would've gone, I still would've needed to say THANK YOU to God, for listening to me . . . even if He would've answered me in a different way. And regardless of how the Lord answers you I pray that you too will say thanks for the simple fact that He, the Lord your God, the Creator of the universe, the Giver of every good and perfect gift, your Savior, your Rock, your Redeemer, your Refuge, your Strength, and your Peace is mindful of you. ***He cares for you. He listens to you and always acts in love and faithfulness.***

May you remember that you are the apple of the Lord's eye. You are the song of His heart and the firstfruit of His creation. You are His beloved and He will always treat you as such. Therefore, talk to Him today. Roll the stone of doubt, distrust, and self-reliance away from your heart and believe and rely on Him. For when you do, you too will see the glory of God. And even if you do not understand how His glory is revealed, even if you don't understand His ways or His timing, remember that as for God, His ways are perfect (Psalm 18:30, Isaiah 55:9). Just because He doesn't answer as we want Him to doesn't mean He's not listening and acting. He sees the whole puzzle put together; we just see one piece or a few pieces at a time. So go forth today putting your trust in the Lord and having faith . . . be sure of what you hope for and certain of what you do not see (Hebrews 11:1).

Entrust things to Him . . . your heart, your situation, your relationship, your friend or family member—commit *all* things to Him *with confidence*. Give Him a chance to show you that He hears you. Remember His promise above, and no matter how He answers your prayers, may you answer Him as Jesus did, "Father, I thank *you* that you have heard *me*. Yes, I know, you always hear and listen to me."

Thankful,

<>< Jessica

Prayer requests? Praises?

From: Hisword2day
To: Your heart
Sent: Thursday, February 26, 2004 12:50 PM
Subject: Minutemen: dressed and ready–Luke 12:35–38

"Be dressed and ready for service and keep your lamp burning, like men waiting for their master to return from a wedding banquet, so that when he comes and knocks they can immediately open the door for him. It will be good for those servants whose master finds them watching when he comes. I tell you the truth, he will dress himself to serve, will have them recline at the table and will come and wait on them. It will be good for those servants whose master finds them ready, even if he comes in the second or third watch of the night." *Luke 12:35–38* NIV

In the years leading up to the American Revolution, volunteers were organized into military companies and trained to bear arms. These volunteers were most commonly referred to as Minutemen for they were ready for battle "at a minute's notice." They lived up to their name and were apparently quite invaluable! In 1774, the Provincial Congress ordered that 1/3 of all new regiments in the Massachusetts militia were to be made up of Minutemen. The Continental Congress even suggested that colonies train up Minutemen. And then in the night watches of April 18, 1775, Paul Revere and William Dawes made their famous ride to warn "The British are coming!" The following day these men fought the first battles of the Revolution at Lexington and Concord.* They had quite a role!

I really admire these men! First of all, to be ready at a moment's notice! Impressive! (Esp. for me . . . ha ha) More impressive however, is their willingness to fight. These men were *volunteers.* They signed up to fight because they so strongly believed in the cause. This means they were willing to leave their family, friends and life at a moment's notice to go fight for the cause, for freedom from the seemingly oppressive rule of the British crown.

I can't help but wonder if you and I are not called to be Minutemen and women for God's kingdom today. Read the above passage, which I believe is personally directed at us: Be dressed and ready for service . . . keep your lamp burning.

I realize that this passage is reminding us that we never know when Jesus will return. We need not delay when it comes to salvation. Yet to me this passage also seems to be telling us, "Soldiers, remember the gravity of this war . . . it involves eternal life and death and freedom from the oppressive rule of the prince of this world. We don't have time to lollygag. Therefore, train yourselves up. The Lord is saying, "Let *me* train you up and be dressed and ready, keep your lamp burning so that *whenever* I come and knock on your door, you are ready. I may come when you least expect it (in the 2nd or 3rd watch of the night), but whenever I come you should be ready for what I call you to do. And what a blessed reward you shall receive! I will wait on you!" (That's a whole other topic!)

So today I ask you, are you a Minuteman for God's kingdom? Are you dressed and ready to take part in God's service at a moment's notice? Do you stand watch? Or are you one of those in Luke 12:45–47 who lollygags and knows their master's will, yet does not get ready or do what his master wants?

Furthermore, it is for freedom that Christ has set us free (Galatians 5:1). Do you so strongly believe in the Cause that you're willing to do *whatever* it takes to fight for the Cause, for freedom, for life? (I really have to ponder this one!)

And then let us ask ourselves this . . . are we training ourselves up to "bear arms?" How so? How are you doing with fencing? Fencing is the art of fighting with a sword. So how are you doing with learning how to fight with the sword of the Spirit—God's word? Do you regularly communicate with your Commander in Chief in prayer?

Well, friend, I could go on, but I will close with this challenge: be or train to be a Minuteman (or woman) for God's kingdom. May you remember that it is the Lord who keeps your lamp burning and trains you for battle (Psalm 18:28, 30). You are so precious and valuable to Him! Therefore, show up daily for training and take up the full armor of God so that when the day of battle (or skirmish) comes, when Jesus comes knocking or the Holy Spirit is sent on His Paul Revere ride, you may be dressed, ready and able to stand your ground.

Fighting the good fight,

<>< Jessica

Prayer requests? PRAISES?

*The World Book Encyclopedia (by World Book-Childcraft International, Inc., Copyright 1979 U.S.A.)

From: Hisword2day
To: Your heart
Sent: Friday, February 27, 2004 12:16 PM
Subject: Are you willing? Luke 13:34

"O Jerusalem, Jerusalem, you who kill the prophets and stone those sent to you, how often I have longed to gather your children together, as a hen gathers her chicks under her wings, but you were not willing." *Luke 13:34* **NIV**

Okay, so can anyone else sense that this verse is directed at them? Goodness gracious! When I read it I could see it applying to so many different groups of people! But I really saw it applying to myself. Yep, I am definitely Jerusalem in this passage! My sins killed the one sent to save me and boy do I know how to hurl the stones of busyness and preoccupation at Jesus! Therefore, when I read this passage I could just hear Jesus tenderly telling me, "O Jessica, Jessica, you who often shun and avoid me. How often I have longed to gather you under my wing. How I have longed to be gracious to you, but you would not let me. *You were not willing.*"

It's true. I am often simply not willing to let Jesus love on me, be gracious to me, and gather me to Himself. (Notice, *He gathers us, we don't gather Him* . . . awesome!) Yet isn't it just amazing that we have a Savior and friend, a heavenly Father who *longs* for us?! Jesus longs for His people. He longs for this country and others. He longs to gather this world to Him.

And He longs for *you*. Never, ever forget that!

My friend, you are the apple of His eye and the desire of His heart! He desperately yearns to gather you into His loving arms and tuck you in the shadow of His wings! He wants you close to Him for He longs to be gracious to you! (Isaiah 30:18)

Today I just challenge you to ask yourself: Are you willing to let Jesus gather you? Do you let Him draw near? Or is this verse directed to you: so often are you not willing?

May you take this weekend to become willing. Go be in His presence, unveiled. Let the Lord gather you up and shower you with His love for when you do, your face will be radiant with a heavenly glow. And then may you, in return, shower Him with your love.

Have a brilliant weekend! Happy Leap Year!

In His love and grace,

<>< Jessica

Prayer requests? Praises?

From: Hisword2day
To: Your heart
Sent: Tuesday, March 02, 2004 11:57 AM
Subject: Fertilizer–Luke 13:6–9

"Then he told this parable: 'A man had a fig tree, planted in his vineyard, and he went to look for fruit on it, but did not find any. So he said to the man who took care of the vineyard, 'For three years now I've been coming to look for fruit on this fig tree and haven't found any. Cut it down! Why should it use up the soil?' 'Sir,' the man replied, 'leave it alone for one more year, and I'll dig around it and fertilize it. If it bears fruit next year, fine! If not, then cut it down.'" *Luke 13:6–9* NIV

This is an interesting little passage! Here we meet a planter who consistently comes to see if his fig tree is bearing any fruit, which it is not, nor has it been for quite some time—three years to be exact. He's given it ample time to grow and bear fruit, and it's just not doing its job at being a fig tree. Therefore, he's a bit agitated and rationalizes that if it's not going to be bearing fruit that he shouldn't let it take up room and resources in the good soil, not to mention his time.

However, the caretaker feels a bit differently. He has hope for this little tree and realizes that the fig tree simply can't grow on its own. Yes, it's been tended to and cared for, but it might be lacking something that it needs in order to bear fruit. So he decides that he just needs to give it a little extra tender loving care and tells the planter, "Leave it alone for one more year, just give me a little bit more time with it and I'll dig around it and fertilize it . . . maybe that's all it needs to finally bear fruit."

Sounds like how the Lord is with us, doesn't it? He is our gardener and we are His garden. The Lord knows we're dependent upon Him to help us grow so He consistently comes to tend to us and keeps a watchful eye to make sure we're growing and bearing fruit. He prunes us (John 15:2). He also gets agitated with us when He's provided time, nurture, care, and resources for us to grow and we're not. But that's when our caretaker, advocate (Jesus) steps in gives us some extra love and care. He even fertilizes us.

Fertilizer, by definition, is a "substance that is added to soil to help plants grow."* It can be manufactured from minerals or made from organic waste, such as manure, plant matter, or sewage. Either way fertilizers contain nutrients (nourishing substances) that are essential for growth and survival.* Therefore, farmers and gardeners add them to the soils of their gardens not to deprive the plants, but to help them thrive.

Can't you just picture the Lord your God getting down on His hands and knees, to dirty Himself in the soil of your heart and life while He's digging and placing fertilizer around you? He knows what you have need of (Matthew 6:8) and He's going to provide whatever it is whether it be just a little bit more time or some nourishing substances that are essential for your survival and growth. Jesus adds these fertilizers not to deprive us, but to help us thrive.

Yet how often we forget this: we forget that fertilizer is added out of tender loving care. Now fertilizer comes in a variety of ways, as we read above. One of the many forms of fertilizer is manure. Likewise, one form of fertilizer for our hearts is "manure." Trying circumstances, a difficult past, a rough day, devastating news, seemingly impossible situations, frustration, disappointment . . . or whatever may seem like a pile of "manure" in your life. But be encouraged for God can and will use this "pile of manure" to fertilize your heart!

My question to you is how do you react when it seems as though a pile of manure is dumped on your life? Do you feel like God is punishing, abandoning, or depriving you? Or do you see it as an expression of God's love? A way for God to fertilize your heart and provide you with essential "nutrients"? How I pray we would put all our faith and trust in Him and allow Him to meet our needs, in any way He deems necessary. After all, He is the gardener.

With all that said, I just want to remind you that you were planted in the Lord's garden for a reason! You were chosen to be tenderly cared for and to bear certain fruit in His garden! Therefore, I encourage you to ask yourself and the Lord: Are you bearing the fruit you were planted to bear? Or are you the barren fig tree? Is there an area of your life that the Lord would be echoing the planter's frustration? Why? Are you not willing to receive His love and care, His help to grow and bear fruit? Or do you just need some fertilizer?

Secondly, ask yourself and ask the Lord to reveal to you where or how He might be fertilizing your heart and life. Remember the Lord your God loves you too much to just leave you alone! He doesn't want you to be cut down! He wants you to grow and thrive! He wants you to share in the joy of bringing glory to His kingdom!

So go and bear fruit today and remember God knows best how to meet *all* of your needs: spiritual, emotional, mental, and physical. He also knows when, where, and how to fertilize your heart. Trust Him today! Let Him be your Caretaker!

His,

<>< Jessica

Prayer requests? Praises?

*The World Book Encyclopedia (by World Book-Childcraft International, Inc., Copyright 1979 U.S.A.)

From: Hisword2day
To: Your heart
Sent: Friday, March 04, 2004 4:09 PM
Subject: Known and identified by fruit–Luke 6:44

"Each tree is known and identified by its own fruit." *Luke 6:44* **Amp.**

Alright. We're going to pick up where we left off on Tuesday when we were talking about God fertilizing our hearts. We saw that it's extremely important that we grow and bear fruit. Now why would it be of the utmost importance to our gardener (John 15:1) that we grow and bear fruit?

Well, first of all, Jesus tells us that any branch that does not remain in Him will be cut off (John 15:2, 6). But this is so *not* what He desires to do! He desires that none should perish or be cut off (2 Peter 3:9), rather that we would grow and thrive! He longs to be gracious to us, remember? (Isaiah 30:18). We mustn't forget this very important truth. However, there are many more reasons, I believe, why the Lord would desire for you and me to grow and bear fruit. Here are a couple of reasons why I hold such a belief.

First of all, Luke 6:44 reminds us that a thorn bush can't bear figs, nor can a grapevine bear briers. And according to John 15:5, Jesus is the vine and we are the branches. Then shouldn't those connected to Jesus, Christians, be bearing the same fruit as Him?

Furthermore, 1 Peter 5:2–3 reminds us that we are to be shepherds of God's flock which is under our care. We are to be examples. The example we set, the fruit we bear is not only how we are known, but more importantly, it is how Jesus is known. Remember, we have been entrusted with the incredible and amazing task of painting a picture of who Jesus is and what life with Him and in Him looks like.

God wants us to make His name known to the entire world so that none will perish! Well, if a tree is known by its fruit then shouldn't Jesus be known by His fruit? Therefore, He prunes us, His branches, to help us grow and bear HIS fruit so that we are not cut off and so that we can be examples for Him in this world . . . so that we can be fishers of men in the sea of this world.

I pray that each of us would seek to know Jesus better so that we can be branches abundantly bearing His fruit into this world! May you let Jesus prune and fertilize your heart so that His Spirit can accomplish and produce within you *His* fruits, thus allowing you, and more importantly Him, to be known, identified, and recognized by the fruits of His Spirit: love, joy, peace, patience, kindness, goodness, faithfulness, gentleness, and self-control! (Galatians 5:22) Wow . . . to be known for Jesus!

A tree is known and identified by its fruit. How are you known? How are you helping others know Jesus?

Your sister in Christ,

<>< Jessica

Prayer requests? Praises?

From: Hisword2day
To: Your heart
Sent: Friday, March 05, 2004 12:38 PM
Subject: Keep your eyes on Jesus–Psalm 25:15

"My eyes are ever on the Lord, for only he will release my feet from the snare." *Psalm 25:15* **NIV**

Friend, this is my encouragement and challenge to you for this weekend . . . keep your eyes ever on the Lord. Whatever the circumstances, wherever you are, set your eyes upon Jesus, the author and perfecter of your faith. For truly, only He can release you from whatever seems to ensnare you . . . worry, fear, doubt, pain, persecution, busyness, stress, difficulties, relationships problems, work issues, confusion, despair, etc. etc. He has the keys to unlock these chains to set you free so that you may run in the path of His commands unhindered!

Remember the depths of Jesus' love for and towards you. Know that He's gone before (ahead of) you, and therefore, He knows what lies ahead. Trust His guidance and His direction. Keep your eyes ever on the Lord for only He will release your feet from the snares of Satan and the snares of this world.

Have a happy, restful, joyful, and Christ-filled weekend!

Eyes upon Jesus,

<>< jess

Prayer requests? Praises?

From: Hisword2day
To: Your heart
Sent: Monday, March 08, 2004 11:44 AM
Subject: In Him–Acts 17:28

"For in him we live, and move, and have our being." *Acts 17:28* **NIV**

Apart from Him we are and can do nothing (John 15:5). Amen! Have I been learning that one! Yet what a wonderful reminder that in Him, Christ Jesus, and through the strength He provides us by being in Him, we can do all things (Philippians 4:13). Furthermore, in Him we can be all He needs us to be and can be who He created us to be. What blessed reassurance!

Friend, I'm sure that this week will give us a healthy serving of struggles and some amazing joys. So whatever you may experience today, this week, this month, or this year, remember that is it is in Him, under the shadow of His wings that you live, move, and have your very being. May that bring you strength, encouragement, and comfort knowing that you can be *in* Him through a relationship *with* Him! How I pray that relationship is alive and active in your life!

Live a life worthy of Jesus. Know He is your all in all. And have a wonderful week living, moving, and simply being in Him.

In Him,

<>< Jessica

Prayer requests? Praises?

From: Hisword2day
To: Your heart
Sent: Wednesday, March 10, 2004 3:56 PM
Subject: We are going–Luke 18:31

" . . . We are going up to Jerusalem and everything that is written by the prophets about the Son of Man will be fulfilled." *Luke 18:31* **NIV**

At this moment we catch Jesus taking His disciples aside to predict His own death. One word in this passage stood out to me like it was a blinking neon sign! It's a small word, but it has big implications for me—We. "*We* are going up to Jerusalem."

This little word sent me a precious reminder that we too always go with Jesus. He still tells us, "We are going to go workout, go to school, go into this relationship, go work, go into this situation . . . we are going **together**."

Now, we mustn't forget that the disciples didn't understand exactly what Jesus meant by His comments in Luke 18. Yet they had experienced enough to know they could trust Him and knew they wanted to go wherever Jesus was going.

Even when you don't understand exactly what Jesus may mean by something happening in your life or where He may be directing you, do you know you can trust Him? Have you experienced that?

If not, remember those people in scripture whose stories can remind you that indeed you can trust the Lord your God. When God suggests a direction or destination, He always goes along with you. Think of the Israelites in the desert . . . He took them on a very roundabout way out of Egypt, but His presence was **always** with them, guiding them, guarding them, and providing for them (Exodus 13:21–22). In the Psalms, When David would go into battle, the Lord would always fight His battles with Him and would hide David in the shadow of His wings thus delivering him from his enemies. When Jesus suggested to the disciples in Luke 8, "Let us go to the other side of the lake," He didn't send them alone; rather He got in the boat with them and calmed the storm when it arose.

So if we know the Lord is with us and we can trust Him, we must ask ourselves do we *want* to be with Him? Do we want to be wherever Jesus is? If yes, then are we going to go where we see Him going?

I pray that you will, and I pray that as each day dawns you hear Jesus telling you, "**We** are going into this day and all of its experiences together. In my unfailing love and strength I am always leading and guiding you. I am your ever present God so whether we face trials or joys, we are facing them together, for I am still in the same boat as you."

My friend, you are never alone. Whatever you're experiencing, trust Him! Even when you don't understand, go *wherever* you see Jesus going and know He is with you always. Go with Jesus! Be led by His Spirit and His presence, both day and night.

For His glory,

<>< Jessica

Prayer requests? Praises?

From: Hisword2day
To: Your heart
Sent: Friday, March 12, 2004 9:53 AM
Subject: May God be gracious to you and bless you–
Psalm 67:1-2

"May God be gracious to us and bless us and make his face shine upon us . . . that your ways may be known on earth, your salvation among all nations." *Psalm 67:1–2* **NIV**

My friend, Rubina, shared this verse with me and I just loved it! So now I'm passing it on to you . . .

How I pray this psalm for us! May God be gracious to us and bless us and make His face to shine upon us so that His ways and salvation may be known *through* us!

Friend, you are blessed in **every** way because of the overflow of God's love towards you. He blesses you to be a blessing, so go into the world around you—go amidst your friends, your family, your workplace, your class, the grocery store—and be a blessing to others. Be an example of Jesus' love and grace! Through you He can indeed make His ways and salvation known among all the nations . . . in every neighborhood, every workplace, every home, every classroom, every relationship, every country! You never know who God is touching through you!

May God be gracious to *you* and bless *you*. May He make His face to shine *so* brightly upon *you* so that you may make His ways and salvation known wherever you go! May you be an effervescent light into this world!

In His abundant love and grace,

<>< Jessica

Prayer requests? Praises?

From: Hisword2day
To: Your heart
Sent: Tuesday, March 16, 2004 9:52 AM
Subject: Lord, I want to see–Luke 18:41

"Lord, I want to see." *Luke 18:41* NIV

As Jesus approached Jericho, a blind man was sitting by the roadside begging. The noises of the crowds passing by got the man curious so he asked what was happening. He was told that Jesus was passing by. Upon hearing this, he called out, "Jesus, Son of David, have mercy on me!" Those in the crowd rebuked him and told him to be quiet. Yet, their reaction did not deter him, rather it made him more determined and he shouted even louder! "SON OF DAVID, HAVE MERCY ON ME!"

It worked; he got Jesus' attention. Jesus stopped and ordered that the man be brought to Him. When he came near, Jesus asked the blind man "What do you want me to do for you?" The blind beggar replied, "Lord, I want to see!" Jesus then said to him, "Receive your sight; your faith has healed you." And immediately he was healed.

For quite some time now, my heart has been crying out for God to open the eyes of people's hearts. I've been praying that God would have mercy on people and would heal their spiritual blindness . . . that He would help them throw aside any hindrances, hesitations, fears, and doubts so that they may see and believe.

And then last night, as I was singing a song of praise, the Holy Spirit triggered something in my own heart that made me realize I'd somehow forgotten to pray this for myself! It was the cry of my **own** heart for I so often allow the "anxieties of life," sin, my own hindrances, hesitations, fears, doubts, a lack of trust and commitment, and many other things to slowly, but surely, close the eyes of my heart! So yes, I've needed to cry out, "Have mercy on me, Jesus! I want to see!" I certainly don't want to fall prey to the "out of sight, out of mind" mentality, which Satan would just love for us to do. To have Jesus out of our minds! Oh gosh, bliss for him!

However, you and I know that faith contradicts this mentality. Faith is being sure of what you hope for and certain of what you do not see (Hebrews 12:1). Therefore, just as the blind beggar's faith healed him, so our faith will heal us and help us to be certain of what we may not always see. Just as Jesus listened to this man's cry for mercy, Jesus listens to our cries for mercy. And just as Jesus restored this man's sight, so Jesus will restore our sight.

I know I have been blinded lately and the blind beggar's cry has been the cry of my own heart. If you too feel blind in any way, cry out to the Lord! You too will get His attention. And when He asks what it is you want, let this be your own plea, "Lord, I want to see."

May we always want to see more and more of Jesus. May we always be on guard and praying so that we do not fall into the traps of dissipation, anxieties of life, sin and other "blinders" to our hearts. How desperately I pray that God would restore our spiritual sight, wherever we may be lacking it, so we may see ever so clearly that Jesus is our Counselor, our Mighty God, our Prince of Peace, the Bread of life (our lives), our All in all, our Rock, our Redeemer, our Healer, our Sustainer, God with us, King of Kings, Lord of Lords, our Everlasting Father, our Alpha and Omega, our Great Physician, our Shepherd, the Author and Perfecter of our faith, the Lamb of God, our Deliverer, the Guardian of our soul, our Comforter, our Advocate, our Sanctifier, our Savior, and our Friend.

"Lord Jesus, have mercy on us. We desperately want to see. Open the eyes of our hearts that we may know you better!" Receive your sight, friend. For your faith has healed you.

In Jesus' name . . .

Prayer requests? Praises?

From: Hisword2day
To: Your heart
Sent: Wednesday, March 24, 2004 11:25 AM
Subject: Enriched in every way–1 Corinthians 1:4–9

"I always thank God for you because of his grace given you in Christ Jesus. For in him you have been enriched in every way—in all your speaking and in all your knowledge—because our testimony about Christ was confirmed in you. Therefore you do not lack any spiritual gift as you eagerly wait for our Lord Jesus Christ to be revealed. He will keep you strong to the end so that you will be blameless on the day of our Lord Jesus Christ. God, who has called you into fellowship with his Son Jesus Christ our Lord, is faithful." *1 Corinthians 1:4–9* **NIV**

Oh what blessed encouragement this passage was for me today! I hope it is for you too!

Have a blessed day knowing your God, who is faithful, will continue to enrich and bless you in every way, lavishing you with grace in Christ Jesus and keeping you strong to the very end. You lack nothing in, by, and through Him! So as you count your blessings today, may you make them count for Him.

By grace your sister,

<>< Jessica

Prayer requests? Praises?

From: Hisword2day
To: Your heart
Sent: Monday, March 29, 2004 11:51 AM
Subject: Within your heart–Luke 17:21

"Behold the kingdom of God is within you, in your hearts and among you surrounding you." *Luke 17:21* **Amp.**

I am terrible at losing my keys. I've made them up in my bed, placed them in the most bizarre places, and simply forgot where I last put them. Sometimes I'll search for half an hour or longer before I ever find them!

Well, a couple of weeks ago I was getting ready to leave for work. I had my purse, a bag strapped to my shoulders, my lunch, a bottle of water, and my laptop computer filling my hands. I had everything and was ready to walk out the door.

Fiddlesticks, where are my keys? I thought. "DAD!" I hollered. "Do you see my keys in the living room?" His witty remark came back, "NO! Oh, wait, it's Wednesday . . . not my day to watch them!"

I knew I'd gotten my keys out so they had to be sitting out somewhere. So putting only my laptop down I started looking in my room—I pulled back the covers on my bed (no luck), checked the bathroom (no luck), and then checked the kitchen. No luck.

On to the living room I went all along thinking, *Where in the world did I put my keys?!* "Dad," I said, "are you sure you don't see my keys?" "No, where did you . . . well, Princess, what are those in your hand?" Yeah, my keys. How quickly I'd forgotten that they were in my hand all along! What a goober I am!

I want you to think for a moment . . . does this scene resemble your search for the Lord at times? Have you forgotten that the kingdom of God and the King Himself was in your heart all along?

I'd have to answer yes to both. So today, I want us to remember that the kingdom of God, His throne of glory is within our own hearts. If you are frantically searching for God, His attributes, or His presence, remember that He is within you and surrounding you! He is ever so near for through the cross and resurrection Christ has come and made your heart His home. Therefore, He truly does go with you wherever you go and is with you always!

Furthermore, He is among you and is surrounding you. (How easy it is to see Him, yet how quickly I forget that!) Take a quick glance around . . . see the trees budding with new life, the squirrels scurrying along, the sun beaming forth light, the rain gently watering the earth, and hear the gentle whisper of His voice in the wind. What great displays of our Lord's presence and creativity!

Know that the Lord your God, the King of Kings in all His glory abides in your heart through the grace and mercy shown us through Jesus Christ! You have the treasure chest of heaven held within your very own heart! Let the Lord unlock all that is within!

Have a blessed day knowing the King reigns in your heart!

By grace, your sister,

<>< Jessica

Prayer requests? Praises?

From: Hisword2day
To: Your heart
Sent: Wednesday, March 31, 2004 11:17 AM
Subject: Let go of your rocks–Matthew 11:28–30

"Come to me, all you who are weary and burdened, and I will give you rest. Take my yoke upon you and learn from me, for I am gentle and humble in heart, and you will find rest for your souls. For my yoke is easy and my burden is light." *Matthew 11:28–30* **NIV**

I've been feeling weighed down by a lot of things lately—nothing bad—I just have lots on my plate right now, and have really been struggling with surrendering them over to God. (I often have a fierce grip on these things!) So I decided that at Sunday School I was going to share with the students I teach what I was learning in my personal life and pray that God would teach them through my learning experience.

For visual effect (and part of the lesson) I went and gathered a bag full of rocks (can we say heavy!) and gave one to each of the students. I explained to the students what each of these rocks represented in my life and asked them to name a few things that the rocks could represent in their own lives. School, grades, sports, friendships, relationships, family issues, work, living situations etc.

Then we talked about this verse, how Jesus wants us to give Him our problems, burdens, and all that weighs us down so that we can find rest for our souls. When we finished I walked around the room and asked the students to give me their rocks.

The first person stuck her hand out, palm up with the rock resting in her hand for me to take. Second, third, and all the way around the room rocks were handed to me hand in the same way—hand outstretched with the rock nestled in their palms.

Now I ask you, as I asked on Sunday, is that how you give your "rocks" to God?

Try this. Put something in your hand, pencil, pen, paper clip, whatever. Hold your hand out with the object resting on the palm of your hand. Now wrap your hand back around the object. Easy to grab back ahold of isn't it? Not really surrendered is it?

Now turn your hand over and release your grip. Pretty hard to grab it back because it's out of your hands.

Now that's surrender. And that's how God desires for us to give our hearts, lives, problems, and burdens to Him. He wants them *fully* surrendered, out of our hands, so we can't "grab back ahold of them," which, if you're like me, you're SO prone to do.

Friend, know that Jesus invites you to let go of **whatever** it is that is burdening you, or weighing heavy upon you. He longs to give you rest and restore your soul! Are you taking Him up on His invitation? I pray that you are!

May you hear Jesus calling this out to you today: *"Come to Me, all you who labor and are heavy-laden and overburdened, and I will cause you to rest. [I will ease and relieve and refresh your souls.] Take My yoke upon you and learn of Me, for I am gentle (meek) and humble (lowly) in heart, and you will find rest (relief, ease and refreshment and recreation and blessed quiet) for your souls."* (Amp.)

As the old saying goes, "Let go and let God." Let go of your rocks . . .

Through Him,

<>< Jessica

Prayer requests? Praises?

From: Hisword2day
To: Your heart
Sent: Friday, April 02, 2004 4:49 PM
Subject: Run your race–Hebrews 12:1

"Therefore, since we are surrounded by such a great cloud of witnesses, let us throw off everything that hinders and the sin that so easily entangles, and let us run with perseverance the race marked out for us." *Hebrews 12:1* **NIV**

Today we're going to continue our discussion about rocks: why is it so important for us to "throw off everything that hinders us?" Why do we need to surrender our "rocks" to Jesus?

Do you remember me telling you that I had brought a bag of rocks with me to Sunday School and that the bag of them was H-E-A-V-Y? Well, guess who had to lug that bag of rocks around everywhere she went for the rest of the morning? ME! Now this particular Sunday was not your regular church experience . . . I had to go from one end of the church to another about three or four different times. I was worn out after dragging those dadgum rocks around all morning! In fact I loathed them by the end of the morning! (ha ha)

Then God reminded me, "Jess, this physical experience of rock hauling is what you do spiritually. So often instead of giving your "rocks" over to me you lug them around. And the same result happens, you're worn out! I don't want that for you! So come to me, my Child and I will give you rest. Let us throw off your sins, burdens, worries, and anything else that hinders you!"

I want you to imagine something. Think of trying to run a marathon. TOUGH! Now imagine running it with a bag of rocks strapped to you. Running a marathon is difficult enough! But with added weight?! Talk about sapping the energy right out of you!!

Well, my friend, life is a marathon, not a sprint. Paul writes about endurance and perseverance and neither of those are too crucial in a sprint; yet in long distance, like a marathon, they're absolutely crucial! And when you don't surrender things to the Lord, whether they be your burdens, your worries, your sins, or something else, you become weighed down making your "race" all the *more* difficult to run. (No wonder Jesus says "Come to me all who are weary and I will give you rest." We're all exhausted from "rock hauling!")

Furthermore, we need to give our "rocks" to God so that we don't throw them at other people or leave them as stumbling blocks in other people's lives.

And of course, ultimately we are to come to Jesus, give Him everything, and throw off all of our hindrances because the Bible tells us to. God asks us to do so. That alone is reason enough!

Today I just pray that each of you would fix your eyes on Jesus and would run your race without dragging a bag of rocks along! Go set your heart at rest in your Savior's presence today and let Him quiet you with His love . . . have a restful weekend!

In Jesus' love and grace,

<>< Jessica

Prayer requests? Praises?

P.S. Remember, just because you surrender something to the Lord doesn't mean it will be out of your life. However, giving it over to Him is such a FREEING experience . . . taking His yoke is so much better! He will give you the strength and ability to endure. How I pray He will teach you how to give things over to Him and run your race at the pace He's chosen for you! What an exciting adventure we are all in for! (Read 1 Corinthians 2:9)

From: Hisword2day
To: Your heart
Sent: Monday, April 05, 2004 12:09 PM
Subject: Visa update–Deuteronomy 32:3–4

"I will proclaim the name of the Lord. Oh, praise the greatness of our God! He is the Rock, his works are perfect, and all his ways are just. A faithful God who does no wrong, upright and just is he." *Deuteronomy 32:3–4* **NIV**

Friend, we serve a faithful God. *All,* not just some, but all of His ways are perfect and just. He has a reason and a season for all things, circumstances, and situations. Again, I was reminded of this fact this weekend.

On Friday evening I received a message from the French Consulate regarding the status of my visa process: it was denied. No explanation was given.

I am reminded that the Lord will not share His glory with another, and maybe if I were to get the visa He wouldn't be receiving the full measure of glory due Him. Ultimately, I want Him *most* glorified through my life . . . if that means having a visa denied, then so be it! It's not a dead end, just a detour.

Now, yes, I was a bit discouraged upon hearing the message. However, the many, many glimpses of His faithfulness that I have seen with my own eyes have shown me that indeed God's ways are not our ways, but they are so much higher and so *much better!* There's always a blessing waiting to happen when you're trusting the Lord!

It's like what God told Habakkuk, " . . . watch—and be *utterly amazed.* For I am going to do something in your days that you would not believe, even if you were told" (Habakkuk 1:5, emphasis mine). Therefore, I can't question Him with doubt, only for understanding. And I know that the understanding will come at the appointed time.

Plus, I mustn't forget 1 Corinthians 2:9, "No eye has seen, no ear has heard, no mind has conceived what God has prepared for those who love Him." Can you imagine the greatness of God that we will all see through this very situation?! I can't wait!!!

Anyway, I just wanted to send you an update on the visa situation and thank you for your prayers! Every single one of them was heard! Not one of them fell on deaf ears! And truly, we are going to see the glory of God! At this point, I am still going to France, I will just have to leave the country every three months and it will make living there a bit more challenging, but it is nothing God can't handle and can't provide. Please keep me in your prayers!

This verse captured what my heart was trying to express . . . this became my prayer and I urge you to pray it for yourself. Have a blessed day proclaiming the name of the Lord. Praise His greatness and trust that He is a faithful God who does no wrong . . . His ways are perfect, even in an imperfect world.

"Yes, Lord, I will proclaim your mighty name! I will praise your greatness! For you are the great God, mighty and awesome! You are my Rock; your works are absolutely perfect and just! Thank you for being my faithful God . . . please remind me daily that you do no wrong and let me not forget your perfection and faithfulness even when I don't understand. Help me to walk by faith, even when I can't see."

His,

<>< Jessica

Prayer requests? Praises?

From: Hisword2day
To: Your heart
Sent: Wednesday, April 07, 2004 12:43 PM
Subject: A lesson from Pilate–Luke 23:24–25

"So Pilate decided to grant their demand. He released the man who had been thrown into prison for insurrection and murder, the one they asked for, and surrendered Jesus to their will." *Luke 23:24–25* **NIV**

Pilate has always been an interesting character to me. His role in history and in Christ's death is intriguing. Historically he was a brutal man, yet he seriously pondered condemning Jesus, a simple carpenter. Yes, there were all kinds of political agendas floating around, but the whole scenario still fascinates me.

Whenever I read the story of the crucifixion and resurrection I try to see myself in all of the characters . . . and it's not too hard! I'm the person in the crowd yelling "Crucify Him!!!" I'm Mary and the other women weeping. I'm denying Jesus as Peter did. I'm Judas as I kiss Him with betrayal. I'm the soldier healed by His hand. And I'm Pilate.

I believe Pilate knew something was different about this Man. I could be seriously wrong, but given Pilate's history of brutality, his interaction with Jesus seems just a bit out of character. Ultimately, however, the crowds and political agendas pressured Pilate to surrender Jesus to their will.

That got my attention: *surrendered Jesus to their will.* How many times have I allowed the "crowds" (this world) to pressure me into surrendering Jesus to their will? Countless! And how many times have I surrendered Jesus to *my* will? Ouch.

So my friend, during this week leading up to Easter, I encourage you to look within . . . Are you surrendering Jesus to the crowd's will? Your will? Or are *you* surrendering to *His* will?

In His love and grace,

<>< Jessica

Prayer requests? Praises?

P.S. Remember that apart from Him you can do nothing (John 15:5) . . .

and that includes surrendering. Ask Him TODAY to help you surrender to His will . . . what a blessing you will receive and how that will make your God smile!

From: Hisword2day
To: Your heart
Sent: Friday, April 09, 2004 8:58 AM
Subject: Some verses for Good Friday

"But he was pierced for our transgressions, he was crushed for our iniquities; the punishment that brought us peace was upon him, and by his wounds we are healed. We all, like sheep, have gone astray, each of us has turned to his own way; and the Lord has laid on him the iniquity of us all . . . Yet is was the Lord's will to crush him and cause him to suffer, and though the Lord makes his life a guilt offering, he will see his offspring and prolong his days, and the will of the Lord will prosper in his hand. After the suffering of his soul, he will see the light of life and be satisfied; by his knowledge My righteous servant will justify many, and he will bear their iniquities . . . for he bore the sin of many and made intercession for the transgressors." _Isaiah 53: 5–6, 10–11, 12_ NIV

Try this . . . make it personal. Put yourself in there, for Jesus endured the cross and rose again out of the overflow of the love in His heart for _you._ (Replace "our" with "my", "us" with "me", "we" with "I", "many" with "you", and "their" with "your".)

"Let us fix our eyes on Jesus, the author and perfecter of our faith, who for the joy set before him endured the cross, scorning its shame, and sat down at the right hand of the throne of God. Consider him who endured such opposition from sinful men, so that you will not grow weary and lose heart." _Hebrews 12:2–3_ NIV

All God had to do as Jesus suffered was show Him a picture of your face and Jesus said, "Oh, this is worth it!" You were the joy that was set before Him that day.

"For all have sinned and fall short of the glory of God, and are justified freely by his grace, through the redemption that came by Christ Jesus. God presented him as a sacrifice of atonement, through faith in his blood . . ." _Romans 3:23–25_ NIV

Indeed, we have fallen short, we've missed the mark, but by the grace given us in Jesus Christ we've hit the bulls-eye of redemption and have been restored to our Creator! **Thank you, Jesus!**

" . . . I have come that they may have life, and have it to the full." *John 10:10* NIV

Oh that we may truly live in the abundance of His love and grace! What a full and rich life it is to know Jesus!

"I have been crucified with Christ and I no longer live, but Christ lives in me. The life I live in the body, I live by faith in the Son of God, who loved me and gave himself for me." *Galatians 2:20* NIV

I pray that today you take a few moments to remember what your Savior did for you so many years ago.

May your knees bow and may your tongue confess again, or for the first time that Christ Jesus is your Lord and your Savior. Feel His passion, share His grace, and abide in His love this Good Friday.

Be joyful today for you are so dearly loved by your heavenly Father! And friend, remember that nothing, nothing, nothing can separate you from the love of God that is in Christ Jesus!

Happy Easter!

Because of Christ Jesus,

<>< Jessica

From: Hisword2day
To: Your heart
Sent: Tuesday, April 13, 2004 7:33 AM
Subject: Leap for joy–Psalm 28:7

"The Lord is my strength and my shield; my heart trusts in him, and I am helped. My heart leaps for joy and I will give thanks to him in song." *Psalm 28:7* **NIV**

Friends, we serve a RISEN Lord . . . how I pray the celebration of our risen Jesus would not end on Easter, but would continue in our hearts every day of the year! Indeed, the faintest memory of His resurrection should remind us that the Lord is our strength, our shield, and our help. Our hearts can trust in Him! When troubles arise we can take heart for Jesus has overcome the world! Talk about reasons for our hearts to leap for joy!

As you encounter your *risen* Savior, may this encounter transform you and cause your heart to bubble over with joy! Remember that the mighty and awesome Lord of Lords has set His affections on *you!* May you give thanks to Him in song for who He is and the great things He has done.

Leaping for joy,

<>< Jessica

Prayer requests? Praises?

From: Hisword2day
To: Your heart
Sent: Friday, April 16, 2004 11:58 AM
Subject: A bird's song to the Lord–Judges 5:3

"Hear this, you kings! Listen, you rulers! I will sing to the Lord; I will sing; I will make music to the Lord, the God of Israel." *Judges 5:3* **NIV**

We had torrential downpours throughout last Easter weekend and it was dreary, miserable weather. I personally love rainy weather (when I don't have to be out and about in it), as it provides perfect opportunities to take a nap, read a book, work on "inside" stuff, clean, watch a good old movie, RELAX etc. However, when I have to get out in the rain, I'm not such a happy camper. My clothes get damp, then I'm cold. And that inevitably leads to me grumbling and complaining.

Well, on Saturday as I sat eating breakfast and watching the rains come down, a joyful noise caught me attention. The birds were chirping away! I mean they were *really* singing out! They were out in the middle of the storm, and yet they were still singing. Wow!

Friend, life brews up a lot of storms. I'm sure you've experienced that, much like stormy weather, life's storms can catch you off guard. Sometimes these storms are like rainy weather: they provide an opportunity for rest and other blessings. Yet at other times you find yourself out in the middle of the storm. And if you're like me, I bet you react much the same way as I do when I'm caught out in a rainstorm: you grumble and complain.

Therefore, when I heard these birds singing away amidst such nasty weather, God got my attention. Now, I'm not a bird expert, but their song didn't sound like a song of distress, rather it sounded like a sweet melody of love, praise, and adoration. It was as if they were saying to me, "Hear this Jessica! Listen up! We *will* sing to the Lord! We will siiiiiiing (chirp, chirp, chirp!) We will make music to the Lord!" And that they did! They made music to the Lord, even though they were out in the middle of the storm.

I don't know about you, but that was a lesson worth learning and an example worth following. We have so very much to praise God for!

We are known, grown, and loved by God . . . the mighty and awesome Creator of the universe! And He has set His affections on us?! WOW! I'll say He's more than worthy of a song! And we should be more than honored to make Him music with our hearts and lives!

My prayer for us today is for the Lord to help us become more like these birds singing a sweet melody of love, praise, and adoration, even when we're in the middle of a storm. For even there He is with us.

With God's help, I *will* sing. I *will* make music to the Lord. Will you?

Praying that you will sing,

<>< Jessica

Prayer requests? Praises?

From: Hisword2day
To: Your heart
Sent: Monday, April 19, 2004 2:27 PM
Subject: Revive me–Psalm 119:107

"I am afflicted very much; revive me, O Lord, according to your word." *Psalm 119:107* **NIV**

It's easy to get bogged down with life, isn't it? Work, relationships, organizations, school, family, deadlines, and personal situations seem to demand a lot from us . . . so much so that we may feel as David did . . . afflicted very much!

I've been there lately. Often times my "afflictions" are simply blessings mistaken or misunderstood. I tend to forget how Isaiah 30:20 refers to the bread of adversity and the water of affliction that the Lord gives. It might just be that this "bread" and "water" are meeting the needs for a very hungry and thirsty spirit within me. Nonetheless, we can all use a little revival, renewal, and rejuvenation every now and then. Well, I'm at that point.

As usual, God's word is *right on* . . ."Revive me, O Lord!" I just love how God allows our paths to intersect with a particular passage *just* when we need it! So was the case with this passage. It reminded me that the Lord can revive me; I just must ask. Furthermore, He will do so . . . according to His word. Therefore, I need to dive into it and soak in it!

I'm going to encourage you with the same Word I received from the Lord: Dive into His word. Soak in it. Let Him revive you according to His word. Get ready for your path to intersect with a word from the Lord that is exactly what you need today!

Know that in Him that you have the strength to persevere, the joy to be hopeful, and the faith to stand firm, regardless of your circumstances. For, if you have a relationship with Jesus, He has come and made your heart His home, and it is there where He is residing *at this very moment.* He is near . . . very near! Take heart in that truth . . . take heart that the Lord your God is with you. And He knows better than anyone how to revive you!

"My precious Jesus, I ask you to please revive my friends today, Lord . . . whatever may seem to be afflicting them, Jesus, revive them according to your perfect word. Open their eyes that they may see wonderful new things in your law. Thank you, God, for giving us your word . . . please revive us according to it . . . renew our hearts and minds . . . restore them to you. Thank you, Lord . . . for who you are and how you love us. We love you . . . In Jesus Christ's name . . . AMEN!"

Revived,

<>< Jessica

Prayer requests? Praises?

From: Hisword2day
To: Your heart
Sent: Thursday, April 22, 2004 1:19 PM
Subject: A windy ride–Romans 8:28

"We are assured and know that (God being a partner in their labor) all things work together and are [fitting into a plan] for good to and for those who love God and are called according to [His] design and purpose." *Romans 8:28* Amp.

Two years ago I was able to spend the summer with my brother, Garrett, in Gunnison, Colorado. During my time there I discovered a new hobby: Road biking. Not only was it GREAT exercise, but it also provided me with an awesome new way to enjoy God's breathtaking creation that surrounded me. I loved to ride down new roads and explore, or head down a familiar path to the river with a book, journal, and pen where I'd sit myself along the riverbank to read, write, or just soak in the beauty of the Lord.

One such ride left an imprint on my heart. The day was absolutely brilliant . . . the sun was shining, the skies were blue, and a wonderful breeze was blowing. It was one of those riverbank days. So I chose one of my favorite routes and off I went!

When you're riding a bike, even a light breeze can make your riding a bit more difficult, hence why my "wonderful breeze" didn't seem so wonderful anymore. It was turning into a rather windy ride, making me strain much harder than I usually had to, which in turn led to a little grumbling match with God . . ."Okay, really, the wind? Why did it have to start blowing so hard when I started riding? Now, I know you can calm the winds, so would you mind doing that for me, please?"

Shortly thereafter, the road had a curve. As I rounded the bend, I was no longer in the wind. HALLELUJAH! The wind had ceased! Praise the Lord! Thank you, Jesus!

But then I started getting hot . . . really hot. *Miserably* hot. I thought the wind was bad! The heat was ten times worse! Before I knew it I was begging for the wind again.

Then it clicked. There was a reason for the wind; it fit into His plan for good, not harm. It was God's provision to protect me from the heat. He had sent it to bless me, not to burden me.

I often think of this ride whenever I encounter fierce winds in life. Maybe these "winds" are to protect me from the heat of something else. Maybe the Lord is sending this wind to bless me and I just haven't turned the curve of understanding to see how.

Whatever the circumstance, my windy ride reminds me that with God's help I can pedal through the winds of life, knowing there's a reason; knowing that somehow even the fiercest of winds are fitting into God's plan for good because I love Him and am called according to His purposes.

I hope and pray we can take this ride together . . . I pray for you to press on today. May the Lord show you and may your heart trust in faith that His plan for you is *good,* not harm . . . *blessings,* not burdens. So my friend, as Paul says, **be assured and know that ALL things work together and are fitting into a plan for good *to* and *for you* who love God and are called according to His design and purpose**.

Pressing on,

<>< Jessica

Prayer requests? Praises?

P.S. Speaking of my brother, I am going to visit him tomorrow so I will most likely be out of touch via e-mail from Friday through Wednesday. I have a few prayer requests concerning my visit . . .

Please pray for our time together to be fun and memorable . . . this will probably be the last time I get to see Garrett before I leave for Paris.

Pray that my conversations with Him are seasoned with wisdom, love, and grace and that his heart would continue to be softened so he may come to know the Lord.

And pray that the Lord would use this time to help me rest, relax, and be renewed! THANK YOU IN ADVANCE FOR YOUR PRAYERS!

From: Hisword2day
To: Your heart
Sent: Wednesday, May 05, 2004 9:10 AM
Subject: Light & mountains–Psalm 76:4

"You are resplendent with light, more majestic than mountains rich with game." *Psalm 76:4* **NIV**

Precious Lord, I pray that today you would remind us of this truth . . . as we see light today may we be ever mindful that it's a reflection of you in physical form in this world. Oh may that make our hearts dance with joy! And Father, thank you for my time in the mountains . . . how perfect that you'd bring this verse to me just after my spending time amidst the majesty of your mountains . . . a vivid reminder that you are still more majestic than even the mountains! Help us to never forget your majesty . . . I know that I can only *begin* to comprehend you and your perfect ways so Jesus, increase my faith today so that I can trust you whole-heartedly. Open our eyes that we may see you resplendent with light today Lord. Remind us that what majesty we may see in this world is only a glimpse of the greatness of your majesty. Help us to know you in all things and help us to share you through all things.

I thank you and love you Jesus!

In your name I pray, AMEN!

(How beautiful is the Lord our God?!)

May light and mountains, valleys and plains, breezes, rain, trees, thunder, lightning, stars, snow, clouds, and more be vivid reminders to you of the Lord's presence and His majesty.

In His love and grace,

<>< Jessica

Prayer Requests? Praises?

From: Hisword2day
To: Your heart
Sent: Friday, May 07, 2004 1:40 PM
Subject: Mountains and valleys–Psalm 23:4

"Even though I walk through the valley of the shadow of death, I will fear no evil, for you are with me; your rod and your staff, they comfort me." *Psalm 23:4* **NIV**

Have you ever been up to the top of a mountain? It's Incredible, isn't it? The experience of reaching the top is invigorating (and relieving). And the view that awaits you is breathtaking! At sunset you'll see the sun dazzling the sky with colors, other mountains in the horizon declaring God's majesty, and lush, green valleys blanketing the earth's floor . . . what beauty for the eyes to behold!

However, if you're on a really high mountaintop, above the tree line, you'll notice that there is very little vegetation. Conditions simply don't permit much growth.

In contrast, if you look down in the valleys you'll see all kinds of vegetation! The conditions are just right for growth, and lots of it!

Yet, how often we forget that when it comes to our lives.

Instead, we tend to glorify our "mountaintops" and shudder at the thought of our life's "valleys." We, or at least I, fail to remember what a dear friend reminded me of: life is much like nature; it is in the valleys where the growth happens . . . and lots of it!

Don't get me wrong, mountaintops in nature and in life are wonderful places to be! The sense of accomplishment and thanksgiving for reaching a mountaintop is exhilarating! And the views are stunning! But we mustn't forget what these views encompass . . . for it is the valleys that help create the beauty that your eyes see in nature . . . and the beauty that your heart experiences in life.

Moreover, you need not fear or shudder when you walk through what seems like a valley of death, for even there the Lord is with you; His rod and His staff they comfort you.

Now this is neat . . . In the Old Testament, a rod is often used as a symbol of authority. Furthermore, a rod was used by shepherds to count,

guide, rescue, and protect sheep. A staff is an instrument of support.*
"His rod and His staff, they comfort me." His authority accounts, guides, rescues, and protects *you*, His sheep . . . and He is your instrument of support.

My friend, know that when you walk through one of life's valleys you are not alone. Even when the Lord doesn't seem present, He is always with you; His rod and His staff, they are comforting and guiding you. And never forget that in your valleys the conditions of your heart are fertile for much growth. God never grows you to harm you, rather to bless you . . . ALL of His ways are loving and faithful (Psalm 25:10 and 145:17).

When you reach one of life's mountaintops, look back over your valley and give thanks to the Lord your God for bringing you to it and through it and growing you as you go . . . and praise His holy name for the beauty it encompasses, and the beauty it creates in your life.

Have a great weekend, whether you're on a mountaintop, in a valley, or somewhere in between!

Your sister through His love and grace,

<>< Jessica

Prayer requests? Praises

*According to the NIV Study Bible Notes

From: Hisword2day
To: Your heart
Sent: Wednesday, May 12, 2004 1:53 PM
Subject: Wherever you go–Joshua 1:9

"Have I not commanded you? Be strong and courageous. Do not be terrified; do not be discouraged, for the Lord your God will be with you wherever you go." *Joshua 1:9* **NIV**

I love airports. They are places of departure, arrival, and transition as you travel to a destination . . . and are *great* places to people watch. Observing people interacting with other people, their own personal world, the world around them . . . and how the world interacts and reacts to people is fascinating to me. I tend to see myself in the role of other people. So at times I'm simply entertained, while at other times I'm learning a lesson.

Well, traveling to visit my brother provided me with an opportunity to be in the Denver airport for a rather extended period of time. My three-hour delay turned out to be a huge blessing!

I was reading to pass the time when the interactions between a mother and her daughter caught my attention. This little girl had just discovered how to run (or waddle a bit swifter, really). It was precious! She was still a little wobbly on her feet, changed her direction in a New York minute, and was so caught up in this "adventure" that she paid little to no attention to her surroundings (namely obstacles—other people and poles). But boy howdy was she having fun!

And her mother was with her every step of the way. Wherever the little girl went, her mom went. When the little girl was about to run into something (or someone) her mom would scoop her up and set her down to "explore" again in a new direction, out of harm's way. And when her daughter lost her balance, she was there to pick her up and set her on her feet again.

Simply put, the little girl's mother always had her eyes on her daughter knowing that her daughter was still too young to watch out for herself. She needed her mother to watch out for her.

And out of love, her mom stayed within an arm's length away wherever her daughter went in order to guide, guard, and protect her. Plus, you could tell her mom was enjoying sharing in this new "adventure" alongside her little girl.

As I watched this parent interact with her child, the Lord brought this verse to mind: "Be strong and courageous. Do not be terrified; do not be discouraged, for the Lord your God will be with you wherever *you* go."

Then I realized . . . I was watching my Father interact with me. For I am still a little child, *His* child, wobbly on her feet, the feet of faith, in an airport called earth enjoying and exploring this adventure called life.

And much like the little girl in the Denver airport, I too am so caught up in my "adventure" that I am often unaware of my surroundings (namely obstacles), and I, too, need my Father to be with me wherever I go. I, too, need Him to keep His watchful eyes on me at all times, to scoop me up out of harm's ways, to set me in a new direction, and to pick me up and set me on my feet again when I lose my balance.

Simply put, I need my heavenly Father to share in this adventure alongside me because I *desperately* need Him to guide, guard, protect, and direct me.

I am so thankful, so deeply, deeply grateful that my heavenly Father does go with me wherever I go. He's always looking out for me, always guiding me into His arms of love, out of harm's way, and so enjoys sharing in this adventure of my life.

Out of the depths of His unfailing love and unending grace, you and I have a Father who stays ever so close to us *wherever* we, His beloved children, go. Simply amazing!

But do you really know that? Do you believe that with all of your heart, regardless of your circumstances?

Whether you believe it or not, He is always close. Therefore, do not be terrified or discouraged, rather remember His command: Be strong and courageous! For the Lord your God will indeed be with you wherever you go. He is with you in this adventure of life guiding, guarding, and protecting you *every single* step of the way.

If you have a relationship with Jesus then you are en route home. How I pray that the Lord would keep this truth at the forefront of our hearts and mind. Remember that the Lord our God is with us *wherever* we go . . . may we seek to serve Him, and only Him, every step of the way, despite how wobbly we may be.

In Jesus' name, love and grace,

<>< Jessica

Prayer requests? Praises?

From: Hisword2day
To: Your heart
Sent: Friday, May 14, 2004 8:21 AM
Subject: Awesome deeds of righteousness–Psalm 65:5–7

"You answer us with awesome deeds of righteousness, O God our Savior, the hope of all the ends of the earth and of the farthest seas, who formed the mountains by your power, having armed yourself with strength, who stilled the roaring of the seas, and the roaring of their waves, and the turmoil of the nations." *Psalm 65:5–7* **NIV**

WOW! Was anyone else incredibly encouraged by this verse! Are we not SO blessed to serve our God and Savior?! He who answers us with AWESOME deeds of righteousness?! Have you seen one of these awesome deeds lately?

If not, check out the sunset tonight . . . or the stars . . . or watch the flowers dance in the wind . . . or watch a child interact with this world . . . or simply take a deep breath knowing He is the breath of life and has breathed life into you today.

I pray that today the Lord will remind you that He is the Lord your God . . . your Savior . . . the hope of all the ends of the earth and the farthest seas. He is *your* hope.

Remember that He formed the mountains by His power and armed Himself with strength. He also formed *you* by His power and has armed *you* with His strength.

He stills the roaring seas and their roaring waves and He stills the roaring seas and waves of your life. The Lord will be with you and the waters and rivers will not sweep over you (Isaiah 43:2).

He stills the turmoil of the nations . . . how we need to pray, in complete faith, for Him to do this *today.* And remember, He can still the turmoil in your personal life, too.

My precious friend . . . the Lord your God loves you with a love so deep and passionate . . . so perfect. His love will **never** fail you! May you see His awesome deeds of righteousness and experience Him as your hope, power, strength, and peace.

Thank you, Jesus, for being our Savior . . . help us to be your faithful servants. Answer us with awesome deeds of righteousness that proclaim your name today and help us to be aware of them. Thank you, Lord, for being our hope, power, strength, and peace . . . may we share you with others so that they will realize you are their Savior.

In Christ Jesus,

<>< Jessica

Prayer requests? Praises?

From: Hisword2day
To: Your heart
Sent: Tuesday, May 18, 2004 7:20 PM
Subject: Encouragement from the Centurion–Matthew 8:5–7

"When Jesus had entered Capernaum, a centurion came to him, asking for help. 'Lord,' he said, 'my servant lies at home paralyzed and in terrible suffering.' Jesus said to him, 'I will go and heal him.'" *Matthew 8:5–7 NIV*

Have you ever gone before the Lord asking for help?

Do you always know exactly what to pray for, or how to pray for a situation or for someone (yourself)? Or, do you sometimes just come before the Lord, needing help, but not really knowing how to pray, what to pray for, or what to lift up?

I find myself in these shoes right now—not sure what or how to pray about certain things. I know and truly do believe that when we don't know what we ought to pray for that the Spirit Himself intercedes for us (Romans 8:26). However, I still find that I get discouraged or frustrated when all I can do is present a situation, person (often myself), or emotion before the Lord and say, "Okay God, here 'it' is," without making a specific request other than "HELP!"

Well, here we read about a man who goes before the Lord and is in my shoes: he presents a situation before Jesus—his servant is ill—but, in this particular account, he never *specifically* asks Jesus for healing. Maybe he would have and Jesus just cut him off before he could ask. Or maybe he didn't know how to ask for what his servant needed.

Regardless, Jesus knew what was needed. All the centurion did was present the situation, and Jesus knew the solution.

Wow . . . how encouraged I was when I read this! Even though I may not always know what to pray for *specifically*—what to ask for or what's needed—*Jesus does.* I just need to follow the centurion's example: present my friend, situation, emotion, or myself before the Lord, and *trust in full faith* that regardless of what I know and understand, Jesus always knows and fully understands . . . the situation . . . *and* the solution.

Friend, remember this story. If ever you come upon a time in your life when all you can do is present something or someone before the Lord and don't know how to pray, what to ask for, or what to lift up, remember that Jesus *always* knows what is needed even *before* you can ask (Matthew 6:8). Therefore, just surrender it.

Furthermore, cling to what Paul reminds us of: when we don't know what we ought to pray for, *the Spirit intercedes for us,* expressing our hearts in ways words simply can't. Just never forget to go before Him and know that your seemingly "simple" plea for "HELP!" does more than you can fathom.

If you have a situation, Jesus has a solution. May you come to Him as the centurion did and seek His help . . . how the Lord loves to help His children! As you come to Him, may the Lord of peace Himself give you peace at all times and in every way!

Blessings to you my friend,

<>< Jessica

Prayer requests? Praises?

From: Hisword2day
To: Your heart
Sent: Friday, May 21, 2004 2:44 PM
Subject: Into the details–Matthew 10:29–30

"Are not two sparrows sold for a penny? Yet not one of them will fall to the ground apart from the will of your Father. And even the very hairs of your head are all numbered. So don't be afraid; you are worth more than many sparrows." *Matthew 10:29–31 NIV*

This story may be very familiar to you: it was part of Jesus' pep talk to "the 12" before sending them out . . . He warned them, taught them, and encouraged them. It's also a pep talk containing a truth of which I needed to be reminded. Maybe you do too . . .

Do you know how many hairs you have on your head? Would you dare count them?

Why not?

I'm guessing your answer is something like mine . . . who cares?! That's a totally irrelevant and pointless piece of information that I certainly don't need . . . makes no difference to me or the rest of the world, for that matter.

Right. It's a pretty insignificant detail to us.

Yet not to your heavenly Father. It makes a difference to Him. Even the hairs upon your head are important enough for Him to count . . . for Him to *create.*

The fact that He cares enough to know how many silly hairs we have on our head speaks loudly to my heart. It tells me that we have a heavenly Father who cares IMMENSELY for us . . . that He is into the details of our lives. From the most insignificant, pointless details of our lives, to the "big" ones, our heavenly Father *knows* of them and has accounted for *each and every* detail.

So friend, whether it's a tiny detail in your life or a seemingly big one, know and believe that your heavenly Father is into **that** detail of your life. You are precious and honored in His sight . . . you are of GREAT worth. You are loved with an unfailing and passionate love deeper than you can imagine! Therefore, He cares about *every* detail in your life.

If God takes care of every need a sparrow has, and you are worth more than sparrows to Him, don't you think He will do the same for you, His beloved child?

What detail do you need to surrender today? I pray that the Lord will give you the faith and strength to trust each detail of your life into His loving care.

Through Jesus, your sister,

<>< Jessica

Prayer requests? Praises?

From: Hisword2day
To: Your heart
Sent: Wednesday, May 26, 2004 12:03 PM
Subject: Thanks–Psalm 138:1–2

"I will give you thanks with all my heart; I will sing praises to You before the gods. I will bow down toward Your holy temple and give thanks to Your name for your lovingkindness and Your truth; for You have magnified your word according to all Your name." *Psalm 138:1–2* **NASB**

May we give thanks to the Lord with ALL of our hearts. May we sing praises before Him with more than our mouths. May we bow down toward His holy temple and give thanks for His loving-kindness and His truth. Indeed the Lord our God has magnified His word according to His name.

Thank you, Lord . . . I give you thanks and sing your praise with all of my heart! Thank you for you! Thank you for your faithfulness, for your loving-kindness, and for your truth. Please continue to send forth your light and your truth, that they may guide me to your holy place . . . to you. I love you and bless your name! AMEN!

Thankful,

<>< Jessica

Prayer requests? Praises?

From: Hisword2day
To: Your heart
Sent: Friday, May 28, 2004 12:56 PM
Subject: The fish's mouth–Matthew 17:25–27

**" . . . When Peter came into the house, Jesus was the first to speak. 'What do you think, Simon?' he asked. 'From whom do the kinds of the earth collect duty and taxes—from their own sons or from others?' 'From others,' Peter answered. 'Then sons are exempt,' Jesus said to him. 'But so that we may not offend them, go to the lake and throw out your line. Take the first fish you catch; open its mouth and you will find a four-drachma coin. Take it and give it to them for my tax and yours.'" *Matthew 17:25–27 NIV*

I am sure that there are some deep theological truths behind this passage; however, based on my limited knowledge of the history and culture surrounding this experience, I'm sure I don't understand it all. Regardless, the Lord spoke to my heart.

Just prior to Jesus sending Simon Peter off on a rather *interesting* mission, the tax collectors came to Peter and asked if his Teacher paid the temple tax, which Jesus did. Then we read the dialogue that follows in the passages above.

Through this story, I was reminded that indeed, the Lord might call us to do something seemingly illogical. I often question and doubt when I sense God telling me something that seems out in left field . . . but we serve a very unconventional God. He loves to do things in His own special way. His glory and power are often displayed much better that way.

Furthermore, I was reminded that our God always provides. Yet often times His provision or the means for Him providing (and I'm not just talking monetarily) come in the most peculiar and unlikely ways. I mean, who'd have thought that money would come out of the mouth of a fish?!

Well, our God hasn't changed. He is the same yesterday, today, and forever, therefore, it's not uncharacteristic for Him to work in unusual and interesting ways in our lives *today. How* He works and provides may vary, but He's always at work and will always provide.

Now I ask you, has the Lord ever told you to do something seemingly illogical and irrational? Do you trust Him over your logic or circumstances? Has He provided time, strength, energy, peace, love, joy, encouragement, friendship, or even financial provision through a most interesting venue?

In other words, what is your "fish's mouth"?

Lord Jesus, open my eyes that I may see you more, may trust you deeper, and may show you more freely. Thank you for working in ways that *only* you can. Thank you that your ways are so much better than my ways! Grant me faith to trust you over logic or my circumstances, and help me to see *all* the ways that you work and provide. You are so loving and faithful! Thank you, Jesus, for you. I love you. AMEN.

In Jesus' love and grace,

<>< Jessica

Prayer requests? Praises?

From: Hisword2day
To: Your heart
Sent: Tuesday, June 01, 2004 10:45 AM
Subject: The time has come . . . headed to Paris

Well, I have exciting news today . . . the time has come for me to leave for the Lord's harvest field of Paris! At 3:00 P.M. (Texas time) I will board a flight bound for the other side of the pond! PRAISE JESUS for all that He has done to make this time arrive!

I'm sorry that I am telling you this with such short notice. Once God gave the "green light" to leave, my life's been like one big roller coaster . . . up, down, and all around! There are still some details to be worked out, such as living arrangement, but fret not though! I have talked to our Master and Commander and He assures me that He is on top of everything and has taken care of all the details. ☺ Your prayers are of course still very much needed and GREATLY appreciated!!!!!!!!

My simple words would never be able to capture the depths of my appreciation for all of your prayers, words of encouragement, financial investments, and acts of kindness throughout this whole preparation stage. I would not be going without you fighting this battle too! The Lord has shown me that this is not a "me" thing, but a God thing . . . it is a body of Christ thing. It takes us all and I'm just so honored to serve with you!

So know that from the bottom of my heart I thank you and give thanks to the Lord with every thought of you . . . for the blessing you have been and for who you are in Him. For as I head out into a foreign mission field, I am reminded that you too are in a mission field and I am excited for what the Lord is doing literally ALL around the world!

"I tell you the truth, a time will come and has now come when the dead will hear the voice of the Son of God and those who hear and believe will live." *John 5:25* NIV

Friend, thank you. Thank you for being the Lord's righteous right hand holding me up when I start to slip. Thank you for setting a hedge of protection around me with your prayers. Thank you for praying for the Lord to open my heart to Him so that I might know Him more and more.

Thank you for praying that ultimately HIS perfect will be done. Thank you for praying over all of the details and for just simply lifting me up in any way! Thank you for sending me and making it possible for me to take the message of Jesus' love and grace into the lives of teenagers in Paris. Thank you for helping the dead to hear the voice of the Son of God . . . you are building the Kingdom one heart at a time.

By grace your sister,

<>< jess

Praise Reports & Answers

First, join me in PRAISING GOD for His goodness, His faithfulness, and for just who He is! Isaiah 26 says that the Lord blesses His people with peace and all that they have accomplished HE has done for them . . . AMEN to that! (Thank you for your prayers as they have been infusing my heart, mind, body and soul with that supernatural peace!) Let's thank Jesus today for His sacrifice and selfless heart . . . for without Him we wouldn't have a message to preach or life to give.

Answers to FAQ

Did the tractor sell? YES! As some of you know a tractor was donated to me to help fund my ministry in Paris. Well, last week it sold! And with quite an interesting twist . . . wow does God work in mysterious ways! THANK YOU so, so, so much for your prayers concerning this! **(Isn't it neat that God gave me a machine used to prepare a field for a harvest to help send me into a mission field to prepare it for a heavenly harvest?!)**

Where will I be living? Upon arriving, I will be staying with my Area Director, David Usrey, and his family until I can find a place of my own. The other intern already in Paris, Lisa, and I might be living together. We're looking for places and just letting the Lord lead and pave the way if He desires for us to be roommates . . . please pray for God to provide a place and make His will VERY clear . . . whether we are to live together or I am to live alone.

How long will I be in Paris? My commitment is for the next 2–3 years; however I will be returning to the U.S. from time to time. I will be back at the end of the year for the holidays and a wedding. And I'll be returning at least once a year thereafter.

Will my e-mail be the same? YES . . . same e-mail address.

Will I continue sending the scripture e-mails? Most definitely! Until I get settled, I can't tell you how frequently they will be coming, but as the Spirit leads and provides I will pass on what He shares with me.

Pray for my flight . . . for safety and just for my heart to be open and available today . . . pray that I get some rest too. ☺

Pray for the kids in Paris . . . for the people in general in Paris . . . for God to soften their hearts and open doors for the message of the Good News! PRAY FOR SALVATION!

Pray for me to decrease and Jesus to increase in and through me.

Pray that HIS WILL BE DONE AND THAT HE BE GLORIFIED!

THANK YOU SO MUCH IN ADVANCE FOR YOUR PRAYERS!!!!! THEY ARE POWERFUL AND EFFECTIVE! (James 5:16).

NOTES

February 14, 2003:
-Max Lucado, *A Love Worth Giving* (W Publishing Group 2002)
    April 11, 2003:
-NIV Study Bible Notes

April 29, 2003:
-NIV Study Bible Notes
    July 1, 2003:
-Philip Yancey, *The Jesus I Never Knew*
    August 25, 2003:
-Merriam-Webster Online Dictionary by Merriam-Webster, Incorporated
-The New American Webster Handy College Dictionary
    September 15, 2003:
-Merriam-Webster Online Dictionary by Merriam-Webster, Incorporated
-Oxford Reference Online (Oxford University Press)
    October 6, 2003:
-Merriam-Webster Online Dictionary by Merriam-Webster, Incorporated

October 28, 2003:
-Merriam-Webster Online Dictionary by Merriam-Webster, Incorporated
-The New American Webster Handy College Dictionary
    January 16, 2004
-*The Passion of the Christ,* a Mel Gibson movie 2004
    February 26, 2004
-The World Book Encyclopedia (by World Book-Childcraft International, Inc., Copyright 1979 U.S.A.)

January 5, 2004:
-Merriam-Webster Online Dictionary by Merriam-Webster, Incorporated

March 2, 2004:
-The World Book Encyclopedia (by World Book-Childcraft
International, Inc., Copyright 1979 U.S.A.)

May 7, 2004:
-NIV Study Bible Notes

Contact author Jessica Sullivan
or order more copies of this book at

TATE PUBLISHING, LLC

127 East Trade Center Terrace
Mustang, Oklahoma 73064

(888) 361 - 9473

Tate Publishing, LLC

www.tatepublishing.com